THE NPT AND THE DEVELOPING COUNTRIES

About the Author

Dr. Jita Mishra is a Senior Lecturer in the Department of Political Science in Sri Venketeswara College, University of Delhi. Her areas of specialisation include International Relations, India's Foreign Policy, Political Theory and Gandhi. She has written a number of articles on contemporary issues and presented papers at several seminars and conferences.

THE NPT AND THE DEVELOPING COUNTRIES

Dr. Jita Mishra

CONCEPT PUBLISHING COMPANY, NEW DELHI-110059

Cataloging in Publication Data—DK
Courtesy: D.K. Agencies (P) Ltd. <docinfo@dkagencies.com>

Mishra, Jita, 1966-
The NPT and the developing countries / Jita Mishra.
p. cm.
Includes bibliographical references (p.)
Includes index.
ISBN 13:9788180695377
ISBN 10: 8180695379

1. Treaty on the Non-proliferation of Nuclear Weapons. (1968). 2. Nuclear nonproliferation—India. 3. Nuclear nonproliferation—Pakistan. 4. Nuclear nonproliferation—Korea (North). 5. Nuclear nonproliferation—Iraq. 6. Nuclear weapons—Government policy—Asia. 7. Security, International —Asia. 8. Asia—Foreign relations. I. Title. II. Title: Non-proliferation treaty and the developing countries.

DDC 327.174 709 5 22

ISBN-13: 978- 81-8069-537-7
ISBN-10: 81-8069-537-9

First Published 2008

Published and Printed by
Ashok Kumar Mittal
Concept Publishing Company
A/15-16, Commercial Block, Mohan Garden
New Delhi-110059 (INDIA)

Phones : 25351460, 25351794
Fax : 091-11-25357103
Email : publishing@conceptpub.com

Dedicated to

To the everlasting memory of my dear grandfather

Late Prof. B. Mahapatra

Principal Burla Engineering College

who had been a constant source of inspiration

to me since my childhood

and my loving mother

Mrs. Bina Dash

without whose support this work could not

have been successful.

Preface

The emergence of new nuclear states in the developing world in the Post-Cold War era has led to the revival of interest in the dominant discourse on Non-Proliferation. The articulation of the conceptual debate on the Non-Proliferation Treaty in significant developing countries, namely, India, Pakistan, North Korea and Iraq, has focussed on providing a critical analysis of the Non-Proliferation Treaty in the light of their geo-political security parameters. The strategic location of these developing countries in extremely volatile regional and extra-regional security environments, have aggravated their security concerns and shaped their perceptions towards the NPT.

This study revolves around the hypothesis that the Non-Proliferation Treaty does not address the security needs of the developing countries whose strategic compulsions are specific and region oriented. A related hypothesis is that the discriminatory nature of the NPT aggravated the anxieties and vulnerabilities of these developing countries.

To test these hypothesis data has been collected from both Primary and Secondary sources. The Primary sources include, Government Documents, International Atomic Energy Agency Reports, United Nations Documents and Parliamentary publications. The Secondary sources include books, journals and newspaper articles.

While this study incorporates a general critique of the NPT from the viewpoint of developing countries, its scope is delimited to perspectives of four developing nations, namely, India, Pakistan, North Korea and Iraq towards the Non-Proliferation Treaty. These four countries are taken as case studies for important reasons. First there has been an attempt examine the perspectives of India and Pakistan, two South Asian countries that are not signatories to the NPT. Secondly from the Korean Peninsula the specific North Korean case is taken that was a signatory to the NPT and has recently withdrawn from the treaty. Thirdly the work attempts to study the perspectives of Iraq in the Middle East that has remained a signatory of the NPT. Finally these developing nations have been subject to tremendous and varying degrees of international pressure, in the case of Iraq extreme punitive measures to confirm to the norms of the NPT. The western debates over the nuclear issues in the developing world have rarely taken into account the psychology underlying the resistance of India and Pakistan to the NPT.

The scholarly literature on proliferation has tended to ignore the motives behind nuclear proliferation in the developing world. This research has probed the motives of weapons proliferation in the four nations and their approaches towards the NPT. These developing nations express deep resentment at the fact that the Non-Proliferation Treaty did not ensure the universal Non-Proliferation of Nuclear Weapons but only stopped the dissemination of nuclear weapons to non-nuclear states. This research attempts to probe new areas concerning national priorities, specific assessment and geo-strategic compulsions of the four developing nations in their approach towards the Non-Proliferation Treaty.

The methodology adopted in this study is by and large historical and comparative analytical. The historical method has been used to trace the developments within the Non-Proliferation Treaty from 1968 to 2003. The comparative method would provide the means through which responses towards the Non-Proliferation Treaty are differentiated according to geo-political specificities in the states of India, Pakistan, North Korea and Iraq.

The study has been structured into six chapters each chapter deals with a specific dimension of the theme.

Chapter 1 studies the conceptual dimensions of Non-Proliferation and traces the historical background of the NPT. The chapter also endeavours to explain the provisions of the treaty in the context of the conceptual debate. This chapter addresses the crucial issues of the developing nations concerns about the export control devices and intrusive verification mechanisms evolved by the developed nations to check the proliferation of nuclear weapons to additional nations. The chapter analyses the role and participation of the developing nations in the various review conferences. The chapter also highlights the discriminatory nature of the NPT and the security concerns of the developing nations security concerns of the developing nations.

The 2nd chapter examines the multiple imperatives behind India's opposition to the Non-Proliferation Treaty. The chapter probes the history of India's concern over the Chinese threat. It then examines India and Pakistan's conflictual relationship that has heightened India's security dilemmas. This chapter provides an overview of India's nuclear tests in 1974 and May 1998 and examines its repercussions on the global Non-Proliferation Regime. The chapter also examines the evolution of the Indian nuclear doctrine.

Chapter 3 attempts to analyse Pakistan's approach to the NPT in the context of its geo-political environment, its threat perceptions and its attempt to achieve parity with India. The chapter acquires substantive importance as an attempt is made to delve into the history of Pakistan's nuclear development. The chapter addresses the crucial issue the US pressure on Pakistan in the post-September 11 period to confirm to the norms of Non-Proliferation.

The 4th chapter attempts to examine North Korea's perceptions towards the Non-Proliferation Treaty. In the first part the chapter deals with North Korea's security dilemma arising out of its hostile relations with South Korea, Japan, China and the US. The chapter examines North Korea's reluctance to ratify its safeguards agreement with IAEA until 1992 and its clash with the IAEA overful access to nuclear sets. This chapter examines the circumstances that were instrumental in North Korea's decision to join the Non-Proliferation Treaty. The chapter then proceeds to analyse that North Korea's recent withdrawal from the NPT and its apparent efforts to accelerate its nuclear programme is a response to adverse changes in the external environment.

Chapter 5 attempts to locate the roots of insecurity of Iraq that led it to pursue a clandestine nuclear programme in 1990's. The chapter investigates the geo-political environment of Iraq, the historical background of its nuclear programme its perspectives on the NPT. This chapter examines its confrontations with the UN inspection teams, its tussle with the US leading to operation freedom Iraq and forced regime change.

And chapter 6 beautifully summarized the whole issue of NPT in light of Developing Countries.

I express a deep sense of gratitude to my supervisor Dr. Shanta Nedungadi Varma for her able guidance, resolute training, calm and encouraging attitude and uncompromising zeal for quality which has inspired me in the pursuit of this academic venture.

I want to give special thanks to Prof. Shusheela Kaushik, for encouraging me to take the topic, for it was really an interesting endeavour. I acknowledge my special thanks all the teachers of the Political Science department especially Prof. Subrata Mukherjee, Prof. M.P. Singh and Prof. Bidyut Chakravarty for the help they have rendered in my work. I also want to give a special thanks to Prof. Ashwini Ray for the support he gave to me at the final stage.

It would be remiss, if I did not add the contributions of the library staff of Institute of Defence Analysis, Delhi University, Teenmurti, who rendered valuable assistance to me during my work.

My efforts would not have been equal to this task, had they not been supported by Dr. A.S. Reddy, Dr. S.K. Mishra, Dr. Vasant Sharma, Mr. Prakash Narayan, Arvind, Nidhi Singh, Mukesh, Dr. Sunil Tiwari, Bittoo, Aparna, Aditya and Mr. S.K. Dash.

New Delhi

Jita Mishra

Contents

Abbreviations

BARC	:	Bhabha Atomic Research Centre
CBW	:	Chemical and Biological Weapons
CIA	:	Central Intelligence Agency
CTBT	:	Comprehensive Test Ban Treaty
DPRK	:	Democratic Peoples Republic of Korea
EMIS	:	Electromagnetic Isotope Separation
HEV	:	Highly Enriched Uranium
IAEA	:	International Atomic Energy Agency
KANUPP	:	Karachi Nuclear Power Plant
KEDO	:	Korean Peninsular Energy Development Organisation
LWR	:	Light Water Reactors
MW	:	Mega Watt
NATO	:	North Atlantic Treaty Organisation
NGO	:	National Government Organisation
NPT	:	Non-Proliferation Treaty
NSC	:	National Security Council
PAEC	:	Pakistan Atomic Energy Commission
PARC	:	Pakistan Atomic Research Centre
PINSTECH	:	Pakistan Institute for Nuclear Science and Technology
ROK	:	Republic of Korea
START	:	Strategic Arms Reduction Treaty
UN	:	United Nations
UNMOVIC	:	United Nations Monitoring Verification and Inspection Commission
UNSCOM	:	United Nations Special Commission
USIP	:	United States Institute of Peace
USSR	:	Union of Soviet Socialist Republic
WMD	:	Weapon of Mass Destruction

1

The NPT: Conceptual Basis and Historical Evolution

Non-Proliferation has occupied a central place in international relations discourse in the Post-Cold War era, which has also witnessed a limited proliferation of nuclear weapons among the developing nations. The developing nations like India, Pakistan, North Korea and Iraq have responded to systemic pressures of their regional security environment and extra regional threats by giving tough resistance to the Non-Proliferation Treaty. There is growing realisation in the developing world that the Non-Proliferation concern of the US is directed towards sustaining its hegemony in the Post-Cold War era and curbing horizontal proliferation. Much to the disappointment of the developing world some nuclear weapons states have acted as self appointed trustees of the international community for promoting their own interests in the name of Non-Proliferation.[1] The Non-Proliferation debate in significant countries of the developing world has focussed on providing a critique to the Non-Proliferation Treaty, taking cognisance of the ground realities of their insecurity dynamics. This research aims at studying the developing nations' perspectives on the Non-Proliferation Treaty, taking four major developing countries as case studies, namely, India, Pakistan, North Korea and Iraq. It attempts to probe the several imperatives, both general and country specific that have led these developing nations' to adopt variant perspectives and policies with regard to the NPT. The developing countries perceive the NPT as a treaty that ensured that no more countries acquired nuclear capability apart from the existing ones, namely, the United States, Soviet Union, Britain, France and China. It was an attempt to lock in place the balance of power as it existed on

January 1, 1968.[2] In this context, it is pertinent to underline the following crucial points.

First, the NPT has the consent of five major nuclear powers because it accommodates their interests. Apart from the five declared nuclear weapon countries, namely the US, Russia, China, France, Britain and 183 states have joined the treaty. The overwhelming majority of the members are from the developing world. The viability of the treaty to a large extent depends on the views of developing nations, which are parties to the NPT. Secondly, while a majority of the developing states have accepted the regime, their reasons to be a party to the treaty do not necessarily stem from its inherent worth. They may be the product of a cynical assessment of the price to be paid for defiance of the wishes of the super power.[3] Thirdly, the Non-Proliferation Treaty lacks the consent of the outer ring of emerging nuclear powers like India and Pakistan. These states are considered as outlaws by the NPT.[4] Further, it is important to ascertain developing nations views on whether the NPT has fulfilled their aspirations.[5] The Non-Proliferation Treaty is unique in the sense that it aims at the prevention of emergence of a sixth nuclear power after United Kingdom, United States of America, China, France and the Russia.[6]

Another anomaly arises from the fact that it is only the actions of the members from the developing nations who are party to the NPT, namely, Iraq and North Korea, that are subject to close scrutiny and accusations of non-compliance. The US Non-Proliferation concern in the new world order era may seem genuine, but in reality it appears to be aimed towards sustaining the US leadership in the post-Cold War world. Furthermore, most of the literature on the subject of the Non-Proliferation Treaty is from the Western perspective. An attempt has been made in this chapter to highlight a non-western or developing nations perspective towards the Non-Proliferation Treaty. For conceptual clarity an attempt has been made to delve into the historical background of the Non-Proliferation Treaty, its provisions, its membership and the outcomes of the review conferences.

The Concept of Non-Proliferation

The term non-proliferation as defined in the Compact Oxford Dictionary "is the prevention of an increase in the number of nuclear weapons that are produced." There are two distinct categories of proliferation vertical and horizontal. Vertical proliferation may be defined as an increase in the number and types of nuclear weapons possessed by nuclear weapon states, whereas horizontal proliferation refers to the spread of nuclear weapons to non-nuclear weapon states or their ability to make them.[7] The acquisition of nuclear weapons by India and Pakistan in 1998 represents an instance of horizontal proliferation. Vertical proliferation involves the expansion of nuclear arsenals by states that already possess some nuclear weapons. The US-USSR nuclear arms race during the Cold War is an example of vertical proliferation.

The relationship of vertical and horizontal proliferation was a central issue in the approach of non-nuclear weapon states to the NPT debate in 1968. India consistently attacked vertical proliferation. It was the central theme in the NPT review conference. The proliferation is constructed both at vertical and horizontal level. Vertical and horizontal proliferation are linked by the fact that the most non-nuclear weapon powers would like to see a reduction in vertical proliferation, while nuclear powers have focussed on reducing horizontal proliferation. The west proliferated vertically with impunity, stockpiling Weapons of Mass Destruction without regard for humanism. The NPT legitimises nuclear arsenals of the Nuclear Weapon States. The treaty imposes control on peaceful activities of non-nuclear weapon states and not on the military activities of nuclear weapon states. It attempts to prevent only 'horizontal' proliferation i.e. increase in the number of countries possessing nuclear weapons and not vertical proliferation i.e. quantitative increase of nuclear weapons.[8]

The Historical Background of the NPT

The NPT has its origin in the international concern for safety from nuclear disasters perceived inherent in the spread of nuclear weapons. The date on which nuclear weapons officially began to proliferate is 16 July 1945, with the explosion of the first nuclear device at Alamogordo (New Mexico) known as the Trinity test. The idea of an atom bomb occurred to number of scientists soon after the discovery of fission of Uranium and it was an accident in history that it coincided with the outbreak of the Second World

War. The British and the American scientists feared that German scientists would develop the bomb. The atom bomb project had for all practical purposes folded up in Germany as early as 1942 even before the Manhattan project started in the United States.[10] Following the discovery of nuclear fission in 1938 scientists and world political leaders sought to prevent the spread of nuclear weapon through surveys and proposed that all of the world's nuclear activities be placed under the control of a single international agency.[11]

The Acheson Lilenthal Report and Attempts to Curb Proliferation

An attempt to control the development and dissemination of nuclear technology as a peaceful source of energy and simultaneously preventing proliferation of nuclear weapons was based on the Acheson Lilenthal Report of 1945. The report emphasised for positive aspects of control and insisted on the need to curtail dangerous activities nuclear energy and development as matters of international ownership and control. On November 15, 1945, the USA, the UK and Canada proposed the establishment of a UN Atomic Energy Commission for the purpose of 'entirely eliminating the use of Atomic energy for destructive purposes.[12]

The Failure of the Baruch Plan

The Baruch Plan of 1946 offered by the US sought to forestall nuclear arms proliferation by putting all nuclear resources under international ownership and control. The creators of nuclear weapons influenced the Baruch Plan. Its aim was to prohibit nations from owning anything that might help them to make a bomb. The plan failed to gain acceptance from the Soviet Union, which feared an American monopoly in nuclear technology. At the time of the Baruch Plan, the US was the only known possessor of the fabrication of explosive nuclear weapons. The United States had conducted the first nuclear test series after World War II in July 1945.[13]

End of US Nuclear Monopoly and onset of Proliferation

The American bomb was a challenge to Russian scientists and

engineers. Stalin needed the bomb as quickly as possible.[14] The nuclear monopoly of the US came to an end with the explosion of a nuclear device by Soviet Union in 1949. Great Britain consequently launched its own military and civilian programmes and succeeded in exploding the first nuclear device in 1952. France exploded a nuclear device in 1960.[15] The Soviet Union for its part initiated close cooperation with China. China carried out its nuclear test in 1964. Therefore the limitation and counter productive effects of the principal denial of technology had been established and horizontal proliferation was a reality at that time.[16] In 1953, evidence of failure of the US policy of nuclear survey was mounting. The UK and Russia had both tested nuclear devices and France was forging ahead with its civilian nuclear programme.[17]

Perspectives on the Origin of the NPT

Two dominant perspectives exist depicting the origin of the NPT. The Western perspective depicts the origins of the NPT as a concerted effort linked to American concern over the issue of proliferation of nuclear weapons to more states. From developing nations' perspectives, there was an equally genuine concern for nuclear disarmament. During the 1960's the US and Soviet Union began to acknowledge their shared interest in preventing more nations from acquiring nuclear weapons, when in February 1960, the first French nuclear test was carried out in Algeria.[18] But the main initiative for preventing the spread of nuclear weapons came form the developing world. Developing nations like India, were in the forefront of non-nuclear countries urging the non-dissemination and non-acquisition of nuclear weapons.[19]

In 1958, at the 13th session of the United Nations General Assembly, Ireland introduced the Non-Proliferation question into the agenda. The Irish Foreign Minister Frank Aipen offered a draft resolution concerning the further dissemination of nuclear weapons before the first committee of UN General Assembly on October 17, 1958.[20] The 15th session of the General Assembly finally accepted the resolution that called upon "all governments to apply all possible efforts for the achievement of permanent agreement to prevent the widespread proliferation of nuclear weapons".[21] This resolution drew attention the dangers of further nuclear weapons proliferation and call for measures to prevent the spread of nuclear technology to additional states.

The approach of the developing nations from the very beginning has been strongly against the legitimacy of nuclear weapons as instruments of policy and correspondingly against and discrimination between nuclear weapon states and non-nuclear weapon states. Nations like India, Pakistan, North Korea and Iraq supported the move to stop the spread of nuclear weapons.

In the matter of Non-Proliferation, the second Non-Aligned Summit at Cairo in 1964 called upon the great powers to desist from all policies conducive to the dispersion of nuclear weapons to states that did not posses them.[22] While individually, several Non-Aligned countries had agreed to join the NPT because of coercive pressure from nuclear weapon countries, but they refused to endorse it because of its discriminatory character.

A landmark was reached on 19 November 1965 when the General Assembly adopted Resolution 2028 (XX) setting forth the principle, on which the NPT should be based.[23] India and seven other nations presented their resolution to the General Assembly of the United Nations. It included the following propositions:

- The treaty should be void of any loopholes, which might permit nuclear and non-nuclear powers to proliferate, directly, or indirectly nuclear weapons in any form.
- The treaty should embody an acceptable balance of mutual responsibilities and obligations of the nuclear and non-nuclear powers.
- The treaty should be a step towards the achievement of general and complete disarmament more particularly nuclear disarmament.
- There should be acceptable and workable provisions to ensure the effectiveness of the treaty.[24]

After much debate and intensive negotiation on collective security arrangements, safeguards and balanced obligations, the United States and Soviet Union submitted a reverse version of the NPT to the Eighteenth Nation Disarmament Commission on March 11, 1960. The global NPT that emerged was not disarmament oriented but arms control oriented. When the NPT was opened for signature, India decided not to put signature.

NPT Opened for Signature

On June 12, 1968 the UN General Assembly approved the final text of the NPT. The treaty was opened for signature on 1 July, 1968 and signed on that date by the US, Soviet Union and 59 other countries.[25] The treaty entered into force with the deposit of US ratification on 5th March 1970[26] China acceded to the NPT only on 9 March 1992 and France even later on 3 August 1992. In 1996 Belarus, Ukraine and Kazakhstan became a party to the NPT as a non-nuclear weapon state. In June 1997, Brazil became a state party to the NPT. [27]

When the NPT was being negotiated in the 1960's the United States and Soviet Union pressed for a treaty of indefinite duration. The non-nuclear states refused to go along, arguing that it might perpetuate the idea that nuclear weapon states could hold on their nuclear weapons for ever while denying non-nuclear states their right to develop such weapons. The impasse was broken by a compromise. The treaty called for the nuclear weapon state parties to negotiate on effective nuclear disarmament and to convene an extension conference in 25 years to determine the duration of treaty. The compromise gave the non-nuclear states some leverage in pressing for nuclear disarmament.[28] The non-nuclear states have objected to the lack of progress in nuclear disarmament and the lack of transparency with respect to P-5 nuclear weapons programmes. North Korea's announcement to withdraw from the NPT raises the issue of the irreversibility of the treaty's commitment, which will continue to shape the future of the NPT.

Security Guarantees to Non-Nuclear States

The nuclear weapon states provided security guarantees to non-nuclear states as incentives to join the Non-Proliferation Treaty. The majority of developing nations who joined the NPT could not anticipate the fact that the nuclear weapon states would go back from their promises on positive security guarantees and negative security assurances.

Positive Security Guarantees

In their efforts to address the concerns of non-nuclear weapon states, the United States, United Kingdom and Soviet Union submitted identical declarations saying that nuclear aggression or threats against any non-nuclear weapons states party to the NPT would require immediate action by the UN Security Council. These are known as positive security assurances. These declarations were incorporated into the draft Resolution 255 on June 19, 1968.

Negative Security Assurances

Negative security assurances were also given by nuclear weapon states to non-nuclear weapon states, members of the NPT, whereby each nuclear weapon state undertook not to threaten, or to use nuclear weapons against non-nuclear weapon states in launching an attack. The five nuclear weapon states through the United Nation Security Council Resolution 984, issued coordinated negative security assurances for non-nuclear weapon states. Their hypocrisy in this regards stands exposed with the recent US attack on Iraq.

The NPT Membership

The Non-Proliferation Treaty saw a continuous expansion of its membership. On June 12, 1968, 63 states had signed the NPT. Today there are 188 members. In the decade of 1960's, 21 nations signed the NPT. These included Iraq, Ireland, Canada, Mexico and Finland amongst others. The 1970's showed a remarkable increase in the NPT membership to 85 nations. Some of the nations that joined the NPT in 1970's were Sri Lanka, Bangladesh, Japan and Republic of Korea. In the 1980's, 28 nations acceded to the NPT, including North Korea, Turkey, Kuwait and Spain.[29]

During the 1990's, 48 nations joined the NPT. After the disintegration of Soviet Union, the various republics joined the NPT like Slovak Republic, Kazakhstan, Azerbaijan and Armenia.[30] Prior to the indefinite extensions of the NPT, more nations were pressurised to join the NPT. A major change that has occurred since the NPT was initiated, is that the US and Russia are no longer adversaries. In the 1990's a variety of nations moved to embrace the norms of the Non-Proliferation Regime. The list of signatories to the NPT has continued to grow with the significant addition of South Africa in July 1991, and the Peoples Republic of China in

9th March 1992. The decision of Belarus, Kazakhstan and Ukraine to accede to the treaty as non-nuclear weapon states avoided a possible crises for the NPT. France has not only joined the NPT, but like Canada it has become one of the strong supporters of the regime.[31] It is to be underlined that China conducted 35 nuclear tests before joining the NPT.[32] The developing nations were concerned that the nuclear powers were reluctant to institute any checks on their own stockpiles. The concerns were articulated in the debates on the NPT. France conducted 204 nuclear test till 1991 after which it acceded to the NPT.[33] The developing nations were naturally tempted to emulate the path of these nations in testing nuclear weapons. France and China's imminent accession to the NPT reflected historical changes of position that would greatly influence the treaty to meet the challenge of 1995.[34] Zambia and Tanzania which had long resisted pressure to join because of the treaty's discriminatory features and concerns, joined when South Africa announced their accession to the treaty. In the decade of 2000, only one nation acceded to the NPT, namely Cuba.

In spite of its widespread support the NPT has been severely criticised ever since it was negotiated and several important global and regional powers had refused to sign it. The developing nations share common concerns for retaining their nuclear option; they are mostly a heterogeneous group as regards their capabilities, motives, aspirations and intent. India, Pakistan, North Korea and Iraq seek security by building a nuclear capability to secure their survival in politically alien surroundings. These nations are disillusioned with the final outcome of the non-proliferation arrangements and have been forced to proliferate nuclear weapons.

Provisions of the Treaty

The NPT is a collection of eleven articles designed to prevent new nuclear countries from obtaining nuclear weapons. It established a system of safeguards and verification. According to the preamble, the purpose of the treaty was to facilitate and guarantee access to peaceful application of nuclear technology and by-products for all parties of the treaty whether nuclear or non-nuclear under the supervision of the International Atomic Energy Agency.

Article I: Prohibits the transfer of Nuclear Weapons or other explosive devices to any state, whether a party to the treaty or not, whether a nuclear weapon states or not directly or indirectly through an alliance. This Article obligates nuclear weapons states not to assist, encourage or induce any non-nuclear weapon state to manufacture or have control over nuclear weapons or explosive devices.

Article II: Prohibits non-nuclear weapon signatories from manufacturing or otherwise acquiring nuclear weapons or devices including peaceful nuclear explosives.

Article III: Obligates non-nuclear weapon parties to accept international safeguards as specified in a special arrangement with International Atomic Energy Agency.

Article IV: States that all parties to the treaty have the right to full exploitation of the use of nuclear energy for peaceful purposes and obligates these parties in a portion to cooperate with other countries in developing nuclear technology.

Article V: Obligates the nuclear weapon parties to make available nuclear explosives for peaceful purposes to non-nuclear weapon parties under international supervisions or as low as possible excluding any charges for research and development costs.

Article VI: Obligates each parties of the treaty to undertake in good faith effective measures to bring about general and complete disarmament.

Article VII: Gives the right to the states to conclude regional treaties to assure absence of nuclear weapons in their respective territories.

Article VIII: Allows any party to the treaty to propose amendment to this treaty, which has to be approved by on majority of votes of all parties.

It also stipulates a conference to be held in Geneva every five years to review the treaty.

Article IX: States that the treaty would be open to all states for signature and be subject to ratification. This Article provides that the depository government pursuant to Article 102 of the Charter of the United Nation should register the treaty.

Article X: Gives the right to the parties to withdraw from the treaty if they feel that extraordinary events leading to the subject matter of the treaty have jeopardised the supreme interests of the country.

Article XI: Emphasises that the text of the treaty shall be deposited in the archives of the depository governments. The duly certified copies of the treaty shall be transmitted by depository governments to the government of the signatory and acceding states.[35]

Export Control Devices and Verification Mechanism— The Developing Nations' Concerns

The developing nations are extremely sensitive to the existing export control and verification mechanisms designed to curb the proliferation of nuclear weapons. The Zangger Committee, the London club of suppliers, the Wassenar arrangement and the IAEA verification mechanisms were specific mechanism for curbing the spread of nuclear technology to developing nations.

Zangger Committee

During 1971, a group of states that were potential suppliers of nuclear items met to establish a consensus on what would trigger safeguards under the terms of the NPT. This group was designated, as the NPT exporters committee became widely known as the Zangger Committee. Following the Indian detonation of a peaceful nuclear device in May 1974, Canada initiated a review of the non-proliferation policy. The Zangger Committee regularly held meetings in Vienna on May 28, 1998, to discuss the implementation of export control requirement of nuclear NPT. The nations are Argentina, Australia, Austria, Belgium, Bulgaria, Canada, China, the Czech Republic, Denmark, Finland, France, Germany, Greece, Hungary, Ireland, Italy, Japan, The Republic of Korea, Luxembourg, Netherlands, Norway, Poland, Portugal, Romania, the Russian Federation, Slovakia, South Africa, Spain, Sweden, Switzerland,

Ukraine, the UK and the US. For many years the work of the Zangger Committee was regarded as somewhat suspect by a large number of developing countries who saw in it a mechanism for restricting nuclear efforts to the developing nations and linked proliferation with it.[36]

London Club of Suppliers

The London Club of Supplier group was formed immediately after India's nuclear tests of 1974 when it was realised that the NPT had failed to regulate the flow of nuclear materials and technology to additional nations. This concern led to the notion of a nuclear supplier group or London Club to further restrict the supply of items that might be used to advance a non-peaceful nuclear programme. The Nuclear Supplier Group insisted on stricter export condition than those supplied in the NPT. Nations importing nuclear materials from Nuclear Supplier Group member states were now required:

- To accept international safeguards on all imported material and technology and on facilities using or replicating sensitive material and technology.
- To provide physical security for transferred nuclear facilities and materials.
- To agree not to transfer the nuclear materials and technology to third party countries without permission of the original exporter. The purpose of these tightened restriction was to prevent the manufacture of nuclear explosives and to prevent nuclear explosions peaceful or otherwise by non-nuclear weapon states.
- For their part, the nuclear weapon states pledged to exercise restraint in the export of sensitive technologies such as Plutonium reprocessing, Uranium enrichment or heavy water production equipment. In April 1992, the 28 nuclear supplier group member states further tightened control over nuclear exports in response to revelations of Iraq's clandestine import of nuclear technology. The group expanded its trigger list to include sixty-five dual use items.[37]

Wassenar Arrangement

One of the means of export control for conventional arms and dual use technology is the Wassenar arrangement. The Wassenar arrangement was designed to prevent destabilising acquisition of weapons and technology through a formal process of transparency and consultation.

IAEA and Intrusive Inspections

The International Atomic Energy Agency was founded in 1957, is the primary mechanism for verifying that the parties to the NPT are complying with its terms. The IAEA safeguards serve as a verification mechanism for the NPT. The non-nuclear weapon states are required to conclude an agreement with the IAEA for the application of comprehensive full scope safeguards. The specification for such agreements is contained in the document known as INFCIRC/153 (Rev2). Safeguards are to be applied on all special fissionable materials in all peaceful nuclear activities of non-nuclear weapons parties. These safeguards agreements enter in force not later than 18 months after the date of initial negotiations. Over the years, members of IAEA have broadened the scope of material and facilities that safeguards cover. In 1997, the IAEA Board of Governors agreed to strengthen the safeguards system called the Model Additional Protocol. The INFCIRC/540 provides the guidelines for the new safeguards. The strengthened safeguards will increase access to all aspect of a country's nuclear programme and will allow for improved verification technologies. The safeguards clauses invariably point out the discrimination against non-nuclear weapon states.

Developing nations argue that they are at a permanent military disadvantage that made them more vulnerable to nuclear intimidation. Non-nuclear weapon states party to the treaty wished to use nuclear energy for peaceful purposes. North Korea and Iraq were willing to fully comply with the safeguards, obligations but they have considered intrusive inspections as a threat to their sovereignty. A fact also not fully appreciated is that by accepting IAEA safeguards, sovereign states also have accepted inspection teams made up of persons of many nationalities, cultural background and political persuasions, despite the fact that most states are very sensitive about the potential impact of foreign presence.[38] As Lewis Dunn put forth, new nuclear weapon states are not likely to allow international inspectors access anything like the freedom enjoyed by the UN in Iraq. North Korea announced that it intended to withdraw from the NPT rather than accede to IAEA inspections regime for introduction of a new nuclear weapons programme.[39]

There are two types of IAEA inspections. Firstly inspections of declared atomic site which target nation reveals and declares to be permitted facilities under the NPT. Secondly inspections on demand-inspection of sites, which target nations, have not revealed but the IAEA has reason to consider suspect as violating the treaty. The IAEA can sometimes act on information supplied by intelligence services of other nations.

NPT Review Conferences

The developing nations had strong reservations on intrusive inspections on their nuclear facilities by the IAEA, in which they did not have much say. However the NPT review conferences provided them a forum of participation to express their grievances.

First Review Conference, 1975

Article 8 (3) of the NPT makes specific provisions for a conference of the NPT parties to be held every five years.[40] The First Review Conference was held in 1975. It was marked by a heated debate, how well the treaty goals were being implemented.[41] The group of non-nuclear weapon states complained that nuclear powers have not complied with Article VI, which requires them to pursue negotiations to end the nuclear arms race and work towards nuclear disarmament. For the non-nuclear weapon states in question, the lack of movement towards these goals is tantamount to a breach of contract.[42]

Second Review Conference, 1980

The Second Review Conference of the NPT in 1980 centred principally on Article VI dealing with nuclear arms limitation and disarmament and to a lesser extent, Article IV, which dealt with peaceful nuclear cooperation. Debate at the Second Review Conference in 1980 was difficult and contentious. This debate centred principally on Article VI and therefore became deadlocked and eventually concluded without producing a consensus in the final document. There were differences agreement between group of 77 and the nuclear weapon states over the issue of lack of progress in nuclear disarmament.[43]

Third Review Conference 1985

The Third Review Conference of the NPT met in Geneva on 21 September 1985. There was article-by-article review of the operation of the treaty. Despite the call of developing nations for greater efforts to grant access to the nuclear material and technology, there was a general acknowledgement that an appreciable level of technical assistance in the area of peaceful uses had been provided both bilaterally and multilaterally. The Third Review Conference took place in the background of continuous political underpinnings of the IAEA/NPT Regime. There was a broad criticism of the nuclear weapon states for the lack of progress on nuclear disarmament. The Third Review Conference noted the destructive potentials of nuclear arsenals of nuclear weapon parties were undergoing continuous development.[44]

Fourth Review Conference, 1990

The Fourth Review Conference began from August 20, 1990. It examined the ways to strengthen the Non-Proliferation Regime and the implementation of the NPT.[45] The question of a Comprehensive Test Ban Treaty was one of the main issues in the discussion at the conference. The United States however opposed the linking of the NPT prospects with the conclusion of the CTBT.[46] Consensus was also achieved on such issues as negative security assurances and positive security assurances, prohibition of attacks on nuclear facilities, cooperation in the peaceful uses of nuclear energy and on nuclear safety. A very important result of the conference was a strong commitment by a clear majority of extending the life of the NPT in 1995.

Fifth Review Conference, 1995

The Fifth Review Conference of NPT, which was held at New York in 1995 in accordance with Article 10.2, had the dual task for of reviewing the treaty and deciding upon its extension. At this conference, on 1 May 1995 the 174 state party to NPT adopted a decision to extend the NPT indefinitely as part of a politically binding package of three decisions, firstly strengthening the review process, secondly principles and objective for Nuclear Non-Proliferation, thirdly the indefinite extension of the NPT.[47]

During the May 1995 NPT Review Conference the non-aligned countries took a tough line on the Nuclear Non-Proliferation Treaty, demanding a strong review mechanism in exchange for their support for indefinite extension. There were three proposals regarding the extension of the treaty. The Canadian proposal backed by 103 countries supported indefinite extension. A group of seven non-aligned states—Indonesia, Egypt, Iran, Iraq, Nigeria, Myanmar and Malaysia supported 25 years rolling extension.[48] The Mexican proposal made three points, it asked for a Comprehensive Test Ban Treaty, no later than 1996; negotiation on a fissile material production cut off, including possible consideration of nuclear stockpile and negotiations and binding international arrangements on security assurances by nuclear weapon states.[49]

As the world prepared for the NPT extension, developing nations expected that talks about the future of the treaty would also be about global nuclear disarmament. But these hopes were dashed when Jayantha Dhanpala, the President of the conference announced the nuclear Non-Proliferation Treaty had become permanent with no legally binding commitment from nuclear powers to get rid of their nuclear weapons. The conference ended in a great triumph for the US and other nuclear powers but a total defeat for the prospect of ending the age of atomic weapons.[50] Some nations like Indonesia, Iran, Egypt or North Korea did not vote for indefinite extension.[51]

The 1995 Review Extension Conference showed considerable division and acrimony between the nuclear weapon states and the non-nuclear weapon states. Many non-aligned states felt cheated by the nuclear weapon states that were not building there specifically on the issue of disarmament. The primary resistance to extending the treaty on 1995 came from non-aligned nations. The non-aligned countries could ultimately muster only 11 countries to sponsor its resolution for a 25 years rolling extension.[52] The primary resistance to extending the treaty in 1995 came from nations which complained about the failure of five nuclear powers to satisfy their obligations under Article VI of the treaty. The absolute failure of nuclear weapon states to meet this commitment is evident.[53]

The 1995 Review and Extension Conference was a major success for the west. The NPT was extended indefinitely. The division on principles and objectives for Non-Proliferation and disarmament and strengthening the review process was made. After the indefinite extension, the weapon powers manoeuvred to designate three meetings mandated by the 1995 conference as preparatory meetings so as not to make any substantive review of the progress made on the implementation of the treaty. The three Preparatory Committees held in the intervening periods between 1995 and 2000 failed to prepare an agreed agenda and discussions became progressively more acrimonious.

On December 10, 1996, the UN General Assembly adopted the dates of April 7-18, 1997 for the first session of the Preparatory Committee at UN headquarters in New York.[54] It headed for a major confrontation between nuclear weapon states and non-nuclear weapon states on both procedural and substantive issues.

While the 1997 Preparatory Committee managed to agree in a report including a Chairman's working paper. The 1998 Preparatory Committee fell apart over disagreement on several crucial issues. This Preparatory Committee failed in part because the nuclear weapon states did not want a substantive discussion on nuclear disarmament or to provide an opportunity to the non-nuclear weapons states to call into account the implementation of Article VI.

The 1999 Preparatory Committee denounced the two rounds of nuclear detonations conducted by India in mid-May and retaliatory test by Pakistan. In the third Preparatory Committee of May 1999, the nuclear powers barring China gave a period of updated fact sheets of figures in the cuts and measures taken as part of fulfillment of obligations under Article VI of the treaty. China, on the other hand also retreated its doctrine of no first use and restraint in building up its arsenals without revealing any detail of the state of its nuclear forces and commitment on reduction. The two signatories North Korea and Iraq violated the norms of the NPT though each was given a different treatment. The NPT thus served as a cover for its signatories to pursue clandestine nuclear programme.[55]

The Preparatory Committee agreed to a number of procedural issues for example the Review Conference will be held in New York from 24 April to 19 May 2000 with Jacob Seleli of South Africa as its President and the failure was due to the basic difference cast between nuclear powers and non-nuclear parties to the NPT.[56]

2000 Review Conference

The 6th Review Conference of the parties to the treaty of the NPT took place at the UN from 24 April to 19 May 2000. The 2000 Review Conference was the first time since 1985 that the states party to the treaty were able to agree on a final document, reviewing the implementation of the treaty. This conference focussed on practical steps for systematic and progressive efforts to implement Article VI of the NPT and paragraphs 3 and 4 (a) of the 1995 decision on principles and objectives of Nuclear Non-Proliferation and disarmament. These were projecting as the 13 steps for disarmament.

13 Steps for Disarmament

1. Entry into force of the Comprehensive Test Ban Treaty.
2. Moratorium on nuclear test explosion.
3. Negotiation to be conducted in the conference on disarmament within 5 years on fissile ban treaty.
4. Establishing subsidiary body to deal with nuclear disarmament.
5. The principle to apply nuclear disarmament.
6. Unequivocal undertaking by nuclear weapon states to accomplish total elimination of their nuclear arsenal.
7. Full implementation to START II, conclusion of START III, preserving and strengthening of the ABM treaty.
8. Implementing trilateral initiative between United States of America, Russia and the IAEA.
9. Steps by non-nuclear weapon states based on the principle

of undiminished security for all to promote international stability.
10. Nuclear weapon states to place excess fissile material under the International Atomic Energy Agency.
11. Reformation of general and complete disarmament under effective international control.
12. Regular reports of the implementation of Article VI para 4 (c) of the 1995 decision.
13. Development of verification capabilities to assure compliance with disarmament agreement.[57]

In providing security benefits for universality the conference urged all states not party to the treaty at that time, namely, Cuba, India, Israel and Pakistan to accede to it without delay. There was concern over India's and Pakistan's 1998 nuclear tests, violations by Iraq and North Korea and criticism by Arab States of Israel's unsafeguarded nuclear programme.[58] While Pakistan had attended all the previous Review Conferences of the treaty as an observer, it did not attend the Sixth Review Conference because of changed nuclear realities in South Asia.[59]

The first session of the Preparatory Committee was at United Nations in New York on April 8-19, 2000, under the Chairmanship of Ambassador Henrik Salander of Sweden in which 137 parties attended. The 1st session of the Preparatory Committee for 2005 Review Conference on NPT ended midway when the US declined to report on the implementation of disarmament provisions of Article VI.[60] The leaked "nuclear posture review" by the USA indicated an even greater diversion from the NPT commitment, the use of nuclear weapons as contemplated against savage non-nuclear weapon states. Mr. Salander threatened to adjourn in the session because of difference of opinion. The Preparatory Committee did succeed in outlining the struggle that would ensure to make nuclear weapon state more accountable. The specific matters were addressed in the 13 steps that were agreed to at the 2000 Review Conference.[61]

The NPT Preparatory Committee in New York concluded on April 19, 2002 after adopting the document containing arrangements for organising future Preparatory Committees at Geneva in 2003 and at New York in 2004 and the next Review Conference in New York 2005. A number of issues were discussed such as implementation the nuclear disarmament commitments in the treaty, the nuclear programmes of India, Pakistan, Israel and associated regional security concerns and lack of compliance by Iraq and North Korea. Iraq expressed "extreme reservation about the paragraph addressing its non-compliance with the NPT".[62] It was recalled that both the 1995 NPT Review and Extension Conference and the 2000 NPT Review Conference scored the importance of security assurances. It was emphasised that negative security assurance was a key basis of the 1995 extension decision and remained essential.[63]

The proliferation concerns dominated the Preparatory Committee proceedings for the 2000 NPT Review Conference with countries highlighting on going problems in Iraq, a new found allegation of an expensive nuclear programme in Iran and North Korea destabilising withdrawal from the treaty.[64]

The Second Preparatory Committee of the treaty on the Non-Proliferation of Nuclear weapons held in Geneva from April 28 and May 9, 2003, and chaired by Ambassador Laszlo Molnar of Hungary can be characterised as a carefully managed meeting that accomplished the adoption of its report, but also as a missed opportunity to address resurgent prolifcration and disarmament challenges collectively.[65] Attended by 106 state parties, the Preparatory Committee was a diplomatic but not necessarily a political success. While the first Preparatory Committee seemed to ponder over widening cracks, the second Preparatory Committee more clearly reflected US priorities in post 9/11 security environment. There was resurgent marginalisation of disarmament. The meeting look place in the shadow of some very serious proliferation challenges. These included North Korea's withdrawal from the NPT on January 10, 2003, the US allegation of clandestine nuclear facilities in Iran, persistent debates in the US about developing new nuclear weapons, with continued threat that the test moratorium would be violated and the Comprehensive Test Ban Treaty ruined. In addition to the US led war on Iraq is viewed by many as a promoter of proliferation due to the dangerous strategy of lumping together the very different threats from nuclear, chemical and biological weapons, showing the power of such capabilities to initiate fear in much better armed governments, and undertaking pre-emptive military action against a non-nuclear weapon adversary. On the other side,

Cuba whose accession to the NPT on November 4, 2002 made it the 188th state party stated reasons for joining in terms of strengthening and consolidation of the United Nations, multilateral and international threats and disarmament.[66] The US focussed on Iran's non-compliance with the treaty. In particular, the state parties to the NPT expressed concern about the North Korea's nuclear weapon programme. North Korea's decision to withdraw from the treaty represented a serious challenge to the global Non-Proliferation Regime. It is hoped that that North Korea's nuclear issue should be resolved peacefully through diplomatic means. State parties welcomed the talks between the US, the North Korea and China held in Beijing from 23 to 25 April, 2003 and hoped that these talks would prove to be an important first step towards the resolution of the North Korean nuclear issue.

The NPT was extended indefinitely on the understanding that member states would agree to forgo acquiring nuclear weapons taking serious steps towards eliminating their nuclear arsenals. This bargain became the 13 steps to disarmament agreed to at the 2000 Review Conference. Yet it is far from happening. There exist strong differences even among states party to the NPT. Mazuri regards the NPT as a system designed to minimise the number of countries that have nuclear weapons capacity and ultimately intended to discourage developing countries from going nuclear and says that it can be regarded "as an extension of the old philosophy of imperialism as a monopoly to inspection". V. C. Trivedi compared the application of safeguard under the NPT to maintain law and order in a society by placing all its law abiding citizens in custody while leaving its law breaking elements free to roam in the streets.[67]

As the Non-Proliferation Regime has grown in strength the number of nations of proliferation concern has multiplied. North Korea's commitment to Non-Proliferation Treaty has been less than complete. Its withdrawal from the NPT and its refusal to allow further inspections raise serious doubts about the peaceful nature of its nuclear programme.[68] Much of Iraq's nuclear infrastructure was destroyed during the Gulf War yet it remained state of proliferation concern. The primitive attack on Iraq finally could not produce any evidence of existence of weapons of mass destruction. India and Pakistan have crossed the nuclear rubicon but do not find any space to be recognised as nuclear weapon powers on the NPT.

India is critical of the US and the other nuclear powers for denying the rights of non-nuclear nations to acquire weapons without giving up their own. Some nations like North Korea have refused to rule out their nuclear option.[69]

NPT Fails to Bring About Global Disarmament

The NPT failed to bring about global nuclear disarmament. The five nuclear weapon states were reluctant to make any meaningful commitment to nuclear disarmament. Although the regime may have made some contribution to global security it is far from ideal. But at the same time the alleged violation of the treaty by Iraq (1991) and North Korea (1993) were met with harsh international response. However there was an element of hypocrisy in the continued imposition of the NPT on these states while the nuclear states have also failed in a scheme to honour their side of the agreement. The bitter reality is the failure of the NPT is multifaced. The NPT has not been able to prevent for the proliferation of nuclear weapons to additional states. The NPT entered into force in 1970 and for most of its history, the nuclear weapons states ignored the commitment to nuclear disarmament. Most non-nuclear states have expressed frustration at the slow pace of disarmament. The three Preparatory Committees in 1997, 1998 and 1999 undertook substantative debate on definitive issues but could not arrive at a consensus.

A careful review of the developments since NPT 2000, indicates the lack of implementation of items approved by the conference especially phase related to Article VI of the treaty known as 13 steps.

The Ministers of the non-aligned states at their meeting in Durban, on April 2002, expressed serious concern that the development of new types of nuclear weapons are being considered and the provision for the use or threat of use of nuclear weapons against non-nuclear weapon states in contravention of the negative security concerns that had been provided by nuclear weapon states.[70]

The proposed use of nuclear weapons against nations that do not possess them is a grave matter. Since 1978 the US has tried to reassure the world that it would not launch nuclear weapons against a non-nuclear weapon nations. The point of this declaration was to encourage the non-nuclear nations to sign and abide by the NPT. The US would have a difficult time pressing other nations to forge nuclear weapons if it reserved the right to blast countries with its own nuclear arsenal. India is critical of the US and other nuclear powers for denying the right to non-nuclear nations to acquire the weapon without giving up their own.

North Korea has undertaken a gradual but determined development of a nuclear programme. By using its present reactors to separate Plutonium production it would produce one or two bombs. New nuclear states are not likely to allow IAEA inspectors access to anything like the freedom enjoyed by the UN in Iraq. North Korea's announcement that it intended to withdraw from the NPT is a consequence of its dissatisfaction with the treaty functioning and its failure to address it immediate security concerns.

NPT—A Discriminatory Treaty

The NPT was an inherently discriminatory treaty imposing different sets of rights and obligations between nuclear weapon states and non-nuclear weapon states. The NPT codified an uneasy bargain among non-nuclear weapon states party to the treaty and the five nuclear weapon states. The essence of this bargain was that if non-nuclear weapons states forgo nuclear weapons they would be assisted in exploiting the peaceful benefits of nuclear technology. The unbalanced obligation of non-nuclear weapon states placed them at a permanent military disadvantage and made them more vulnerable to nuclear intimidation.

The NPT established system of nuclear apartheid by dividing the nations of the world into "nuclear haves" and "have nots". Developing nations expressed inherent distastefulness with the existence of a nuclear club, which by definition was seen as a discriminatory group.

The NPT was discriminatory against non-nuclear weapon states as is evident in Article III. Which specified that only non-nuclear weapons states would subject themselves to IAEA safeguards.

The main concern of the developing nations is that the five nuclear weapon states have not honoured their legal obligations enshrined in Article VI of the treaty dealing with complete disarmament and Article I relating to non-transfer of nuclear technology. China's continued event nuclear assistance to Pakistan has made a mockery of Article I of the NPT. At the 2002 Preparatory Committee the United States announced that it only generally agrees with the conclusion of the 2000 NPT Review Conference and no longer supports some of the Article VI conclusions in the final document from the 2000 NPT Review Conference.[71] It shows the hypocritical attitude of the Nuclear Weapon States who are pursuing their own national interests and neglecting the security concerns of the developing nations.

The Assessment of the NPT requires a developing nations dimension and depends upon the question of equality. It looses its relevance without it since the entire world order is based on unequal tenets and the NPT regime is a part of it. The logic of inequality cannot be sustained without a developing nations dimensions.[72] The west is very critical of developing nations acquiring nuclear weapons. Deputy Secretary of states Richard Armitage accused North Korea of starving its people at the same time pursuing a nuclear weapons.[73] Nuclear weapons are increasingly seen in North Korea as instruments to resist US imperialism and aggressiveness.

There are two distinct views that have dominated the Non-Proliferation discourse in international relations. First, there is the West Centric approach premised on the discriminatory principle of distinguishing between horizontal and vertical proliferation as exemplified by the Non-Proliferation Treaty. Second is the non-western perspective to the NPT premised on rational national security concerns of the developing nations which also is focus are universal disarmament. This thesis would deal with the developing nations perspectives on the NPT. This thesis would look into the specificities of approaches of four nations India, Pakistan, North Korea and Iraq towards the NPT. These nations have their own rationalisations for acquiring nuclear weapons, arising out of their security considerations that shape their approaches to the NPT.

NPT and the Security of Developing Nations

The NPT does not serve the security concerns of developing nations like India, Pakistan, North Korea and Iraq. The presence of a nuclear neighbour is a powerful incentive to develop nuclear weapons. This is evident in the case of South Asia where the China—India—Pakistan equation exists. The case studies of India, Pakistan and North Korea clearly illustrate that measures taken to stop attempts at nuclear proliferation could not yield the expected results. The NPT is a treaty that has generated conflicting opinions and contradictions between different states. The similarities and dissimilarities need to be probed in these groups in the context of the treaty. Their security concerns have shaped their approach to the NPT. North Korea and Iraq belong to a separate category of states, commonly known in US terminology as "Rouge States". Both have been direct victims of US hegemonic ambitions North Korea and Iraq had joined the Treaty due to their compulsions and soon expressed dissatisfaction with the treaty's functioning. India and Pakistan belong to a different category of states that had not signed the NPT and were in the forefront of the developing nations who had crossed the nuclear Rubicon in defiance of the treaty. Developing nations have reason to believe that the nuclear powers hardly understand or care about their security problems. The tensions of the developing nations have multiplied in the post Cold.War period as the US is making diplomatic efforts to organise the international community to contain the nuclear programme of new nuclear weapon states.[74]

To sum up, the NPT, which was concluded on 1968 and entered into force in 1970, established an international framework for preventing the proliferation of nuclear weapons. It's membership stood at 188. The five nations, namely, US, USSR, UK, China and France were allowed to retain a stockpile of weapons in order to maintain "global" security. It is seen that the permanent extension of the NPT makes disarmament an illusory goal. The NPT may be considered as a valuable arms control agreement in the developed world, but is perceived in the developing world as a treaty ridden with inherent contradictions. An assessment of the Article II and Article III of the NPT clearly illustrated the discriminatory features of the NPT especially in reference to the developing countries. The indefinite extension of the treaty has endorsed the possession of nuclear weapons exclusively in the hands of five nuclear weapon powers. An analysis of the review conferences revealed the overriding gap between nuclear weapon states and non-nuclear weapons states on the issues of horizontal and vertical non-proliferation. Further, to tighten their hold, the developed nations have evolved stringent export control mechanisms through the Zangger Committee, London Club of Suppliers, and Wassenar Arrangement to control the diffusion of nuclear technology to developing nations. It was argued that the developing nations oppose the western desire to keep the developing world both insecure and underdeveloped through their policies of coercive diplomacy and technology denial. The newly nuclear empowered nations like India, Pakistan, have strong reservations against the NPT. Although the NPT became effective in 1970 some countries that remain outside the treaty (including Israel that has not been dealt with in the study), have become *defacto* nuclear countries. Without the entry of these countries the NPT will remain an incomplete treaty. Therefore it is pertinent to examine the geo-strategic compulsion of these countries, which have shaped their perceptions towards the NPT.

NOTES

1. Manpreet, Sethi, "Post-Cold War Nuclear Proliferation, Patterns and Possibilities", *Asian Strategic Review,* (New Delhi: Institute for Defence Studies and Analysis, 1997-98), p. 199.
2. D. R. Sardesai, Raju, G.C., Thomas, *Nuclear India in the Twenty First Century,* (England: Palgrave, Macmillan, 2002), p. 121.
3. Caroline, Thomas, *In Search of Security the Third World in International Relations,* (Britain: Wheat Sheaf Books Ltd., 1987), p. 121.
4. Ashok, Kapur, "Dump the Treaty", *The Bulletin of Atomic Scientist,* Vol. 46, No. 7, (The Educational Foundation of Nuclear Science, Chicago August 1990.) < http://www.bulletin.org/issues/1990/ja90 /ja90kapur. html>
5. Jayantha, Dhanpala, "Disappointment in the Third World", *The Bulletin of Atomic Scientist,* Vol. 46, (The Educational Foundation of Nuclear Science, January 1990) <http://www.thebulletin.org/ issue/ 1990/ja 90 dhanpala.html>.
6. "Preventing Nuclear Weapons Proliferation, An Approach to the Non-Proliferation Treaty Review Conference", *SIPRI Publications,* 1975, p. 24.

7. T. T. Poulose, *Nuclear Proliferation and the Third World,* (ABC Publishing House, 1982), p. 3.
8. Uttara, Sahaserabddhè, India's Nuclear Policy, Usha, Thappar, Mangesh, Kulkarni (Ed.), *India in World Affairs Towards the 21st Century* (Mumbai: Himalaya Publishing House,1999), p. 276.
9. Charles, Krauthahmer, "The Unipolar Moment", *Foreign Affairs,* Vol. 7, No. 1, 1991, p. 30.
10. Joseph, Rotblat, The 50th Anniversary of Hiroshima in Joseph, Rotblat, Michiji, Konuma, *Towards a Nuclear Weapon Free World,* (Singapore: World Scientific Co. Pvt. Ltd., 1997), p. 105.
11. George, Rathjens, Rethinking Nuclear Proliferation, Brad, Roberts (Ed.), *Weapons Proliferation in the 1990s,* (Cambridge: MIIT Press, 1995) Uttara, Sahaserabddhe, India's Nuclear Policy, Usha Thappar, Mangesh Kulkarni ed, *India in World Affairs Towards the 21st Century,* (Mumbai: Himalaya Publishing House 1999), p. 276.
12. Henry, D. Sokolski, *Best of Intentions America's Campaign Against Strategic Weapons Proliferation,* (USA: Prager Publishers, 2000), p. 15.
13. Martin, Zuberi, "Operational Crossroads"; Meeting the Bomb at Close Quarters, *Strategic Analysis,* IDSA, Vol. 22, No. 11, February 1999, p. 1667.
14. Martin, Zuberi, "Stalin and the Bomb", *Strategic Analysis,* IDSA, Vol. 23, No. 7, October 1999, pp. 1145-1146.
15. Treaty on Non-Proliferation of Nuclear Weapons, Department of State, USA <http://www.state govt./www/gloal/arms treats/npt.html>.
16. R. Imai, and R. Press, *Nuclear Non-Proliferation Failures and Prospects,* (New York and London: International Consultative Group on Nuclear Energy, 1980), p. 3.
17. Bertrand, Gold, Schmidt, *The Atomic Complex, A World Wide Political History of Nuclear Energy,* (La Grange Park III: American Nuclear Society, 1980), pp. 250-25.
18. Treaty of NPT, *History Monterey Institute of International Studies,* <http://cnsohl.miis.edu/npt/npt_3/history.htm>.
19. Dr. Savita, Pande, *The Future of the NPT,* (New Delhi: Lancer Publication, 1995), p. 6.
20. "Further Dissemination of Nuclear Weapons, 1958", US Department of State, *Documents of Disarmament,* 1945-59, Vol. 2, pp. 1185-1186.
21. UN General Assembly Resolution, 1576 (XV), 20 December 1960.
22. Bhalchandra, Udgoankar, "Beyond Non-Proliferation", MP Fry NP Keatinge, J. Rotblat, *Nuclear Non-Proliferation and the Non-Proliferation Treaty,* (New York: Springer-Verlag Berlin, Heidelberg, 1990), p. 174.
23. David, Fischer, *Towards 1995, The Prospects for Ending the Proliferation of Nuclear Weapons,* United Nations Institute for Darmouth Research, Darmouth Publishing Company Ltd. 1993, p. 24.

24. Bhalchandra, Udgoankar, *Op cit.*, p. 169.
25. "Indefinite Extension of the Treaty, Risks and Reckoning", *Acronym Report*, September 1995 <http://www.acronym.org.uk/acrorep/acro7. htm>
26. Nuclear Non-Proliferation Treaty, <www.fas.org/nuke/control/npt/-7k>.
27. William, Epstein, "Indefinite Extension with Increased Accountability", *The Bulletin of Atomic Scientist*, (Chicago, The Educational Foundation of Nuclear Science, January1995), <http://www.thebulletin. orgl/issues/ 1995/ja95/ja95.npt.html>
28. Jayantha, Dhanpala, "The NPT-Yesterday, Today and Tomorrow", UN, New York, <http://disarmament.UN.org/speech/29 April 2003.htm>
29. "Signatories and Parties to the Treaty on Non-Proliferation of Nuclear Weapons", *US Arms Control and Disarmament Agency Fact Sheet*, October 14, 1994, <http://www.iaea.org/world atom/documents legal/ npt status.html>.
30. *Ibid.*
31. Munir, Ahmad, Khan, Towards a Universal Framework of Nuclear Restraint, in Joseph, F. Pilat and Robert, E. Pendley, *1995 A New Beginning for the NPT;* (New York: Plenum Press, 1995), p. 33.
32. Know Your Nuclear Tests World Wide, 1945-1998, *The Bulletin of Atomic Scientist*, Vol. 54, No. 6, November/December 1998.
33. Robert, S. Norris, Bill, Arkin, "Know You Nuclear Test World Wide" 1945-1955, *The Bulletin of Atomic Scientist*, Vol. 52, No. 3, May-June 1996.
34. China Acts on Non-Proliferation Pact, *International Herald Tribune*, 30 December 1991, p. 2.
35. Treaty on Non-Proliferation of Nuclear Weapons, Department of Disarmament Affairs, United Nations 2000, <http://disarmanent.un.org. 8080/wmd/npt/npt text.html>.
36. Gary, T. Garner, *Nuclear Non-Proliferation A Primer*, (London: Lynne Reinner Publishers, 1994), pp. 89-90.
37. R. Timerbaev, A Major Milestone in Controlling Nuclear Exports, *Eye on Supply*, p. 8.
38. David, B. Dewitt, *Op cit.*, p. 83.
39. Douglas, Jehl, US seeking UN Pressure to Compel North Korea to Honour the Treaty, *New York Times*, March 13, 1993, p. 3.
40. See Provisions of the NPT.
41. David, B. Dewitt, *Op cit.*, p. 16.
42. Garry, T. Garner, *Op cit.*, pp. 89-90.
43. Emily Bailey, Richard Guthrie, Darryle Howlett, John Simpson, *The Evolution of the Nuclear Non-Proliferation Regime* (UK: Mountbatten Centre for International Studies, 1990).

44. *Ibid.*
45. Brad, Gordon, Prospect for Further NPT Review Conference Called Good, *Testimony Before The House Foreign Affairs Subcommittee,* <http: www.fas.org/nuke/control/npt/news/9007/2-147084/18k.htm>
46. David, Fischer, Harald, Muller, "The Fourth Review of the NPT", *SIPRI Year Book,* 1991, No. 31, p. 560.
47. Fawzi, Hammad, "Taming the Trigger Happy", *Al Ahram Weekly,* Issue No. 481, Cairo, 11-17 May 2000.
48. Nirmal, Mitra, "NAM Countries Take a Tough Stand on NPT", *Hindustan Times,* May 6, 1995.
49. *Ibid.*
50. C. Raja, Mohan, "The Bully has its Way", *The Hindu,* May 14, 1995, p. 10.
51. Sujit, Datta, "Perpetuating of the Divide", *The Pioneer,* May 17, 1995.
52. *Document NPT/CONF 1995/L. 4* (May 10, 1995).
53. Eugene Carroll, The NPT Review Test Chance, *The Defence Monitor,* Vol. XXIX, No. 3, (Centre for Defence Information, 2000).
54. Tariq, Rauf, "View Point, Preparing for April 1997 NPT Prep.Com", *The Non-Proliferation Review,* Winter 1997, <http//cns/miis.edu/ pubs/npr/ vol 104/42/ rauf 42 pdlf>.
55. Neil, Joeck, *Strategic Consequences of Nuclear Proliferation in South Asia,* (London: Frank Cass and Company Limited, 1986), p. 9.
56. Mitchell, Reiss, Arms Control Failure in Francine Frankel (Ed.), *Bridging The Non-Proliferation Divide, The US and India,* (Delhi: Centre for Advanced Studies, Konark Publishers, 1995).
57. Senator Doughlas, Roche, *Status of Implementation of 13 Steps and Nuclear Disarmament,* <http://www/reachingcriticalwill.org/npt/ ngo res/Roche 13 pts.htm>.
58. Historical Consensus, *Fact Sheet,* Released by the Bureau of Proliferation, US Department of State, Washington DC, July 1, 2000.
59. Abdul, Sattar's, *Pakistan Foreign Minister Statement* on the 6th Review Conference of the NPT held in New York from 24 April to 20 May 2000.
60. Widening Gulf evident at the first Preparatory Committee, *Disarmament Times,* Vol. XXV No. 2, <http://disarm.igc.org/dt 2002.2pdf, pp. 1-2.
61. *Ibid.*
62. Rebecca, Johnson, Low key NPT Meetings Mark Deep Disagreements Over Treaty Implementation Especially on Nuclear Disarmament, *NPT Prep-Committee,* April 8-19, 2002.
63. *Ibid.*
64. Christine, Kucia, NPT Meeting Controls New Nuclear Threat, *Arms Control Today,* Arms Control Association, June 2003, <http:// www.arms control.org/oct/2003-06/npt-June03 asp?>.

65. Rebecca, Johnson, Rouges and Rhetoric, The 2003 NPT Preparatory Committee Slides Backward, *Disarmament Diplomacy,* Issue No. 71, June-July 2003, <http://www.acronym.org. UK/dd/dd71/71 npt.htm>.
66. Jorge, Ivan, Mora, Godoy, Permanent Representative of Cuba, General Debate, April 29, 2003, <http: www.npt/conf.2005/DC II/ wp. 10>.
67. T. T. Pouiose, *Op cit.,* p. 87.
68. Gary, T. Gardner, *Op cit.,* p. 105.
69. Randall, Forsberg, William, Driescoll, Gregory, Webb and Thomas, Dean, *Non-Proliferation Primer, Preventing the Spread of Nuclear, Chemical and Biological Weapons,* Cambridge, the MIIT Press, 1995, p. 10.
70. Randall, Forsberg, *Op cit.,* p. 10.
71. See Ambassador Norman, A. Wulf, *Statement the Representative of USA* to the First Session of the Preparatory Committee Meeting in the 2005 NPT, Review Conference of the Parties to the Treaty on Non-Proliferation of Nuclear Weapons, April 8, 2002.
72. D. Shyam, Babu, *Nuclear Non-Proliferation Towards a Universal NPT Regime,* (New Delhi: Konark Publishers, 1992), p. 15.
73. Armitage, North Korea Starving its People for Weapons, *US Department of State,* <http://USinfor.state.govt/regional/ea/e asec/ starting.htm>.
74. Robert, D. Blackwill, Albert, Carnesale, *New Nuclear Nations and Consequences for US Policy,* (New York: Council in Foreign Relations, 1993), p. 32.

2

India and the NPT

India has expressed vociferous protest against the intrinsically discriminatory nature of the Non-Proliferation Treaty, ever since the conclusion of the Non-Proliferation Treaty in 1968. By detonating its nuclear devices, India has operationalized the verbal protest into an international challenge. India is a post-colonial state with a democratic state structure and a strong industrialized base including technological capabilities. There has been a paradigm shift in India's nuclear posture from the time of independence. Earlier India's nuclear programme lacked transparency but today India has come out of the posture of nuclear ambiguity after it's five nuclear tests on 11th May and 13th May 1998.The Nehruvian idealism has been followed by successive governments and therefore India has exercised considerable nuclear restraint. The Indian Government at the time of the test was vocal in highlighting the capability and strength in the context of nuclear weapon's pointing to the deteriorating security environment. This chapter aims to focus attention on the substance of the Non-Proliferation Treaty in the context of India's security. This chapter probes the history of India's concerns over the Chinese and Pakistani threats to its security. It also analyses India's role at the time of the inception of the NPT and examines the historical background of India's nuclear programme. It further deals with India's nuclear doctrine. It is to be noted that Prime Minister Nehru hoped that India would develop atomic power for peaceful uses but warned that, so long as the world was constituted as it was, every country would have to develop and use the latest scientific devices for its protection.[1] Jawaharlal Nehru was a genuine supporter of nuclear disarmament, but at the same time he aspired for a modern India that would develop in science and technology.

Nehru recognised that nuclear weapons capability would enhance India's status and power in a western dominated world.[2] Nehru saw nuclear power in its peaceful capacity as providing India with the ability to leapfrog many technologies. India could go from dung power to nuclear power in a single step. Nehru said "I think we must develop it for peaceful purpose of course if we are compelled, as a nation to use it for other purposes possibly no pious sentiment of any of us will stop nation from using it that way."[3] Under Nehru Government of India projected an image that it was devoted to high principles and the cause of global nuclear disarmament. At the same time Indian scientists were given a free hand to develop scientific agenda in the approach formulated by Dr. Homi Bhabha and Dr. Sarabhai. Indian nuclear programme is a paradox to many. India is a strong advocate of genuine nuclear disarmament, at the same time it has opted for nuclear weapons for it's security reasons.

India's Position at the Time of NPT's Inception

However India refuses to be a signatory to the Non-Proliferation Treaty. India was an active member of United Nations 18 nation disarmament committee, which negotiated nuclear and conventional disarmament before the superpowers began the bilateral arms control process. The proposals that India made at that time included a standstill agreement on nuclear testing and a non-discriminatory Non-Proliferation Treaty. India signed the partial test ban Treaty in 1963 in the hope that the treaty would lead to universal disarmament. India took further initiative in the United Nations to place the item of Non-Proliferation of nuclear weapons on the agenda of the United Nations. In 1965 India and along with several other countries submitted a joint memorandum towards achieving a solution to the problem of proliferation. The memorandum called for negotiation of an international treaty based amongst others, on the following principles:

- The Treaty should be devoid of any loopholes, which might permit any nuclear, non-nuclear nation to proliferate directly, or indirectly nuclear weapons in any form.
- The Treaty should embody an acceptable balance of

mutual responsibilities and obligations on nuclear and non-nuclear powers.

- The Treaty should be a step towards the achievement of general and complete disarmament and more particularly nuclear disarmament.[4]

The principles constituted the basis of the Resolution 2028 (XX) adopted in November 19, 1965 by the United Nation General Assembly with an overwhelming majority, which included UK, USA and Soviet Union.

Unfortunately instead of working on the basis of these agreed principles the present Non-Proliferation Treaty devoid of these principles was sponsored in 1968. India believed that the treaty was seriously flawed and did not really aim to bring about Non-Proliferation of Nuclear weapons. India therefore did not accede to the Treaty and continues with this position till date. There were specific articles, which were objected to by India in the Non-Proliferation Treaty for significant reasons. These were:

Article I: Prohibits the transfer of nuclear weapons or other nuclear explosives to any state whether a state is party to the treaty or not, whether a nuclear weapon state or not, directly or indirectly through an alliance.

Article II: Prohibits non-nuclear weapon signatories from manufacturing or otherwise acquiring nuclear weapons or devices including Peaceful Nuclear Explosives.

Article III: Obligates non-nuclear weapon parties to accept international safeguards as specified in a special arrangement with the International Atomic Energy Agency.

Article IV: States that all parties to the treaty have a right to full exploitation of the use of nuclear energy for peaceful purposes and obligates these parties to cooperate with other countries in developing nuclear technology.[5]

Article V: Obligates the nuclear weapon parties to make available nuclear explosives for peaceful purposes for to non-nuclear weapon parties under international supervision or as low as possible excluding any charges for research and development costs.

Explaining India's stand, the Indian Ambassador Azim Hussain made the following statement at the 1567th meeting of the first committee of the United Nations on May 4, 1968:

- The treaty did not ensure the Non-Proliferation of nuclear weapons but only stopped the dissemination of weapons to non-nuclear weapon states without imposing any restriction on the continued manufacture, stockpiling and sophistication of nuclear weapons by existing nuclear weapon powers.
- The treaty did not do away with the special status of superiority associated with power and prestige confined to these powers, which possessed nuclear weapons.
- The treaty did not provide a balance of obligation and responsibilities between nuclear weapon states and non-nuclear weapon states.
- The treaty did not constitute a step-by-step approach towards nuclear disarmament.
- The treaty did not prohibit one nuclear weapon state from assisting another nuclear weapon state by providing technical aid.
- Article X of the treaty appears to legitimise the present state of affairs and legalise if not encourage an unrestricted vertical proliferation by present nuclear weapon powers.
- Article VI did not create a judicial obligation in regard to cessation of nuclear arms race at an early date. The treaty imputed a false sense of security to the world.

It was discriminatory in regard to safeguards and control, which were all imposed on non-nuclear weapon states, which the nuclear states had not accepted any. The security assurances could not be a quid pro quo for acceptance of the treaty. These safeguards must be obligatory for nuclear weapon states.[6]

In a conference in New York on 27 September 1956 Dr. Homi Bhabha welcomed president Eisenhower's initiative on proposing the formation of the IAEA and said that such an agency should be set up under the aegis of the United Nations. Prime Minister Jawaharlal Nehru, focused on the particular significance of the new proposals to the less developed areas of the world. He said "the use of Atomic Energy for peaceful purposes is far more important for a country like India than it may be for other advanced country.[7]

Threat Perceptions from China

China is India's largest neighbour and a rising major power. India has sought cooperative ties with Beijing since independence. But the relation has been difficult and prone to tension. Clearly much of the source of friction lies in the clash of Asian nationalism and political strategic interest. India had an unhappy relationship with China. Having being defeated by China in 1962, relations were frozen until 1998. China defeated India in the 1962 Himalayan border war. India claimed that China occupied 14,000 km^2 of her territory. China does lay claim to some 90,000 km^2 of Indian Territory in the eastern sector, and occupies parts of the Askai Chin that within the Northern Indian state of Jammu & Kashmir. The more valuable real estate claimed by China in the eastern state of Arunachal Pradesh is already under effective Indian control.[8] The 1964 Chinese test intensified India's nuclear debate which was driven by four considerations, the nature of the threat posed by Chinese nuclear weapons, the availability and implications of external nuclear guarantees vis-à-vis China, the quest of nuclear weaponisation, and the morality of nuclear weapons.[9] The Chinese action nonetheless altered India's immediate strategic environment profoundly.

Andrew Koch says that "China's nuclear and missile outstrip those of India which has neither the nuclear fire power nor the delivery system to pose a serious threat to Indian heartland. The Chinese tests gave India's nuclear establishment the opening it needed to successfully argue for a nuclear weapons programme. China possesses the ability to wreck intolerable devastation on India at all levels of nuclear escalation. If these security considerations are then extrapolated to include ramifications of the Non-Proliferation Treaty India could find itself in a permanent inferior position vis-a-vis China and without credible minimal nuclear deterrent. Such an outcome would prove intolerable for India".[10]

Chinese Capabilities

There is little doubt that Chinese nuclear capabilities are significant.

Beijing already possesses a rudimentary strategic triad consisting of long-range bombers, one nuclear ballistic missile ranging from theatre to intercontinental systems. Chinese Intermediate Range Ballistic Missiles are deployed in Tibet. China has medium range intermediate range intercontinental ballistic missiles deployed on the Tibetan Plateau at Da Qaidam Xiao Qaidan Delingha along the Quinghai Siachin border.[11]

Sino-Pak Axis

India has faced strategic encirclement through nuclear missile collusion between Pakistan and China. There is a fairly strong conviction within India that Pakistan's nuclear build-up and technical know-how is largely of China's making. The Sino-Pakistani connection which has steadily strengthened since early 1980s is seen in the context of Pakistan's relations with China which grew closer as tensions between India and China flared,[12] placing Islamabad at an additional advantage. China has also helped Pakistan to acquire reasonably efficient missile delivery system and weapons that Islamabad desired because of the high degree of assured penetrability, they represented in the face of India's relatively superior air defence framework. This assistance reached high point in 1992. Beijing sold 34 M11 ballistic missiles to Islamabad.[13] China sold ring magnets to help Pakistan run its Uranium purification centrifuges. An American report in mid 1989 pointed out that China had tested a Pakistan bombs at Lop Nor.[14] The continued Chinese nuclear weapon and missile build up and its collaboration with Pakistan in spite of China signing the NPT has seriously undermined India's external security.

The Doctrine of Deterrence

Indeed the doctrine of deterrence continues to captivate strategic thinkers in India. India has asserted that it needs nuclear weapons for self-defence. India will not accept a treaty that creates a division between nuclear haves and have-nots. India believes that it is the sovereign right of every nation to make a judgment regarding its supreme national interests and exercise it's sovereign choice. China has historically exhibited a relatively consistent hard real politic strategic culture. Chinese strategic behaviour exhibits a preference for offensive use of force.

Mediated by a keen sensitivity to relative capabilities, India sees nuclear capability as necessary for dealing with a large nuclear neighbour China that Indians perceive as a source of long-term threat to their national security. China's support to Pakistan in India-Pakistan war of 1965 increased concern about China, which was now actively supporting its enemy. India an original promoter of the nuclear Non-Proliferation Treaty refused to sign the Non-Proliferation Treaty in 1968 and has since opposed Non-Proliferation proposals for South Asia. Brahma Chellaney has argued in terms of the nuclear issue India has always been concerned about China.[15]

The protracted conflict between India and China is unique because it placed India where an extra regional power became a rival state. Beijing is capable of performing computer stimulated tests and posses enough missiles and weapons to destroy India. India has never trusted China in a protracted conflict situation and has tried to redress its military situation since 1962.[16] The Chinese threat to Indian security must remain foremost in the minds of India's security planners. Chinese Inter Continental Ballistic Missiles at Shvng Chenggi could strike any part of India. Nearly 90 IRBM of China are located in Tibet.[17]

India's concern over the Chinese threat has been consistent and was reflected in its stand over the nuclear Non-Proliferation Treaty. India refused to sign the Non-Proliferation Treaty not only because it was discriminatory but also because the Non-Proliferation Treaty and nuclear free zone proposals did not resolve the problem of nuclear threat posed by China.[18] For 34 years after Chinese emergence as a nuclear power, India kept its nuclear capabilities restrained. India curbed weaponisation and searched for a pragmatic way to match its security interests with nuclear Non-Proliferation agenda of major powers. China's increasing activity in the Indian Ocean is a concern to India. Indian coastal guard succeeded in intercepting a Chinese trawler in the Indian Ocean close to Indian coastline. The trawler was installed with modern electronic surveillance equipment.[19]

The Pakistani Threat

The two states India and Pakistan were also locked into bitter and acrimonious relationship dating back to the partition of India and the creation of Pakistan in 1947. India and Pakistan have significant border disputes and have high incidence of terrorist violence.[20] Religious differences, territorial disputes particularly over Kashmir province have added further to the distrust. As two sides have fought wars against each other in 1948, 1965, 1971 and 1999 it is hardly surprising that they should define their national security interests in terms of military prowess with nuclear weapons being seen as the ultimate military insurance policy.[21]

India viewed the partition as unnecessary and tragic, but essentially complete. Pakistan viewed partition as inevitable and necessary but fundamentally incomplete because Kashmir, a Muslim majority state, remained with India.[22] It is widely acknowledged that the Kashmir dispute has been a catalyst of confrontation between the two countries and a scene of friction and conflict for over half a century. The security studies in Pakistan present Kashmir a core as issue and an unresolved problem of the partition of the subcontinent. India has a volatile border with Pakistan and is wresting with a Pakistan sponsored terrorism in Kashmir.[23]

The Chinese Assistance

In 1983 a new dimension was added to the South Asian nuclear scenario that was the evidence of Chinese assistance to Pakistan's bomb programme apart from nuclear programme. It is clear that Pakistan's nuclear programme has relied enormously on China's help and its nuclear weapons have been designed by Chinese nuclear engineers.[24] In 1983 there was Yakub Khan's presence at Lop Nor at a Chinese nuclear test site but in late 1983 came a US intelligence report of the transfer of a complete bomb design and enough Uranium for two implosion devices. The report estimated that the device was meant to produce 20 to 25 kt yields and weighed 400 kg. In mid 1985 the Indian army Chief corroborated the US intelligence report that China was about to conduct nuclear test on behalf of Pakistan. The international press however reported that China had already tested Pakistan's bombs. The information was taken seriously in India and an Indo-Pak agreement not to attack each other's nuclear establishments was concluded.[25]

The Indian Response

The reports of Pakistan acquiring nuclear technology through overt and covert means during 1970s and 1980s were of great concern for India. In March 1978, Indian External Affairs Minister A. B. Vajpayee told the Rajya Sabha that it would be a matter of concern for India if Pakistan's nuclear programme is aimed at purposes other than peaceful. In April 1981 the then Prime Minister, Mrs. Indira Gandhi stated that if Pakistan went nuclear, India would respond in an appropriate way to such a development.[26]

Pakistani nuclear arsenal is India specific and designed to offset India's conventional and nuclear weapon superiority. India swears by the no first-use principle, Pakistan is averse to it.[27] To begin with India's traditional challenger Pakistan is clearly a nuclear weapon power, whatever uncertainties may have existed about Islamabad's nuclear capabilities in the subcontinent and beyond were permanently laid to rest in May 1998.[28] India believes that Pakistan's nuclear arsenals are even more firmly under military control and Pakistan continues with weapons acquisition well beyond its legitimate security interest.

According to K. Subrahmanyam although India tested its nuclear weapons in 1974, its nuclear programme remained dormant until 1988 and was resurrected in the context of Pakistan's nuclear weapons capability.[29] India a dominant power in the South Asian region has been attacked by Pakistan, a conventionally inferior power in the region on four different occasions in 1948, 1965, 1971 and 1999.[30] The overt nuclearisation of India and Pakistan is inseparable from the fierce nuclear rivalry and muscle flexing over assumed technological prowess and claims of military superiority. It is widely believed that Pakistan's nuclear weapons are it's weapons of first strike but India has declared no first use posture.[31] Pakistan's claim of superiority came from the top. In January 1999 Abdul Qadeer Khan, the father of the country's uranium enrichment programme and the Ghauri missile asserted that Pakistani missiles are far superior than what India had.[32]

Historical Background

In 1965 among a small group of non-aligned countries India put forward the idea of an international Non-Proliferation agreement under which the nuclear weapon states would agree to give up their arsenals provided other countries refrained from developing or acquiring such weapons. This balance of rights and obligations was absent in the Non-Proliferation Treaty, which emerged in1968. In the 1960's our security concerns deepened.[33] The more the Non-Proliferation Treaty negotiators met, the more apparent became the differences between India and nuclear weapon powers, on four main issues of concern i.e., for ending further production of nuclear weapons and delivery systems securing commitment to nuclear disarmament, obtaining security guarantees and retaining the right to conduct peaceful nuclear explosion.[34]

By late 1966 the public debate on whether India should move decisively to build nuclear weapons had acclaimed. Major General Som Dutt indicated the strengthening of bonds between Pakistan and China, which intensified India's security concerns. The threats from China emanated from its capacity to stimulate crisis in Nepal, Bhutan and disputed regions in the North-East. Against these potential security challenges India was tempted to develop nuclear weapons.[35]

On March 27, 1967 the Lok Sabha convened a debate on nuclear policy. The Minister of External Affairs M.C. Chagla stated that as a non-aligned nation India was not under any nuclear umbrella. India would not accept a treaty that impeded further development and peaceful uses of nuclear energy. He added that the government would accord security the highest priority in its final consideration of the treaty. In late April 1967, the emergency committee of the Indian cabinet dispatched Prime Minister's secretary L.K. Jha to Moscow, Paris, Washington and London to explore the issues. Two meetings revealed India's desire to escape from hard choices inherent in the Non-Proliferation Treaty.[36] In April 18, 1967 meeting with the Defence Secretary Robert Mac Namara, L.K. Jha cited two obstacles to the signing of the Non-Proliferation Treaty. One is security problem vis-a-vis China and the other was the fact that India had developed nuclear technology, which contributes to Indian confidence and prestige. Sarabhai added that the US and the Soviet Union were not prepared to make nuclear disarmament the next step. And as China's position on NPT of not signing it was very clear. If China would not sign the Non-Proliferation Treaty, India's reluctance to give up the option of building the bomb is quite understandable.

The Lok Sabha debated the Non-Proliferation on 5 April 1968. The then Prime Minister, late Smt. Indira Gandhi assured the house that "we shall be guided entirely by our self enlightenment and considerations of national security."[37] She highlighted the shortcomings of the Non-Proliferation Treaty while re-emphasising the country's commitment to nuclear disarmament. The Governments position to nuclear Non-Proliferation remains unchanged. On the other side of the debate was the view that security issues were involved and the Chinese were supplying nuclear materials as well as missile technology and equipment to Pakistan.

India's security policies are driven by its determination to be recognized as the dominant power in the region, it's increasing obsession with Pakistan's nuclear weapon capability to deliver such weapons deep into India. Nuclear China, to its North is clandestinely helping to create a nuclear Pakistan to the North-East, India's old ally the Soviet Union is in tatters and the US shows little interest in India's security concerns. India's nuclear rationale becomes clear when you add the mix. It is a post-colonial psyche which bears scars and sensitivities born of centuries of subjugation. China must be a factor as a nuclear political rival and India should make its nuclear preparations accordingly. Indians are concerned about Sino-Pakistan nuclear axis and its implications.

Pokharan I

India, the world's largest democracy conducted its first nuclear test in 1974. It was Nehru who approved the plutonium reprocessing capability from where came plutonium, which was used for the 1974 Peaceful Nuclear explosion. It was during Indira Gandhi's tenure that Pokhran I Peaceful Nuclear Explosion took place. India's 1974 detonation of a peaceful nuclear explosion marked a watershed in Indo-American nuclear relations and in US Non-Proliferation policy.[38]

The explosion also shock the international Non-Proliferation regime that had been based on the 1968 nuclear Non-Proliferation Treaty and the IAEA safeguards system. The blast was seen as demonstrating the Regime's abysmal failure to prevent the emergence of new states with nuclear explosive capability.[39] The shock wave also led to a virtual trade embargo against India and provided a major impetus to the US to review its contractual fuel supply obligations under the 1963 Indo-US nuclear cooperation agreement.

India then displayed public contempt for Non-Proliferation Treaty. It viewed it as a system of "atomic colonialism" and its open defiance of the treaty by conducting a nuclear test may have helped to diminish legitimacy of the treaty and to make more respectable further acts of defiance of the treaty.[40] Indira Gandhi's decision to explode a nuclear device reflected overwhelming public opinion in the country to defy the NPT because the nuclear weapon powers had urgently flouted Article VI, which compelled the nuclear weapon states to achieve disarmament at an early date.[41]

The US Response

The United States, as the conductor of the global Non-Proliferation orchestra, took Pokhran I as a challenge to the established nuclear order and began concerted efforts to reshape the Non-Proliferation regime and tighter technology controls. The United States unilaterally changed the objectives of safeguards. Not only nuclear weapons but even enrichment and reprocessing facilities were prohibited to non-nuclear states. And the objective of safeguards was no longer detection and diversion of nuclear material from peaceful to military pursuits, but prevention of nuclear explosive capability from peaceful to military pursuits but prevention of "nuclear explosive capability".[42]

The Post Pokhran Indian Posture

India's refusal to sign the NPT and the detonation of a peaceful nuclear device aptly reflected its determination not to overlook its security needs and not to become a party to any discriminatory arrangement which is designed to give it to a second class status and a dependent position.[43] India's position on the NPT is that, it is a discriminatory and a flawed treaty. India continues to be guided by the imperative of India's strategic autonomy and the need to maintain a credible minimum nuclear deterrent.[44]

China's possession of nuclear weapons has acted as a determined catalyst for India to use nuclear technology as a complementary source to produce energy for its domestic needs.

China had provoked India to build its nuclear capability, and conduct tests in 1974 so that it does not lag behind its powerful neighbour.[45] India has replaced its old rhetoric against the NPT with a more sophisticated position that called for India's own security interests in return for opposing global Non-Proliferation rules. A major objective of the new US was psychological denuclearisation, that is to dissipate the growing sentiment that saw nuclear power as salvation for resource starved nations.[46] India's public contempt for the NPT, viewing it as a system of "atomic colonialism".[47] and its open defiance of the treaty by conducting a nuclear test may have helped to diminish legitimacy of the treaty and to make more respectable further acts of defiance by itself and others.

Pokhran II

In May 1998 US Non-Proliferation efforts suffered a setback. On 11 May and 13 May, India denoted five nuclear devices. Its bitter rival Pakistan conducted its nuclear tests on 28 May, 1998.[48] The government said that the nuclear environment in India's neighbourhood had necessitated the test to provide a "reassurance to the people of India that their national security interests are paramount." In letter to president Clinton dated May 11, Vajpayee stated that the threat from China motivated the tests "we have an overt nuclear state on our borders." A state, which has committed armed aggression against India in 1962.[49] Meanwhile, in the aftermath of the 'proliferation trauma' inflicted by India's Peaceful Nuclear Explosions a London club of key nuclear supplies nations has been established with a three-fold purposes:

- To prevent the export of sensitive technologies in reprocessing and Uranium enrichment.
- To evolve a system of strict safeguard, physical protection standards.
- To master proliferation related activity.

On May 11, India conducted three simultaneous tests at the Pokhran test range; a desert site located about 350 miles South West of Delhi. Each shot was said to be in its own shaft. The test site, was built, in early 1980's. However, a series of Indian governments had decided not to conduct tests despite growing pressures from leaders of nuclear weapon establishment.[50] In late 1995 US intelligence agencies detected preparation for a test that led the US government to confront the Narsimha Rao led Indian government. Rao cancelled the planned tests. Finally Vajpayee government organized the test, which surprised the entire world scientists. The May 17, Indian press conference he stated that the three tests were a fission device with a yield of 12 kilotons, a thermonuclear device with a yield of 43 kilotons and a third device of less than one kilotons. India conducted two more tests on May 13 with yields between 0.2 and 0.6 kilotons.[51]

Considerations of national security were important factors in the decision to undertake the nuclear tests. According to Abdul Kalam 'when nuclear technology and defence technology met, they get transformed into nuclear weapons technology. This is what the nation witnessed on May 11 and May 13. India said the test provided "critical data for validation of our capability in the design of nuclear weapons of different yields for different application and different delivery systems". P. K. Iyengar, former chairman of AEC and a key player in the development of the 1974 device, said in an interview that the test showed that India had three categories of nuclear weapons, designing a low yield tactical weapon, a full size fission weapon and a thermo nuclear weapon.[52]

India's nuclear test gave a blow to the Non-Proliferation regime. The Non-Proliferation Treaty gave legitimacy to five nuclear weapons states to stay nuclear forever. It was through the Non-Proliferation Treaty, the nuclear weapon states were eliminating the nuclear weapons of Rogue states. By testing five devices of increasing complexity India has in one stroke resorted the asymmetry. Pakistan matched for show but not technically in terms of infrastructure. President Musharraf clearly said that India's bomb deterred Pakistan from launching a conventional war. Abdul Kalam was equally emphatic that India's bomb made Pakistan stop it's nuclear sabre-rattling from going beyond a short rattle. Pakistan claims to have denoted five simultaneous nuclear tests on May 20th of boosted device with highly enriched Uranium which Samar Moharik Mane, head of their nuclear test programme claimed to have produced total yield in the range of 40 to 45 kilotons. Pakistan conducted additional test on May 30, 1998. It claimed that the yield was in the range of 15 to 18 kilotons.[53] The

Indian nuclear tests were regarded as a major scientific achievement and a breakthrough for developing nations. Indians strongly felt that it was an assertion of national sovereignty and independent decision-making in security related matters. In the election manifesto the Bhartiya Janata Party had declared that-it would revaluate the country's nuclear policy and exercise the option to induct nuclear weapons. It also declared that the Bhartiya Janata Party rejected the notion of nuclear apartheid and would actively oppose attempts to impose a hegemonistic nuclear regime. We will not be dictated by anybody in matters of security and the excessive of nuclear option. India and Pakistan's testing of nuclear devices in May-June 1998 signalled the end of nuclear ambiguity in South Asia.

Pokhran II was an expression of the Indian challenge to the discriminatory nuclear regime. More importantly the act showed New Delhi's determination to force itself into an exclusive club of nuclear weapon states. In forging entry into the club, India played according to the membership rule prevailing that might is right. Pakistan replied on May 28 and May 30 as a show of its own ambition to achieve parity with its archrival.[54]

The International Response to the Nuclear Tests

India's and Pakistan's nuclear tests were universally criticized and condemned by the international community. They appealed to India and Pakistan to adhere unconditionally to nuclear Non-Proliferation Treaty and to participate constructively in negotiation of Fissile Material Cut,Treaty in Geneva, are informed by the logic of Non-Proliferation. The tests spurned immediate global condemnation. In all, 152 nations large and small developed and developing voiced their opposition. Forty-six nations attending the extraordinary meeting of 61 nations conference on disarmament issued a joint statement condemning nuclear tests by India and Pakistan and urging them to join the Comprehensive Test-Ban Treaty and the Non-Proliferation Treaty. These nations strongly felt that actions of India and Pakistan threaten and undermine the process of disarmament and the goal of eliminating nuclear weapons altogether. Arundhati Ghose stated that the indefinite extension of the NPT followed by nuclear testing by some nuclear weapon states are required to examine the situation within which developing nations are placed.[55]

The Security Council adopted Resolution 1172 on June 6, 1998. In its resolution the Security Council condemned the nuclear tests of both the countries and called forth each to sign the NPT and the Comprehensive Test-Ban Treaty, while at the same time affording the need for increased international cooperation on disarmament and nuclear Non-Proliferation.[56]

The US Concern

The development of India and Pakistan nuclear programmes raises immediate long-term concern for the United States. The two nations should not use their nuclear weapons in a crisis, that their nuclear weapons should not add to regional instability and that the technology to produce these weapons not be transferred to any other nations or non-sovereign rogue groups. In the last decade India and Pakistan have had two serious crises and in both cases the United States played an important role in defusing the tension. The first incident in Kashmir occurred in 1990 when each of the two countries possessed a few unassembled nuclear devices and the American diplomacy helped calm the situation. Then in the summer of 1999, India and Pakistan were engaged in a short but bitter war in the Kargil region of Kashmir.[57] The United States sees India's continuing opposition to signing an inherently discriminatory NPT as symptomatic of India's tendency to distrust global arms control efforts.

The Zangger Committee

The Zangger Committee also known as the NPT Exporters Committee consists of nuclear supplier states, which are parties to the NPT. The Zangger Committee held a meeting in Vienna on May 28, 1998 to discuss the implementation of the export control requirements of the Non-Proliferation Treaty. Members of the Zangger Committee strongly deplored the multiple nuclear tests recently conducted by India and Pakistan to refrain from further testing to exercise maximum restraint.[58]

The NPT and the Developing Nations Position in May 1995

In May 1995, 175 out of 178 nations who were parties to the NPT extended the treaty indefinitely and unconditionally. This was done through a process of consensus. The voice of developing nations for rolling extension was sidelined. This came as a surprise to India subjected as they were in the last few months to a long debate in the media regarding the discriminatory nature of the treaty. They thought that somehow the indefinite extension could be averted. India's tests effectively lay to rest the NPT as an instrument of nuclear denial.

The indefinite extension of the NPT in 1995 in fact turned out to be the first step in what India perceived to be a growing constriction of its ability to maintain its nuclear option.[59] In effect, the NPT's indefinite extension implied the world would be permanently divided into nuclear haves and have-nots, Indian security planners saw the permanent ratification of this divide as a strategic threat.

In taking security-linked decision based on compelling and valid national interest, India has acted as a responsible member of the international community. India has not violated any international agreements through these tests neither in 1974 nor in 1998. India's nuclear tests are solely for assuming its own security. India was reacting rationally to a nuclearised environment.[60]

The Post 1998 Scenario

The 1998 tests proved that five legal nuclear powers the US, Russia, China, Britain and France could not indefinitely retain their monopoly over one class of weapons. India and Pakistan also had become declared and defiant powers possessing nuclear weapons.[61]

The Chinese President, Mr. Jiang Zemin accused India of targeting both China and Pakistan by conducting nuclear tests. He emphasised that India conducted its nuclear tests in an attempt to establish its hegemony in South Asia and insisted that India should accede to the NPT and the CTBT.[62]

The NPT preparatory committee meetings held in 1997 and 1998 have clearly demonstrated the reluctance on the part of states possessing nuclear weapons to take steps towards a speedy progress of global nuclear disarmament. India has consistently maintained that nuclear Non-Proliferation and disarmament have to be discussed within a global framework and in a comprehensive and non-discriminatory manner. Indian and Pakistani nuclear tests gave a blow to the NPT regime though, the Indian leaders especially predicted that the decision to test would make the country more respected more secure and more firm in the control of events in South Asia.

Indian and Pakistani tests have major implications for global arms control and disarmament regime. The tests illustrated the step-by-step approach to arms control and disarmament which has failed.[63] By signing the NPT the countries of the world established a new norm. The NPT established a deadline in 1967. For those who could have nuclear weapons for the time being the five were the ones who had them in 1967, India did not have India participated actively in the conference in which the deadline was set. Since China had tested nuclear weapons in 1964 it was classified as a nuclear weapon state under the treaty.[64]

The Polarisation of Debate in South Asia

The nuclear tests by India and Pakistan seem to have polarised much of the debate on the security of South Asia. On the other hand Non-Proliferation proponents and peace activists consider the region to be tethering on the brink of disaster and on the verge of a nuclear conflicts.[65]

On the day of India's second set of nuclear tests, the US Assistant Secretary of State for South Asia, Karl Inderfurth laid out a broad response by Washington. He rejected India's claim of a security threat from Pakistan and China as unpersuasive.[66] The nuclear nations rejected India's claim to be a nuclear weapon state by citing the NPT's time bound definition of the phrase.

Prof. Samuel P. Huntington, the celebrated author of the "Clash of Civilizations", during his New Delhi visit on 19 January 1998 suggested that India stood isolated and should seek an alliance with the US. But the US also wanted India to sign the NPT, as a nuclear have not. This was not acceptable to the younger self-confident generation of Indians. So far as Indo-US relationship is concerned India has been realistic and an attempt has been made to establish a strategic relationship with the US. Selig Harrison suggested that a nuclear bargain is possible between India and the United States. This would reduce the tension over Non-Proliferation that has poisoned Indo-American relations.[67]

In 1995 the NPT came up with its twenty-five year review. The US sought an "unconditional and indefinite extension" of the treaty. India, which had chosen to stay outside the NPT regime, decided not to participate in proceedings in New York and did not even seek an observer status. After the treaty was extended, only India, Pakistan and Israel remained outside its scope. The indefinite extension of the treaty came as a dramatic shock to the Indian security policy establishment, which now realized that India would come under acute pressure to sign the NPT.[68] The conversion of the NPT into a permanent unjust international nuclear regime was definitely directed against the emerging geo-strategic self-confidence of the Indian elite.[69]

India's position on the NPT came into sharp focus yet again with the Sixth Review Conference of the states party to the NPT. In line with previous effort the conference has predictably called upon India to be a member of the treaty as a non-nuclear weapons state. External Affairs Minister, Jaswant Singh, has informed the nuclear weapons states that India would not join the treaty. This follows the previous line that discrimination was at the heart of India's rejection of the NPT. At the NPT review conference the nuclear weapons states have issued a statement refusing to acknowledge India as a nuclear weapon state despite its nuclear tests. They have urged India to abide by the UN Security Council Resolution 1172 passed in June 1998 in the wake of South Asian nuclear tests.

India has emerged as a leading critic of the proliferation image as articulated by the US and its allies. India made no secret of its opposition to the indefinite extension. In terms of the proliferation control agenda the marginalisation of the NPT became glaringly apparent in 1998 when India chose to test a series of nuclear weapons. Momentous changes have been taking place in the global and Asian security parameters in recent years.

India and Pakistan Cross the Nuclear Threshold

The transition of India and Pakistan across the nuclear threshold in May 1998 followed by limited border war in Kargil in May–July 1999 are only source of some urgent issues of security that need to be evaluated comprehensively. While China is recognized as a nuclear weapon power under the NPT, India and Pakistan have generally been accepted as one of the three undeclared nuclear weapon powers.[70] The Indian and Pakistani tests are not cases of new nuclear proliferation but the assertion of long existing and long acknowledged situation. The crossing of the nuclear threshold by India and Pakistan confronts the world with a peculiar dilemma. On the one hand the two have become nuclear weapon states and on the other hand, officially inter state nuclear order cannot concede nuclear status to them. India detonated five nuclear devices in Pokhran on May 11 and 13 with a view to gain what the Prime Minister characterized as 'Shakti', "Strength" and 'Self Confidence'. Before dust could settle in Pokhran Pakistan detonated six nuclear devices as on May 28 and May 30 at Chagai.[71]

The Transformation of the NPT

The NPT through its permanent and indefinite extension has been finally and fully transformed into a little more than a centralized institutionalised mechanism for ensuring Non-Proliferation and reinforcing the exclusivity of the nuclear club.[72] The fact that France and China finally joined the NPT regime in the post-Cold War period did not reflect a newfound commitment on their part to obey Article VI that calls the nuclear weapon states, which are signatories to the NPT to pursue negotiations in good faith to complete disarmament. They joined the NPT after legitimising their own formal entry and status into the nuclear club. The post Cold War has seen the Chinese placing a great emphasis on their role as responsible member of the global community as a major upholder of the global Non-Proliferation regime. They, therefore, have been reiterating that India should sign the NPT and in effect roll back its nuclear programme. The dominant paradigm in which India and Chinese relations are analysed is essentially of competitive power politics. India a non-signatory has long been an outspoken opponent of the two-tier structure of the regime denouncing it as a nuclear apartheid because it does not require a time bound framework for disarmament by nuclear weapon states.

India has maintained effective export controls on nuclear materials as well as related technologies even though India is neither a party to the NPT nor a member of Nuclear Suppliers

Group. India is committed to Non-Proliferation and maintains stringent export controls to ensure that there is no leakage of the indigenously developed know-how and technologies.[73]

In a statement in Parliament in the context of the Sixth NPT Review Conference, External Affairs Minister, Jaswant Singh said, one of the basic obligations of the nuclear weapon states under the NPT was to prevent further proliferation. The nuclear weapon states had been active collaborarators, not silent spectators to on proliferation, including export on nuclear weapon related components and technologies.[74]

The two South Asian states were non-signatories of the NPT but their claim to the nuclear status would give serious blow to the Non-Proliferation Treaty. In itself this development demonstrated the NPT failure to turn the idea into an acceptable objective for all states and dissuade them from pursuing their ambitions nuclear. More importantly, it showed the inability of the NPT to create reliable barriers to prevent non-member states from achieving nuclear capability. It was a failure because it demonstrated in general the NPT's inability to turn itself into an acceptable regime for all states and in particular the weakness of the NPT in creating enough incentives to persuade India and Pakistan to join the Non-Proliferation regime.[75]

The Transfer of Technology Clause and India's Position

India is critical of the NPT because it also prohibits the transfer of technology for peaceful development of nuclear energy. The NPT and the associated trade controls have been directed against the developing world and against India in particular. The NPT confirms power in a small minority of states while denying it to a large majority. A number of specific arrangements restrict the transfer of nuclear related technology e.g. the London Suppliers Group.[76] India as the principal opponent of the nuclear Non-Proliferation Treaty has become a major target of American export controls and US led multilateral cartels, such as the Wassenar Arrangement, London club and Missile Technology Control regime.

Foreign ministers of G-8 countries who met in London on June 12, after the second nuclear test in a joint communique pointed out that inspite of the recent tests, India and Pakistan would not be granted a nuclear status in accordance with the NPT.[77]

The NPT was a discriminatory treaty as the nuclear powers were free to manufacture unlimited number of nuclear weapons under the Non-Proliferation Treaty. This meant that the expansion of nuclear weapons by the nuclear weapon states would not be considered proliferation, while similar activity by non-nuclear weapon states will be regarded as proliferation. The net result was that they haves can have more and they haves not can have nothing.[78]

Under the NPT only non-nuclear states were subject to inspection verification, by the International Atomic Energy Agency. India, which had developed nuclear technology independently, therefore rejected the NPT.[79]

India decision to build her own nuclear arsenals is response to an environment in which nuclear weapon states have not meaningful steps towards nuclear disarmament. Unless genuine assurances with regards to nuclear disarmament are forthcoming from nuclear weapon states and confidence created any the non-nuclear weapon states, the proliferation of nuclear weapons to more countries is bound to take place sooner or latter.[80]

The security assurances given to non-nuclear weapon states in the context of the NPT, under Security Council Resolution 255 of 19 June 1968 are inadequate. "Considering that only these powers could use nuclear weapons, it could not be expected that an aggression would consent to a collective action being taken against itself".[81]

The Catch in the NPT

The thickest cobweb is the strange NPT definition of a nuclear weapon state, not one which has and deploys nuclear weapons but one which has conducted tests before January 1, 1967.[82] By any objective analysis both India and Pakistan have justification for going nuclear. It is a vicious circle. Because China is the principle long-term security threat to India because of China, and Pakistan because of India. India wouldn't surrender the option of acquiring nuclear weapons. Advocates of nuclear option argued that nuclear weapons would enhance India's international status, ensure its strategic autonomy, erode great power hegemony, reinforce India's, leading role in the developing world and would expand its diplomatic choices in global affairs and would stabilize relations with China.

India cannot be expected, for all times to come, to practise a self denying evidence with regard to nuclear weapons in a strategic environment, which serves the security needs of only a few countries and threatens the security of all others.[83] Nations who have been loudest in advocating sanctions against India are themselves armed with thousands of nuclear weapons or have the protection of nuclear umbrellas.[84] For India, the NPT is illegitimate and non-rational because it is a denial of the equality of opportunity to proliferate, for most the regime is enable to providing security from proliferation and the promise of eventual disarmament.[85]

Pressure through NGO's

In the post 1998 scenario pressure was mounted on India even through the NGO's. The Pugwash workshop on the abolition of nuclear weapons was held in 11-13 October 1999 in New Delhi. It focussed on the fact that the disappearance of the bipolar world did not imply abandonment of cold war strategic concepts. Nuclear powers still think that the first use of nuclear weapons and extended deterrence is their exclusive privilege. One problem that drew the attention of all participants was the nature and the impact of the NPT. It was noted that India supports the Non-Proliferation regime, but disagrees with the Non-Proliferation Treaty. The view was also expressed that the NPT itself implies that 188 nations have decided that nuclear weapons are going to stay for the foreseeable future. Indefinite extension of the NPT has been equated as indefinite legitimisation of nuclear weapons. India's nuclearisation has been justified on the ground that in contrast with Japan and Western Europe India cannot count on any sort of nuclear protection while at the same it faces a powerful nuclear country like China. In this sense India was compelled to nuclearise.

In considering the security motivation behind any decision to acquire nuclear weapons it was focussed that countries fall into five following categories: (1) nuclear weapon states, (2) states that are allied with nuclear weapons and protected by these states, (3) states that belong to nuclear weapon free zones for which some form of international guarantee is available, (4) parties to the NPT that don't belong to any previous category. (5) countries that did not sign the NPT. It was emphasized that the security concerns were the highest for the last two categories of states. The dominance by the nuclear weapon states in world affairs with the help of nuclear weapons has a racist connotation and India is just drawing the relevant consequences. With China directly engaged in South Asia, some felt that India had no alternative but to weaponise.

India, US and the NPT

The US sponsored stability talks with India and Pakistan began after their nuclear tests in May 1998. These talks ran out of steam after President Clinton's landmark trip to India and Pakistan in March 2000. America's transformed relationship with both India and Pakistan would give the US strong leverage in recalibrated and re-energized talks on regional confidence building and restraint.

The US had long been concerned about the prospects of India's nuclear tests. It had received high-level public and private assurance that India would continue to show restraint in Non-Proliferation field. As a result the timing of the test took the intelligence community by surprise. President Clinton and secretary of state Madeleine Albright asked Strobe Talbot who had arms control expertise to develop an American response. He assembled a core group of state department and White House officials whose first agenda item focussed on persuading Pakistan not to respond in kind to India's nuclear tests — a difficult task given a decade of deterioration in US Pakistan relations.

US policy then shifted to promoting restraint in the sub-continent through a series of high level and expert meetings with India and Pakistan. India selected Jaswant Singh to be Talbot's partner at the talks. No one realistically expected India or Pakistan to move quickly or easily give in their nuclear programme after tit for tat nuclear test explosions amid recurring tensions over Kashmir. Although India and Pakistan have now both demonstrated a nuclear capacity the future direction of their nuclear and missile programme is still very much open.

The US has failed to prevent India and Pakistan from developing and testing nuclear weapons but it still has important interest for arms control in the region. These include ensuring New

Delhi and Islamabad to maintain a nuclear test moratorium and eventually sign the NPT. The US is likely to lift economic sanctions upon signing but there are powerful voices in both the countries that oppose the treaty.

Right to a Credible Nuclear Deterrence

The US has an interest in balancing any further Chinese expansion in Asia and India can play an important role in this respect.[86] The sustained dialogue over the past two years between Deputy Secretary of State Strobe Talbot and India's Foreign Minister Jaswant Singh has prompted a greater US efforts to understand legitimate Indian concerns about a wide range of strategic issues. However, there still exists distrust among the Indian elites about US intentions based on the country's past support to Pakistan and the behaviour of China. The Indian officials have insisted on the right to retain India's nuclear option as long as other countries retain their nuclear armaments. India has reviewed its insistence that India unilaterally renounces the right to produce nuclear weapons as hypocritical and this difference of opinion was magnified after India's nuclear tests. Since then India has insisted on the right to maintain a credible nuclear deterrent.

The Glenn Amendment India's stand to maintain a credible minimum deterrence has evoked response from the US, which has imposed sanctions under the Glenn Amendment. Within the US Congress Non-Proliferation advocates like representative Dan Burton voiced outrage at the nuclear tests by India and called for immediate triggering of sanctions under Section 102 (of the Arms Export Control Act universally known as the Glenn Amendment). New Delhi's action were reckless shameful and irresponsible. Markey insisted to halt India's nuclear progress by cutting US economic assistance to New Delhi.[87] Only days after the tests, President Bill Clinton responded as he was obligated under the Glenn Amendment slapping wide range economic and military sanctions against New Delhi and Islamabad. No sooner, had Washington taken this stand on behalf of global Non-Proliferation norm, than it began to move away from its position within 18 months, the US Congress swung from applauding strict sanctions to urging the President to waive not only Glenn Amendment but also Pressler and Symington Amendment which mandate further penalties for states engaged in certain nuclear activities. Congressional anger over South Asian tests had given way to acceptance even understanding, Congress, it would appear had abandoned 25 years of Non-Proliferation activity.

The Brown Back Amendment and the US Gesture to Pakistan

The US Congress harsh response to the South Asian test gradually softened after a period of time, it led to the passing of the Brown Back Amendment. The Brown Back Amendment formally known as India Pakistan Relief Act of 1998 was incorporated into fiscal 1999 omnibus appropriation bill and passed as law in October 1998. Clinton also lifted restrictions on US commercial loans and credit to both countries and announced that Washington would support a pending Pakistani request before the International Monitory Fund. Clinton then moved to eliminate another longstanding irritant in US Pakistan relationship by agreeing to pay Islamabad $140 million in goods as compensation for 28 F-16 aircrafts that Pakistan had earlier bought but whose delivery had been prevented by 1990's triggering of the Pressler Amendment. In October 1999 Congress took a step further by adopting as part of defence appropriation bill Brown Back. This measure gave the President permanent authority to waive with respect to India and Pakistan all the provisions of the Glenn Amendment. In addition it authorized the President to waive Symington and Pressler Amendment sanctions, which had prohibited all US economic and military assistance to Pakistan since 1990.

Brown Back represented an extraordinary reversal of American policy. The measure handed the President the authority to lift all sanctions imposed upon India and Pakistan, as a result of their 1998 nuclear tests. Initially expressing concern for the global Non-Proliferation Regime the Congress in less than 18 months had moved to the position that it should not jeopardize its own interests in pursuit of unobtainable Non-Proliferation objectives. Security considerations have contributed to this newfound interest in the US-India partnership. The US recognized that as important as Non-Proliferation was, it had other critical interests in South Asia that deserved protection as well. India and Pakistan occupy a strategic corner of the globe and regional instability would threaten American political and security interests in the Middle East,

Central Asia and the Indian Ocean. The South Asian experts realized that the use of sanctions failed to advance American national interests. In a speech on April 3, 1999, representative Gary Ackerman said sanctions are too blunt a weapon to be used by us against a sister democracy such as India. "Sanctions aren't good for India they aren't good for America either". The publication by India in mid 1999, of a draft nuclear doctrine envisioning the creation of a nuclear triad of air-sea and ground launched nuclear weapons had absolutely no effect for congressional support for Brown Back.

The 2000 Review Conference and the South Asian Test

The 2000 Review Conference of NPT focussed on the impact of nuclearisation of India and Pakistan. There was no question of recognizing their nuclear status and at the same time if they signed the NPT as non-nuclear weapon states again there would be asymmetry. Some NPT members believed that they were more secure by signing the treaty giving up the nuclear option because other regime members were severely constrained. Therefore, if states with nuclear arsenals are allowed under the NPT the existing members would question the security value of the treaty. Further more, addition of members with special status would create asymmetry in rights and obligations between State parties.

The Non-Proliferation oriented global order is founded upon a flawed and unequal bargain that lies at the heart of the NPT, not just objectively but in the eyes of vast majority of signatories too, notwithstanding the party's self serving Indian objection to the treaty. According to the President K.R. Narayan "this event is a major breakthrough in the realm of national security."[88] Brajesh Mishra said that the test on 11 May 1998, focussed "these that India has a proven capability for weaponised nuclear programme. This will also provide a database, which is useful design of nuclear weapons of different yields for different applications for different delivery systems."[89] India is looking for an opportunity to put itself on equal footing with China. Indians feel that they are denied a natural right by not being acknowledged as a nuclear weapon state, since they have an advanced economy and are the world's largest democracy. The NPT divided the nations into those that were allowed to retain and develop nuclear weapons and those who were forbidden for the same right. It was also in balanced and imposed virtually no obligation on nuclear weapon states and they did not honour even those limited obligations. As a developing country India hopes that the developing world notices that the countries, which have vehemently criticised the tests, are either nuclear weapon states that like to preserve their exclusive position or are those who have addressed their nuclear related national security concerns of the kind India had.

To the US the bedrock of its policy towards nuclear India is the NPT. According to Deputy Secretary Strobe Talbot "We don't and will not concede even by implication that India and Pakistan have established themselves as nuclear weapon powers under the NPT. Until they disallow nuclear weapons and accept safeguards on all their nuclear activities they will continue to forfeit the full recognition and benefits that accrue to members in good standing of the NPT".[90]

The US policy has been to persuade India and Pakistan to first cap, then reduce, and eventually eliminate their capabilities to produce nuclear weapons. For India, the NPT is meant only to promote atomic monopoly. It is widely perceived in the developing world especially in India to be a device to promote atomic colonialism. After India's nuclear tests the NPT became an umbrella under which supplier controls were strengthened. By mid 1970's the orientation of the NPT had decisively shifted towards a strategy of denial and away from nuclear disarmament.

Indian Emphasis on Reciprocal Obligations

The philosophical and legal basis of India's argument against the treaty maintains that reciprocal obligations should be the basis of international relations and contract must be respected not changed unilaterally. At present there are strong incentives in both India and Pakistan against accepting full scope safeguards in favour of an extended nuclear option stance and against a nuclear weapons posture.[91] While Washington always wanted India to concede to Non-Proliferation, it has adopted a soft and permissive approach towards Pakistani nuclear development.[92] To pursue a credible Non-Proliferation strategy in South Asia the US will need to adopt a policy that doesn't appear discriminatory.

While redefining its nuclear weapon capabilities and keeping its deployment option open, India remained aloof from the NPT. Despite strategy pressure it did not sign the nuclear NPT in spite of intense diplomatic activity by proceeding the treaty's indefinite extension on May 1995.[93] Its longstanding position on the NPT remains intact, India regarded the treaty as fundamentally discriminatory document, which separated the world into legitimate and illegitimate nuclear states, solely on the basis of when countries first acquired a nuclear explosive capability.[94]

Disclosers of Chinese transfer of nuclear technology and materials to Pakistan and the inability of the US to take any action against China has further complicated Non-Proliferation dilemma in South Asia. India has insisted time and again that Non-Proliferation Treaty should be able to end both vertical and horizontal proliferation. The US non-acceptance of the inherent linkage between vertical and horizontal proliferation is a matter of grave concern for Indians. The US has ignored the important linkage between vertical and horizontal proliferation that could have really brought about genuine universal disarmament. The linkage between nuclear proliferation and sale of conventional weapons has been ignored.[95] The US proliferation concerns have often been compromised with other security concerns and strategic manoeuvres. A 'win-win' settlement of the current impasse will solve the India and Pakistani Nuclear capable status. A win-win settlement is one that leaves each party to the negotiation better off from its point of view than it would be in the absence of settlement. This is visible in case of softening of sanction by US as a part of a win-win strategy since nothing can be done as India and Pakistan have already crossed the nuclear rubicon.

Two parts of the problem must be dealt with following the nuclearisation of South Asia, how to stabilize the post-test environment in the region and how to restrict the international fallout from these tests. India and Pakistani proposals differed in their emphasis. India proposed a declaration of no first use of nuclear weapons by both states Pakistan rejected the proposal because in a purely conventional conflict the asymmetry of forces favoured India. Pakistan made three different proposals that Kashmir be made the core issue in resolving Indo-Pakistani relationship that India and Pakistan work towards conventional force reductions, that both countries neither weaponise nor deploy nuclear arsenals. As a consequence negotiations between two countries made little headway.

Mutual Steps for Nuclear Restraint

After almost a year of false starts the two countries were able to initiate the first set of measures to formalize nuclear restraint in South Asia. US pressure, domestic, political and economic concerns brought the two countries to the negotiating table. In February 1999 in the Lahore summit between the two countries a memorandum of understanding was reached to develop a set of confidence building measures. The two countries agreed to exchange strategic information about their nuclear arsenals and to give each other advance notice of ballistic missile tests.[96]

When India tested Agni on 2 in April 1999 and Pakistan followed by testing the Shaheen and Ghauri missiles, both countries notified each other about the launch. There were obvious gaps in the declaration, New Delhi's no first use proposal remained unendorsed and Islamabad was unable to get conventional areas talks to the table and to get India to agree to a no war pact. Moreover Pakistan would have liked India to exercise strategic restraint whereas India agreed that it required a credible minimum deterrent against China.[97] A threat perception that led to full weaponisation of India and the fear of Chinese encirclement with the belief that a significant nuclear capability is required against China. India appears to have realized that Pakistan has adopted an unstable nuclear posture by maintaining the option to be able to be first to use nuclear weapon. India's Defence Minister George Fernandes has pleaded with Pakistan for 'Cooperative Security' and a firm commitment to 'no first use policy to eliminate the risk of accidental, miscalculated use of nuclear weapons. Pakistan's refusal to adopt such a policy has placed India in a precarious security environment.[98]

India's Security Concerns

Ever since independence India has tried to harmonise its security with disarmament. It has viewed nuclear weapons as instruments of power and coercion and has argued that their presence anywhere in effect threatened others security. India faces a doubled edged nuclear threat to its security one from China and other from Pakistan. Both have collaborated and identified India as their common adversary and their foreign policy goals are directed towards trimming India's wings. Both China and Pakistan are nuclear powers having conflicting relations with India. India's nuclear capability was a reaction to the Chinese nuclear programme and its antipathy and subsequent patronage of Pakistan.

India's five nuclear tests in May 1998 were ostensibly impelled by security consideration. Prime Minister Vajpayee's letter to President Clinton after the event stated "we have an overt nuclear weapon state on our border, a state which committed armed aggression against India in 1962. That country has materially helped another neighbour of ours to become a covert Nuclear Weapon State. At the hands of these bitter neighbours we have suffered three aggressions in the last 50 years. And for last 10 years we have been a victim of unremitting terrorism and militancy sponsored by it in several parts of our country.[99] The ideological predilections of Hindu fundamentalist Bhartiya Janata Party government were founded on conviction that state power equates with military power and nuclear weapons also informed India's decision.[100]

William Walker has recently stated "It is a mistake to view Indian actions just as reactions to Pakistan or even to China...." Perversely India's deepening affection for nuclear weapons has also been propelled by its hatred, of the Non-Proliferation Regime, by its intense grievance over being locked into what is seen as an inferior status.[101]

The Bhartiya Janata Party's decision to go nuclear reflected changes that occurred in the subcontinent, which ranged from the escalation of insurgency in Kashmir, the test firing of Ghauri missile by Pakistan, to overt expansion of Chinese military presence in Myanmar, the construction of naval facilities in the Coco Islands by the Chinese and their reach to the Andaman Islands. These were the emerging threat perceptions that India had to contend with.[102]

Drafting the Nuclear Doctrine

The present tone and tanner of India's nuclear doctrine can be traced to the Bhartiya Janata Party's election manifesto, issued before March 1998 general elections, which first brought the Bhartiya Janata Party into power for a brief 13 days period. It promised that the Bhartiya Janata Party if elected would establish a National Security Council to undertake India's first ever-strategic defence review to study and analyse the security environment and to make appropriate recommendations... revaluate the countries nuclear policy and exercise the option to include nuclear weapons.[103]

An Overview of the Draft Doctrine

The draft nuclear doctrine begins with a preamble. This first highlights the threat of nuclear weapons, inadequacies of the NPT and non-attention by the nuclear weapon powers to nuclear disarmament. It then proceeds to express India's commitment to a peaceful and equitable international order while retaining its autonomy in strategic decision-making. The preamble finally notes that nuclear doctrine outlines the broad principles of development and implementing of India's nuclear forces.[104]

The Cabinet Committee on Security (CCS) adopted and made public the key elements of its nuclear doctrine and command structure on January 4, 2003. A National Command Authority (NCA) will be set up in which a political council headed by the Prime Minister who will be the sole authority for ordering a nuclear strike. Though India sticks to the no-first-use policy announced earlier in the draft policy, it has now been made more flexible to extend the scope for use of nuclear weapons. The Cabinet Committee on Security said that a nuclear strike would be ordered if India or its forces anywhere in the world were attacked with nuclear or biological weapons. The Cabinet Committee on Security also approved an all services strategic forces command to manage and administer all strategic nuclear weapons and delivery systems under the Commander in Chief T.M. Asthana. The Cabinet Committee on Security discussed all doctrinal and operational details including alternative chains of command for retaliatory strikes. The CCS also reiterated New Delhi's commitment to nuclear disarmament. There is a basic difference between India and Pakistani's nuclear doctrines. The Indian doctrine has three unwritten clauses. One, the bomb won't be used against an enemy who doesn't have nuclear capability. Two, it would only be used only after the enemy uses nuclear weapons against India. Third, a conventional war can be waged against a nuclear-armed enemy. Pakistan's doctrine is premised on its belief that nuclear weapons have given it an equalizer against India's conventional superiority. Therefore its doctrine, that when a conventional Indian strike reaches an unacceptable threshold; it will nuke India. Musharaf warned Prime Minister Vajpayee that if Indian troops moved across the international border, or the line of control, they should not expect a conventional war with Pakistani forces.

In 1962 when Leonard Beaton and John Maddox wrote a book on the spread of nuclear weapons they could hardly foresee that Israel and India would become nuclear weapon states, since then we have seen Pakistan joining the group. But now the international community must decide how to fit these three *de facto* states Israel, India and Pakistan into the NPT as their perceived need for deterrence could be considered greater than joining the NPT. The US should change its policy towards India and Pakistan, which needs to be shaped by relation not orthodoxy. The US cannot afford a uni-dimensional nuclear policy and the US cannot afford to rely so heavily on the sanctions.

The NPT and the New Categories of Nuclear Armed States

The Non-Proliferation objectives have so frequently lost out strategic interest especially of great powers. India is one of the rare examples of a state that has exercised self-restraint in this respect. The threat perceptions of different countries vary a great deal and are specific to technological and geo-political environment. In India's perception, proliferation issue is not related to one country or sub region but can hardly be separated from larger and more universal developments. India's strategic perceptions have also been influenced by great power strategies especially those related to intervention on the developing world. India's strategic posture is based on defensive defense, that leaves the initiative to the aggression.[105] At the same time geo-political and geo-strategic factors since 1962 had heated potential threat of exhorbitantly expensive two front conflicts. The debate over the future of the NPT that necessarily surrounded the NPT extension decision provided a locus of alternative framing of the security problem of specific nations. In this counter image the security focus is on the weapons particularly their possession, and the emphasis is placed on civilian side of the dual use the technology. The proliferation image constructs suppliers, recipients and rogues. India doesn't fit into any of these category. India has developed nuclear capability, which it made public in a service of tests in 1998. The US on the other hand promotes its proliferation on agenda that enables it to retain its privileged status as a nuclear weapon states and primary supplier.[106]

India has refused to sign the NPT since its inception because the treaty allows the five nuclear weapon states to retain nuclear weapons without a specific schedule for nuclear disarmament. But initiatives during the Rajiv Gandhi's tenure for a phased manner of nuclear disarmament by 2002 have never attracted support or even serious attention from the nuclear weapon states. India repeatedly urged that NPT's nuclear apartheid be remedied by serious commitment to nuclear disarmament by the declared nuclear weapon states, as required by Article VI of the treaty. India was repeatedly ignored. The fact that a few nuclear aristocrats retained for their own security was precisely the reason why India abandoned the road to NPT and has followed the path led by nuclear weapon states.

Subrahmanyam's formula is now widely accepted India will acquire nuclear weapons in order to pressurize nuclear 'haves' to disarm and to protect itself against nuclear blackmail. The Indian bomb would be an instrument of resistance to the blackmailing tactics of Nuclear Weapon States while affirming India's concern with welfare of all nations. The logic could also be applied to various schemes for disarmament proposal by the Superpower and other nuclear weapon states. The nuclear blasts in Pokharan (India) and Chagai Hills (Pakistan) brought South Asia to the main focus of international attention. The five established nuclear power refused to acknowledge India and Pakistan's joining the 'club' and both governments have been repeatedly pushed towards signing the Non-Proliferation Treaty. The international reaction in the Indian sub-continent and subsequent Pakistani nuclear tests was single out the region for destroying the established and accepted Non-Proliferation regime. India's quest for nuclear weapons was caused not only by regional factors but also by extra regional considerations. The nuclear weapon powers continue to stock piling their nuclear technology for security reasons. At the same time they oppose India and Pakistani nuclear tests, and put pressure on them India to sign the NPT. The geo-strategic environment, regional and extra regional factors do not allow India to accept the discriminatory NPT.

The NPT and the Post-Soviet Union Scenario

The breaking down of the Soviet Union and the emergence of a single dominant power, with the ability to strike conventionally and in nuclear terms, accentuated the insecurity of India and led it to advocate for genuine nuclear disarmament. The key element of the action plan laid by Rajiv Gandhi in the UN Special session on Disarmament was the call for Superpower commitment to complete nuclear disarmament. It is ironical that in the international public opinion, India's and Pakistan's 11 nuclear tests could not be tolerated. Even though both the countries were not the signatories of the NPT, did not violate them formally, these tests posed a grave threat to international security, thus further adding the prevailing insecurity and instability in South Asia. India has been a supporter of genuine nuclear disarmament where both vertical and horizontal proliferation are curbed and is opposed to the discriminatory regime advocated by Non-Proliferation Treaty.

The nuclear testing by India and Pakistan shook the world and provided a setback to global disarmament and Non-Proliferation efforts. The nuclear test posed a bold challenge to the international community and threatened to undermine the very foundation of the nuclear Non-Proliferation regime based on the treaty on NPT. Nuclear Non-Proliferation could only be promoted if it guaranteed simultaneously the promotion of nuclear disarmament.

The indefinite extension of the treaty is regarded as a stumbling block in the effort to promote nuclear disarmament. The confidence of non-nuclear weapon states has been eroded by the failure of nuclear weapon states to keep their obligations under the terms of the treaty. The NPT was not a framework under which nuclear weapon states could perpetually possess nuclear weapons, while the possession of those weapons was prohibited to other countries. The nuclear testing was the right response to India's security concerns considering the global and regional security environment.

India has emphasized that it will not use a first strike and Pakistan reserves the right to "the first strike". So now India has to face asymmetrical nuclear deterrence, therefore India is being forced to create a command and control system to avert any threat or aggression from its neighbours.

In April 1998 the Indian Government constituted a task force to recommend the establishment of a National Security Council (NSC). The task force submitted its report in June 1998 and in November 1998, the government constituted a three tier National Security Council with a National Security Advisor and a National Security Advisory Board. The National Security Advisory Board submitted a Draft Nuclear Doctrine Paper to the government, which was released for the public for wider debate on August 17, 1999. The key features of the proposed nuclear doctrine are produced below:

India shall pursue a doctrine of credible minimum deterrence. In this policy of 'retaliation only' the survivability of our arsenal is critical. This is a dynamic concept related to our strategic environment, technological imperatives and needs of national security. The actual size, components, deployment of nuclear forces will be decided in the light of these factors. India's peacetime posture aims at deterring any potential aggressor.

Any threat of the use of nuclear weapons against India shall invoke measures to counter the threat. Any nuclear attack on India and its forces shall result in punitive retaliation with nuclear weapons to inflict damage unacceptable to the aggressor. The fundamental purpose of India's nuclear weapons is to deter the case and the threat of use of nuclear weapons by any state or entity against India and its forces. India will not be the first to initiate a nuclear strike but will response with punitive retaliation if deterrence fail.

As expected the draft doctrine initiated a major debate in the country about its nuclear policies. Amitabh Matoo called it "an unapologetic real politic articulation of the principal *raison d'etre* of India's nuclear weapons and the requirements needed to lend credibility to the countries deterrent posture".[107]

According to Jasgit Singh the following essential elements constitute the key features of India's nuclear doctrine. Firstly, India's nuclear weapons are meant to deter the use and threat of use of nuclear weapons against India. The orientation of the doctrine is quite narrowly focussed on the need to defend India through deterrence against nuclear weapons threat. India recognizes that nuclear weapons cannot provide deterrence in all circumstances and limited conventional conflict remains impossible. This was borne out by the 1999 Kargil conflict between India and Pakistan.

Secondly, India's nuclear doctrine is firmly anchored on the principle of 'no first use' even against threat or use. It will only be used when an adversary uses nuclear weapons against India. This severely circumstances the potential development, deployment and employment of the nuclear arsenal.

Thirdly, India's no first use doctrine is a defensive doctrine, which limits the use of nuclear weapons to retaliation only.

Fourthly, the doctrine is based on the concept of minimum deterrence, which implies that India's nuclear policy; strategy and posture would.be guided by the minimalist principle. The emphasis on 'minimum' deterrence clearly defines the principle in relation to the capability and not the size of the arsenal.[108]

Finally India's nuclear doctrine emphasizes, that global, verifiable and non-discriminatory nuclear disarmament, is a national security objective and India's desire to develop a credible minimum nuclear deterrent against nuclear blackmail and the threat of use of nuclear weapon, is an eminently justifiable national security imperative.[109] India's no first use retaliation as only nuclear doctrine is not only morally befitting and worthy of India's civilization heritage but is operationally a sound strategy.

India's position on arms elimination was well established and advanced in 1967 at the time of the NPT treaty. This had been reiterated at the time of the 1974 test, in the early 1980's by Indira Gandhi, in 1988 by Rajiv Gandhi and most recently at the renewal conference of the NPT treaty at New York in 1995. Passionately committed, to the need to move towards global nuclear disarmament, New Delhi has been continuously frustrated by the reluctance of the Nuclear Weapon states to disarm. At the New York session, the Indian delegation berated the international community for not capitalizing on the end of the cold war and pursuing total nuclear disarmament to the front of the agenda. In 1996, the Indian delegation at the going on conference in disarmament at Geneva pointed out that attempts to press ahead with nuclear disarmament had stagnated because of the realization by the nuclear weapons states that nuclear weapons still had political and military utility in the chaotic and unpredictable post Cold War environment.[110]

To sum up, it is clear that the nuclear Non-Proliferation Treaty, which is based on differential standards of security is not acceptable to India. While the present nuclear powers justify nuclear weapons even against perceived threats from non-nuclear states, a regime of international nuclear apartheid becomes operational whenever India claims for space in the nuclear area. India regards the treaty as a fundamentally discriminatory document, which divides the world into legitimate and illegitimate nuclear weapon states, solely on the basis of nuclear capacity. It is further noted that India's security environment was further worsened by accumulation of nuclear weapons and missiles in its neighbourhood. India as a nation always wanted to independently pursue its foreign policy. It could not accept a semicolonial and inferior status as a nation, whose security prescriptions were to be determined by others. India could participate in the global arms control negotiations as a nuclear weapon state, thereby continuing its activism for the elimination of nuclear weapons. However, as seen, the five nuclear weapon states are unwilling to recognise India as a nuclear weapon state, despite its nuclear tests, confirming it's nuclear status. India cannot be a party to a treaty that is not only unequal, but also further cannot legally accept it as a nuclear weapon state.

NOTES

1. Lorne, J. Kavic, *India's Quest for Security: Defence Policies 1947-1965*, (Berkeley and Los Angeles: University of California Press, 1967), pp. 27-28.
2. George, Perkovich, *India's Nuclear Bomb, The Impact on Global Proliferation*, (Oxford: Oxford University Press, 2000), p. 14.
3. Zia, Mian, "Homi Bhabha Killed a Crow" in Zia Mian and Ashis Nandy, *The Nuclear Debate, Ironies and Immoralities*, (Colombia: RCSS, 1998), pp. 12-13.
4. M. I. Shaker, "The Third Review Conference Issues and Prospects", David B Dewitt, *Non-Proliferation and Global Security*, (London: Croom Helm Ltd., 1987), p. 3.
5. Lewis, A. Dunn, *"The NPT and the Future of Global Security"*, in David B. Dewitt, *Ibid*, p. 204.

6. Jasjit, Singh, "India's Nuclear Policy—A Perspective", *Strategic Analysis,* Vol. XII, No. VII, November 1989, p. 789.
7. Gopal, Singh and SK Sharma, *"Documents in India's Nuclear Disarmament Policy"*, Vol. 1, (New Delhi: Anamika Publishers, 2000), pp. 76-77.
8. Sumit, Ganguly, "The Sino-Indian Border Talks 1981-1989, A View from New Delhi," *Asian Survey,* 29 : 12 (December, 1989), pp. 1123-1125.
9. Mitchell, Reiss, *Without the Bomb: The Politics of Nuclear Non-Proliferation,* (New York: Columbia University Press, 1988), p. 211.
10. Andrew, Koch, "Nuclear Testing in South Asia and the CTBT", *The Non-Proliferation Review,* Spring Summer, Vol. 3, No. 3.1 1996, <http://cns.miis.edu/pubs/npr/vol 103/33/Koch 33.pdf>
11. Vijai, K. Nair, *"Nuclear Proliferation US Aims and India's Response, Studies in Conflict and Terrorism"*, (New Delhi: Lancer Publishers, 1999), p. 69.
12. Ziba, Moshaver, *"Nuclear Weapon Proliferation in the Indian Sub-continent"*, (London: Macmillan, 1991), p. 17.
13. Jeffry, Smith, Report sites China-Pakistan Missiles Links, *"Washington Post"*, June 13, 1996.
14. Sujit, Dutta, *India's Nuclear Gambit: Rationale and Repercussions,* A Briefing held at the US Institute of Peace, May 14, 1998.
15. Saira, Khan, *Nuclear Proliferation Dynamics in Protracted Conflict Regions Comparative Study of South Asia and the Middle East,* (England: Ashgate Publishing Ltd.), p. 171.
16. Saira, Khan, *Ibid* p. 169.
17. Colonel Ravi Nanda, *Indo-Pak Détente,* (New Delhi: Lancer Books, 1989), p. 226.
18. R. K. Kilhani, *"Nuclearisation in South Asia"*, (New Delhi: Commonwealth Publishers, 2000), p. 27.
19. M.V. Rappai, *India-China Relations and the Nuclear Rhetoric,* <http://www.Idsa-india.org/an-apr9-2.html>.
20. Brahma, Chellaney, "South Asia's Passage to Nuclear Power", *International Security,* Vol. 16, Issue I, p. 43.
21. Fareed, Zakaria, *Newsweek,* 8 June 1998.
22. Ashley, J. Tellis, *Stability in South Asia,* (Dehradun: Natraj Publishers, 2000), p. 11.
23. Dr. Sanjay, Badri, Maharaj, *"The Armageddon Factor, Nuclear Weapons in India-Pakistan Context"*, (New Delhi: Lancer Publishers and Distributors, 2000), p. 22.
24. Amitabh, Matoo, *India's Nuclear Deterrent Pokhran II and Beyond,* (New Delhi: Har Anand Publishers, 1999), p. 22.
25. Raja, Menon, *A Nuclear Strategy for India,* (New Delhi: Sage Publications, 2000), p. 96.
26. P. L. Bhola, "India's Perception and Response to Pakistan's Nuclear

Programme" in Surendra Nath Kaushik, Rajan Mohan, Ramankant (Ed.), *India and South Asia,* (New Delhi: South Asia Publishers Pvt. Ltd., 1991), p. 148-9.

27. "India Evolves Nuclear Doctrine", *The Times of India,* August 5, 1998.
28. Ashley, J. Tellis, *India's Emerging Nuclear Posture,* (New Delhi: Oxford University Press, 2001), pp. 39-40.
29. Saira, Khan, *Op. cit.,* p. 105.
30. Christopher, A. McNally, Charles, E. Morrism, (Ed.), *"Asia Pacific Security Outlook"*, Japan Center for International Exchange, New York, 2001, p. 70.
31. Arpit, Rajain, "Nuclear Deterrence in Southern Asia", Article No. 616, *Institute of Peace and Conflict Studies,* 16 October 2001, <s.org/ ipcs/issue index 2jsp?action = show view& kvalue = 1788 issue = 1009% status = article & 'mod = b>.
32. Praful, Bidwai, Achin, Vanaik, *South Asia on a Short Fuse,* (New Delhi: Oxford University Press, 2001), p. 76.
33. The Statement by Ambassador Savitri Kunadi, *Permanent Representative of India in the Plenary Meeting of the Conference on Disarmament Embassy of India.*
34. George, Perkovich, *India's Nuclear Bomb: The Impact on Global Proliferation,* (New Delhi: Oxford University Press, 2000), p. 129.
35. *Ibid,* p. 136.
36. *Ibid,* p. 134.
37. Indira, Gandhi," Reply in the Lok Sabha ", 5 April 1968, quoted in Gopal Singh and S.K. Sharma (Ed.) *Documents on India's Nuclear Disarmament Policy Indira Gandhi era,* Volume II, (New Delhi: Anamika Publishers), p. 739.
38. Brahma, Chellaney, *Nuclear Proliferation: The US-India Conflict,* (New Delhi: Orient Longman Limited, 1993), p. 31.
39. Hedly, Bull, "Rethinking Non-Proliferation", *International Affairs,* Vol. 51, April 1975, p. 175.
40. T. T. Poulouse, "Atomic Colonialism", *Bulletin of the Atomic Scientist,* October 1978, p. 60.
41. Raja, Menon, *A Nuclear Strategy for India,* (New Delhi: Sage Publications, 2002), p. 86.
42. Martin, Zuberi, "India's Nuclear Leap Forward", in Major Sulakshan Mohan, *India's Nuclear Leap,* (Delhi: Indian Publishers Distributors, 2000), p. 10.
43. J. P. Jain, *Nuclear India,* Vol. I, (New Delhi: Radiant Publishers, 1974), p. 161.
44. 'Withdrawal of Sanction Parliament Question and Answer, March 15, 2000, <http://www.meadev.nic.in/govt/parl-qa>.
45. Jatin, Desai, *Nuclear Diplomacy, the Art of The Deal,* (New Delhi: Commonwealth Publishers, 2000), p. 135.

46. Brenner, Nuclear Power and Non-Proliferation, p. 67.
47. T.T. Pouluse, *Op cit.* p. 60.
48. Ashok, Kapur, Y. K. Malik, Harold, A. Gould, Arthur, G. Rubinoff, *"India and US in a Changing World"*, (New Delhi: Sage Publications, 2002), p. 315.
49. Raj, Chengappa Manoj Joshi *"Hawkish India"*, India Today, June 1 1998<http://www.india-today.com/itoday/oro61998/cover2.html>.
50. David, Albright, "The Shots Heard Round The World", *The Bulletin of Atomic Scientist*, July/August, 1998, Vol. 54, No. 4, <http:www.the bulletin. org/issues/ 1998/ja1998/ja1998albrigt.html>
51. "Joint Statement by The Chairman of The Atomic Energy Commission and The Scientific Adviser to The Defence Minister", *The Hindu*, 18 May 1998.
52. David, Albright, *Op cit.*
53. Steve, N. Dolly, "India and Pakistan Nuclear Test", *Nuclear Control Institute*, June 9, Washington, DC 1998<http://www.nci.org>
54. Iftekharuzzaman, "Living with a Nuclearised South Asia", *Asian Security in the 21st Century*, Jasgit Singh, (New Delhi: Knowledge World Publisher, 1999), p. 147.
55. Arundhati, Ghose, Statement in the First Committee of the General Assembly on 17 November, 1995, *quoted in* Gopal Singh and S.K. Sharma (Ed.) *Documents on India's Nuclear Disarmament Policy*, Vol. III (New Delhi, Anamika Publishers), p. 1360
56. Security Council Resolution 1172 (1998), June 6, 1998, <www.un.org/ Docs/sc. htm>.
57. Stephen, Cohen, "A New Beginning in South Asia", Policy Brief No. 55, *Brooking Institution*, January 2000, p. 2, <http:// www.brook.edu/comm/policybriefs/pbo55/pb55.htm>.
58. "Zangger Committee Statement on India's and Pakistan's Nuclear Tests", <http://project.spriel/expc on/Zangip.htm>.
59. Jasgit, Singh, "India, Europe and Non-Proliferation, Pokhran II and After", *Strategic Analysis*, November 1998, pp. 1111-22.
60. Brief on India's Nuclear Tests, Ministry of External Affairs, *Disarmament and International Security Affairs Division*, 1998, <http:// www.indiagovt.org/pic/nuclear/brief on nuclear tests.htm>.
61. Ramesh, Thakur, "The Best Solution to Nuclear Proliferation is Nuclear Disarmament", *The International Herald Tribune*, Paris, April 22, 2000.
62. N. Kunju, *Indo-Pak Nuclear Cold War*, (New Delhi: Reliance Publishing House, 2002), p. 149.
63. Guy, Wilson, Roberts, *"An Asian Pacific Security Crises New Challenges to Regional Stability"*, Center for Strategic Crises, p. 189.
64. Selig, Harrison, *"Armed India can Help Stabilize Asia,"* September 12, 2000. <http: www.la times.com>.

65. Robert, Windrem, *"Critical Mass: The Dangerous Race of Superpowers in a Fragmented World"*, (London: Simon and Schuster, 1995), p. 351.
66. Karl, Inderfurth, *"Statement Before US Senate Foreign Relations Subcommittee on Rear Eastern and South Asian Matters"*, May 13, 1998, <http://www. mtholyoke. edu/acad/intrel/senprol.htm>
67. Selig, Harrison, "Idea of a Nuclear Bargain Between India and US", *Asian Age*, 9 December 1997.
68. Raju, G. C., Thomas and Amit Gupta, *India's Nuclear Security*, (New Delhi: Vistaar Publication), 2000, p. 53.
69. Eva, Maria, Hexamer, "Nuclearisation of South Asia and Consequences for the International System", in B. M. Jain, Eva Maria Hexamer (Ed.), *Nuclearisation in South Asia*, (New Delhi: Rawat Publications, 1999), p. 59.
70. Jasgit, Singh, *Asian Security in the 21st Century*, (New Delhi: Knowledge World, 1999), p. 18.
71. *Ibid.*
72. Praful, Bidwai, Achin, Vanaik, *Op. cit.*, p.23.
73. Jaswant Singh, "India Committed to NPT Regime-Short of Joining it", *Indian Express*, 10 May, 2000.
74. "Evolution of India's Nuclear Policy", Lok Sabha Debate, 27 May, 1998.
75. Hooman, Peiman, *Nuclear Proliferation in the Sub-continent: Superpowers and Emerging Alliances*,(London: Westport Connection), p. 125.
76. Praful, Bidwai, Achin, Vanaik, *Op. cit.*, p. 239.
77. Soumgajit, Pattnaik, *"India Willing to Accept De-facto Nuclear Weapons Status"*, <http://www.fas.org/news/India/1998/07 1980 706 pin.htm>.
78. R. Venbrat, Raman, "Nuclear Explosion and its Aftermath", *India's Nuclear Leap*, Major Sulakhan Mohan, (Delhi: Indian Publishers Distributors), 2000, p. 25.
79. *Ibid.*
80. J. M. Jain, *Op. cit.*, p. 131.
81. Joseph, Goldblat, "The UN Security Council Resolution of 19 June and the Security of Non-Nuclear Weapon States", in SIPRI, *Nuclear Proliferation Stockholm*, 1974, pp. 236-8.
82. Ramesh, Thakur, "South Asia's Nuclear Tests Accentuating the Positive," *UNU Nexions*, June 1998 <http://www.UNU.edu/hq/ginfo/nex/jun98>.
83. J. P. Jain, *Op. cit.*, p. 163.
84. Andrew, John, Tabler, *"India: Tests are Legitimate Security Measures"*, <http://www.metimes.com/issue 98-22/reg/india_tests.htm>.
85. Ramesh, Thakur, "Envisioning Nuclear Futures", *Security Dialogue*, Vol. 31 (1): Sage Publications, p. 78.

86. Stephen, P. Cohen, "The Economic and Geo-Strategic Stakes in South Asia", *Oxford Analytica, Daily Brief*, 23 March, 2000.
87. Robert, M. Hathaway, "Confrontation and Retreat: The US Congress and South Asian Nuclear Tests", *Arms Control Today*, January-February 2000, <http://www. armscontrol.org/act/2000-01-02/rhjfoo.asp>.
88. K. R. Narayan, " Hailing the Test at Pokhran on 11 May, 1998" *quoted* in Gopal Singh and S.K. Sharma, *Documents on India's Nuclear Disarmament Policy*, Vol. III, (New Delhi: Anamika Publishers, 2000), p. 1468.
89. Statement made by the Principal Secretary to the Prime Minister, Brajesh Mishra on Nuclear Tests on 11 May, 1998 and in, *Documents on India's, Nuclear Disarmament Policy*, Vol. III, Gopal Singh and S.K. Sharma, (New Delhi: Anamika Publisher's 2000), p. 1469,.
90. Arundhati, Ghose, "Taming India", *Times of India*, 26 February, 1999.
91. Ashok, Kapur, "The NPT a View from the Indian Sub-continent in Nuclear Non-Proliferation and Global Security" (Ed.) *David B. Dewitt Nuclear Non-Proliferation and Global Security*, (Australia: Croom Helm Ltd.), 1987. pp. 206-9.
92. Aftab, Alam, *US Policy Towards South Asia*", (Delhi: Raj Publications, 1998), p. 91.
93. Lewis, A. Dunn, "High Room for the NPT", *Arms Control Today*, (Washington DC: Arms Control Association, July/August 1995), pp. 3-9.
94. Devin, T. Hagerty, *The Consequences of Nuclear Proliferation Lessons from South Asia*, (Cambridge: Belfer Center for Science and International Affairs, 1998), p. 176.
95. Aftab, Alam, *op cit*, pp. 96-97.
96. The Lahore Declaration, <http://www.medev.gov.in/govt./Lahore.htm>.
97. Amit, Gupta, "A Nuclear Arms Control Agenda in Raju G. C. Thomas and Amit Gupta, *India's Nuclear Security*, (New Delhi: Vistaar Publications, 2000), p. 284.
98. Ben, Sheppard, "South Asia Ballistic Missile Ambitions" in "Raju G. C. Thomas and Amit Gupta's, *India's Nuclear Security*, (New Delhi: Vistaar Publication, 2000), p. 184.
99. Prime Minister Vajpayee's, Letter to President Clinton, which Leaked to the Press, *Hindu*, May 14, 1998, New Delhi.
100. Raj, Chengappa, *Weapons of Peace: The Secret Story of India's Quest to be a Nuclear Power*, (New Delhi, Harper Collins Publisher, India 2000), p. 35 -35.
101. William, Walker, "International Nuclear Reactions After India and Pakistani Nuclear Explosions", *International Affairs*, Vol. 74, July 1998, p. 511.

102. W. Lawrence, S. Prabhakar, "Security Studies in India: Continuity and Change in The Post Cold War Era", in Dipanker Banerjee (Ed.) *"Security Studies in South Asia: Change and Challenges"*, (New Delhi, Manhoar Publishers, 2000), pp. 64-65.
103. Bhartiya Janata Party Election Manifesto, *"Our National Security"* <http://Bhartiya Janta Party.org/manifes/ chap 8.htm>.
104. P. R. Chari, "India's Nuclear Doctrine Confused Ambitions", *The Non-Proliferation Review* Fall-Winter, 2000, <http://cns.miis.edu/pubs/npr/vol 107/ 73/73 chari.pdf>
105. Jasgit, Singh, "Arms Control and Proliferation of High Technology Weapons in South Asia and The Middle East a View from India", In Shelley, A. Stahl, Arms, Kemp, Geoffrey, *Arms Control and Weapons Proliferation, South Asia*, pp. 123-24.
106. David, Mutimer, *Proliferation and the Framing of Security*, (USA: Lynne Reiner Publisher Inc. 2000), p. 119.
107. Amitabh, Matoo, "India's Nuclear Doctrine in Search of Strategic Autonomy", *Times of India*, August, 1999.
108. Jasgit, Singh, "India's Nuclear Doctrine: A Framework for Restraint and Strategic Satiability", Paper presented in *International Conference on Nuclear Weapons and Global Security*, Challenges for the New Millennium the Hague, 10-12 May, 2000.
109. Gurmeet, Kanwal, *Nuclear Defense Shaping the Arsenal*, IDSA, Knowledge World, April, 2001, p. 71.
110. Vernon, Hewitt, "Containing Shiva India Non-Proliferation and the Comprehensive Test, Ban Treaty" *Contemporary South Asia*, 2000 9(1), pp. 25-39.

3

Pakistan's Perspectives on the Non-Proliferation Treaty

The convergent and divergent interests of India and Pakistan on the NPT and their official positions on this issue form the main plank of the nuclear debate in South Asia. As was evident in the second chapter, the actual reasons for US discomfiture against a nuclearising India, was its failure to stop the spread of nuclear weapons to a developing nation. The deftly cajoled global US campaign and the argument designed to project South Asia as the potential flashpoint of nuclear conflict was challenged by India on the ground of its hollowness. The US has been the keen interpreter of the importance that the NPT bears on South Asia. This shall become a little clearer in this chapter, in the process of unfolding the intersections and concentricity of the Pakistan–United States foreign policy interests on the NPT. This chapter examines Pakistan's perspective on the Non-Proliferation Treaty. It acquires substantive importance as an attempt is made here to delve into the history of Pakistan's nuclear programme and its actual linkages with the security environment of Pakistan. A range of positions taken by Pakistan foreign office, Pakistani intelligentsia including stands of political analysts and statesmen and the military establishments are analytically discussed. This chapter further explores the international response to the nuclear tests undertaken by Pakistan.

Nuclear weapons are an integral part of the strategic discourse in Pakistan. The national consensus in nuclear weapon as epitomized by the Chagai explosions in May 1998, is an article of faith of the nuclear hawks in the country. Even as the United States, while emphasizing its partnership with Pakistan, in the war against terrorism, has given Pakistan a non-NATO (North Atlantic Treaty

Organisation) ally status, Pakistan's controversial nuclear weapon programme has ultimately proved disastrous to this chapter of partnership. The conflicting civil military relationship, weak economy, fragile social cohesion ridden with fundamentalist ideologies, lack of credible command and control mechanism raise the vulnerability of the risks related with the nuclear and strategic assets of Pakistan.[1]

Western analysts predict the dire consequences of the likelihood of a nuclear catastrophe in the region. In the backdrop of the rising nuclear tension in South Asia the question of signing the NPT has acquired special significance. Pakistan is being pressurised to sign the Non-Proliferation Treaty by the P5 nations. This chapter undertakes a comprehensive study of Pakistan's nuclear policy with special emphasis on the geo-political environment that it faces. The dominant discourse on the NPT here is based on the Pakistani perspective. A look at Pakistani contemporary security, thinking and behaviour brings out Pakistan's perception towards the NPT. Pakistan's disarmament policy has been overwhelmingly indocentric. Initially Pakistan supported the US sponsored NPT, but did not sign it because India hadn't signed it. However, the central concern had been that the NPT did not provide any security guarantees to Pakistan to induce it, to sign it, to join it. The underlying motivations of Pakistan's stance on the NPT are far more complex. Pakistan did not sign the NPT because it had decided to develop the nuclear option. Moreover, in its public statement about the NPT, Pakistan referred to its concern with geopolitical realities as the reason for not joining the NPT regime.[2]

THE GEO-STRATEGIC ENVIRONMENT AND PAKISTAN'S INSECURITY

Pakistan's geographical location presents its security planners with serious strategic problems. Pakistan is situated between Iran to the West and India to the East, and Afghanistan to the Northwest and China to the Northeast.[3] The quest for security has been at the heart of Pakistan's foreign policy since independence. A brief purview of its security perception can be analysed after examining its relations with its neighbours.

Iran and Pakistan's Security

Iran shares its border with Pakistan in the West, which stretches about 830 km[4]. Pak-Iran relations are in a state of flux and have become conflict-ridden over a number of issues. Pakistan has majority Sunni population while Iran is Shia in composition.

In the past decade there have been strains in their relationships when Pakistan suspected Iranian support for sectarian violence that plagued the country. Iran is sympathetic to the Shia minority in Pakistan; therefore, Pakistan is suspicious of its neighbour in the West.[5] Iran has been designated by US president George W. Bush as 'Axis of Evil' in January, 2000. Iran is critical of Pakistan's cooperation with the United States in the war against terrorism and has been exerting pressure on Musharaf to back out of the US Camp and actively campaign for the pull out the US forces from Iraq. Iran is party to the NPT and the comprehensive safeguards regime and is deeply concerned with Pakistani nuclear tests. Iran has cultivated close relationship with foreign suppliers that are not allied to nations like Russia, China and North Korea to develop its nuclear weapon in December, 2002. The US experts reveal that Iran was building two nuclear sites at Artak and Natanz that would be useful for nuclear weapon programme.[6] Iran's effort to build nuclear weapon is a matter of great security concern for Pakistan.

The Indian Threat

The Indian threat is described as single most pervading factor that has dominated the Pakistan's landscape.[7] The violence accompanying the partition leading to the emergence of two independent states of India and Pakistan generated hostility, which continues to afflict relations between countries mainly because of the unsettled issue of Jammu and Kashmir. Tension between India and Pakistan from the outset was ascribable partly to difficult and divisive legacy, adverbial perception of history, difference of religion and culture, the clash of political aims and ideologies Between the Muslim League and the Congress. The leaders of Indian National Congress accepted Pakistan grudgingly and anticipated that the new state would collapse.

Pakistan was a state in search of a National identity. It was always apprehensive about India's hegemonic ambitions.

Addressing the UN General Assembly in 1965 Zulfiqaur Ali Bhutto described Pakistan's security dilemma in no uncertain terms by asserting, "It was a small country facing a great aggressor always given to aggression." "The ultimate objective of monster" that is how India was referred to "was to annihilate Pakistan."[8] Ambassador Munir Akram stated, "Since its independence, our nation has confronted the endemic hostility of our neighbour." We have twice been subjected to aggression by this country, which dismembered our state in 1971 and is even now engaged in an eight year brutal war to suppress the right of self-determination of the people of occupied Jammu and Kashmir.[9]

Pakistan sees national security, as an extension of regional security in the broadest sense. At the regional level, the pursuit of domination by one state over its neighbour is a recipe for insecurity and instability. The prevailing asymmetry with regard to both strategic objective and relationship between military forces between the largest countries in South Asia and its small neighbours is a limit in factor for instability and has been exacerbated by Indian desire to dominate.[10]

India's possession of the Muslims core of the former Kashmir state, is perceived to keep Pakistan incomplete and fosters radicalising of grievances in Pakistan's domestic politics. Instances of India's successful use of force to cut Pakistan down to size as in the 1971 and dismemberment of the country is viewed as a proof of the lengths India will go with its superior military force. India's unilateral seizure of Siachin in 1984, and Pakistan's narrow escape from border war in the Brasstracks crisis of 1986-87, and successive military mobilizations since over Kashmir or the border with China in 1990 and most recently during Kargil crisis of 1999 are seen as reflection of India's dark side, its proclivity for military intimidation and its underlying threat to Pakistan's survival.[11]

Explaining the importance of nuclear capability the Pakistan's national security, General Mirza Aslam Beg former Chief of army staff wrote, that to give up the nuclear capability would be tantamount to committing a national suicide. To acquire this capability is totally in congruence with our defence requirement.[12] According to Chris Smith Pakistan's nuclear programme is rooted in the basic insecurity, namely profound conventional military imbalances, a chronic lack of defence in depth and a concern over India's hegemonic intention.[13] The arguments in favour of a nuclear option for Pakistan are interlinked with India's nuclear capability as well as providing protection to Pakistan's covert operation in Kashmir. K.M. Arif retired vice chief of the army staff and Munir Ahmed Khan who was the former chairman of the Pakistan Atomic Commission articulate such views.[14] Both of them believe that India's nuclear capability is a threat to Pakistan's national security and Pakistan's nuclear option is for a defensive purpose to forestall nuclear blackmail and hegemony of India.[15]

Pakistan's perception of threat to its national security is not imaginary; it is grounded on the experience of India's recurrent use of force to impose solutions of its own preference upon less powerful neighbours. Pakistan's concern are aggravated by the growing power, disparity and compounded by its lack of territorial depth for defence by conventional means.[16]

Pakistan views its own effort to acquire a nuclear capability as deterrence against a real military threat from its larger and hostile neighbour. This pursuit is born out of the need for self-defence in response to Indian nuclear explosion of 1974 and May 1998. If India had not introduced nuclear weapon into South Asia, Pakistan would have no reason to acquire them. Pakistan's case is univocal and is rationalized exclusively in term of India's nuclear test.[17]

Afghanistan and Pakistan's Threat Perceptions

With the threat of India perpetually looming from the West, and Afghan pressure on the western flank has been always a matter of anxiety for Pakistan. On the eve of the establishment of Pakistan, Afghan government denounced the 1893 treaty establishing the Durrand line as the boundary with British India and launched an irredentism in the guise of support for 'Pakistan'. Afghanistan was the only nation to vote against Pakistan's admission to the United Nation.[18] The Soviet invasion of Afghanistan made Pakistan a country of permanent geo strategic importance. In a matter of days the United States declared Pakistan as a frontline state against Soviet aggression. Pakistan received 3 million Afghan refugees who poured across the border. It provided a conduit for weapons and gave a safe haven to the Afghan Mujahidin. The Afghan crisis underscores the close relationship between Pakistan's internal and external security. The terrorism as well as cross-border drug trade, arms trafficking and other criminal activities that involve both Pakistan and Afghan elements, have adversely affected Pakistan's internal security. Pakistan's policy-makers are therefore pursuing strategies aimed at containing hostile Afghan activities in Pakistani soil while retaining a dominant role in Afghan politics to enhance Pakistan's regional influence and acquire sufficient geostrategic importance to balance that of India.[19] US pressure forced Pakistan into abandoning the Taliban. The United States regards Pakistan as an important ally and frontline state in the battle against the global terrorism.[20]

China-Pakistan Nexus

For Pakistan in particular, the time-tested friendship with China has been a critical factor of security and reassurance in facing up to the aggressive policies of India. With the enforcement of the Pressler law from October 1998 and the cessation of US economic and military aid, Pakistan's dependence on China's political and strategic support increased the importance of Pakistan's relation with China whereas, the western developed countries continued their ban on the supply of sensitive technology to Pakistan; China agreed to provide two nuclear power reactors in 1989 and 1996, though these were to be placed under institutional safeguards under the Pressler law and Russia resuming its strategic partnership with India, made China's friendship and support emerged as a cornerstone of Pakistan's security.[21] However, the position has changed since the Chagai nuclear test. The Chinese ambassador to the UN Security Council called on India and Pakistan to exercise restraints, stop all further nuclear tests, and abandon their nuclear weapons development programme, be committed to the CTBT and NPT immediately and unconditionally.[22]

Pakistan's Views on the NPT

Pakistan supported the draft nuclear Non-Proliferation Treaty and its representative described it as a 'landmark' and by far the most important agreement yet reached on disarmament. It had voted in favour of the resolution commending the NPT in 1968.[23] However, after India declined to sign the treaty Pakistan also refused to put its signature on it. Pakistan has perceived it's joining the treaty without reciprocal move on the part of India as a serious threat to its national security.

Pakistan had supported the Irish draft resolution[24] pertaining to stop the dissemination of nuclear weapon and the then present danger of the spread of these nuclear weapons and the knowledge of their technology to states which do not posses them. This imminent peril demands that the General Assembly gives an urgent consideration to the conclusion of the treaty to outlaw the further spread of nuclear weapon and knowledge of their manufacture.[25]

At the 20th session of the General Assembly, the Pakistani delegate Shahi opposed the Indian demand for an acceptable balance of mutual responsibilities and obligations of nuclear and non-nuclear powers. According to him the effect of such a demand was to make the conclusion of the treaty on Non-Proliferation impossible since its imposed conditions had raised a host of problems in which wide difference had existed between the East and the West for nearly two decades.[26]

The Indian opposition to the NPT was misinterpreted by Pakistan as a delaying tactics to further her nuclear ambition. In his criticism Shahi emphasized that India represented the *n*[th] country problem particularly in view of the fact that it had refused to open its nuclear establishment to international inspection and safeguards and already a chemical separation plant in its territory.

During the period 1965-68 Pakistan continued to support the superpower manoeuvres to affect a ban on the wider spread of the nuclear weapon. Thus in the General Assembly Resolution 2373 (XXII) adopted on 12th June, 1968, commending the Nuclear Non-Proliferation Treaty, Pakistan cast a positive vote. It was in contrast to Indian voting behaviour.[27]

Pakistan has already made it clear that its decision about the Non-Proliferation Treaty will be guided by the attitude of India to this issue and it was Indian policy which largely determine Pakistan's action in this sphere and Pakistan would not commit itself to NPT unless India did the same.[28]

Bhutto categorically rejected the NPT on the ground that it would limit Pakistan's future need for a deterrent Bhutto saw the NPT as a deception and an intrusion in Pakistan's nuclear activities. He stressed the importance of national security measures as a back up of Pakistan's diplomacy.[29] Pakistan's attitude to the Non-Proliferation of nuclear weapon is mainly determined by the fear of a nuclear India. Its position on the NPT, which it had not singed, demonstrates the interaction of security interest in a sensitive region.[30] Usmani expressed along with other Pakistani officials that Pakistani policy on the NPT is linked with India's position on the treaty.[31]

According to brigadier Siddiqi (retd.) there are two major factors pushing Pakistan into nuclear race, these are the urge to keep up with Jones (India) and the NPT, which is discriminatory against the nuclear have nots. Prestige and security needs push countries into nuclear race and vertical proliferation of nuclear weapons adds fire to the fuel and leads to horizontal proliferation of nuclear weapons.[32]

Pakistan realized that a number of NPT members paid only lip service to the treaty and joined it for reasons of convenience. It acknowledged that nuclear weapon states did not provide any security guarantee to non-nuclear weapon states. In face of these realities Pakistan decided to keep its nuclear option open. Unlike India, Pakistan was concerned with horizontal rather than vertical proliferation, especially weapons proliferation in India. The pre-occupation with an arrangement to secure this objective impelled Pakistan to initiate a proposal as early as 1966, for a conference to discuss the security of non-nuclear weapon states.[33]

Pakistan felt, the imbalance of the obligation in the treaty should not prevent countries accepting Non-Proliferation measures, neither was it realistic to impose obligations on nuclear weapon states. Instead non-nuclear states should be given adequate security guarantees against the threat of use of nuclear weapon. The same argument went for the application of the safeguards on civilian nuclear activities ever if such measures were applied equally, the imbalance would persist as along as nuclear weapon states are permitted to retain their nuclear capabilities.[34]

Pakistan maintained that its position on the NPT was dependent on the geographical context of the region in which it was situated. Pakistan tried to build the image of a restrained small power suffering from hegemonic tendencies of the bigger power in the South Asian region.

The NPT provides for a verification provision. Pakistan has shown considerable sensitivity to foreign inspection safeguards.

There is little prospect that Pakistan will unilaterally agree to US inspectors to verify its nuclear status. Such inspection would not only hurt Pakistani status but also carry sensitive security implications, which would benefit India.

The Pakistani representative in the UN stated "we believe that the concern for Non-Proliferation should not militate against the inherent rights of developing countries to benefit from the peaceful nuclear technology in a universal and non-discriminatory basis."[35]

In May 1981 Agha Shai reiterated the position, "why should only nuclear power have the privilege of carrying the nuclear explosions...we shall see if and when we get the capability. We will find out what the international regime has envisaged."[36]

A SIPRI study maintains that 'Pakistan is likely to sit on the fence over the NPT until there is change in India's position.'[37] This study goes on to assert that Pakistani government has taken a positive attitude to the Non-Proliferation Treaty as such, but has indicated that it feels unable to adhere to the NPT because of the apprehension of Indian policies in particular the fact that India is not prepared to accept the NPT.[38]

According to a Pakistani government statement on 13 May 1968, "all the near nuclear countries would have to join the NPT before Pakistan did it". Pakistan was equally concerned about Israel's possession of nuclear weapons. In the name of Non-Proliferation of nuclear weapons and projecting their elimination as the ultimate objective, this treaty actually aims at securing permanent monopoly of nuclear technology by five nuclear powers. The objective of the treaty was to 'cleanse' the world except those countries that already had acquired the capability of nuclear weapons and to restrict the use of nuclear technology to peaceful purposes only.

Unlike the proclaimed objective of the NPT the actual underlying motive seemed to perpetuate nuclear apartheid at a global level. It implied that nuclear deterrence should remain monopolized with nuclear powers. Secondly the nuclear capability of the rest of the countries is frozen up at the level where it stood at the time of any agreement. Third the possibility of any emerging nuclear power is eliminated. Fourth whatever the scope there was for the peaceful use of nuclear technology it should be further limited and particularly left at the mercy of nuclear powers. In today's world balance of power depends on nuclear deterrence and if the Muslim world remains devoid of it, it would be at the mercy of others. Pakistan is the first Muslim country that has acquired the nuclear capability. Pakistan has challenged the western monopoly. Therefore, the nuclear doctrine of Pakistan cannot be de-linked from the non-discrimination at the world level and from the risks of Indian aggression.[39]

In the 1980's Pakistan was under the increasing pressure from the United States to move towards Non-Proliferation and make a unilateral commitment on the NPT. Pakistan refused to do so. However, to prove its seriousness about Non-Proliferation and to prevent the nuclearisation of South Asia it offered a regional approach to Non-Proliferation.

Pakistan has always believed that a regional approach to Non-Proliferation and disarmament is complementary to international endeavour towards those objectives. Pakistan believes that without taking into consideration the regional aspects of Non-Proliferation it would not be possible for such states like Pakistan that face strategic security threats to adhere to the provisions such as the NPT. Since the first Indian nuclear test in 1974, Pakistan made several proposals to keep the regime free of nuclear weapons.

These proposals included:

- Establishment of a nuclear weapon free zone in South Asia 1974.
- A joint declaration in 1979 renouncing the acquisition or manufacture of nuclear weapons.
- Simultaneous adherence if the International Atomic Energy Agency safeguards all nuclear facilities, 1979.
- Bilateral Regional Nuclear Test Ban, 1987.
- Conference on Non-Proliferation in South Asia, 1991.
- Zero Missile Zones in South Asia, 1973.
- No war pact in South Asia, 1973.

All these proposals have been rejected by India because it does not take into account India's security interests. India has reservations to the concept of zonal Non-Proliferation in isolation from the global nuclear disarmament.[40]

Any attempt to comprehend Pakistani perspective on NPT might go amiss if the views of various statesman and foreign policy analysts are not included. These views from various sections of the intelligentsia and leading statesman are governed by the underlying concern for national security.

Bhutto described the NPT as "an international treaty limiting this deterrence to nuclear powers. Making Pakistan's attitude towards the NPT conditional upon India's nuclear ambitions Bhutto argued that Pakistan should not allow herself to be deceived by the treaty because India will proceed with its nuclear programme inspite of the Non-Proliferation regime.[41]

Pakistan's Foreign Minister Sartaj Aziz has said that the signing of the Non-Proliferation Treaty is not possible because it recognizes only five countries as nuclear powers. "There is no question of signing it because we cannot join the NPT in its present shape." In the present shape of the NPT only five countries are nuclear powers and they do not accept others within their arena. "Therefore either they amend the treaty or allow us entry as nuclear power, only then we may join it."[42]

Pakistani Prime Minister Nawaz Sharif emphasized that established nuclear weapon states had double standard on nuclear Non-Proliferation. The Nuclear Non-Proliferation Treaty is discriminatory. In an interview with dailies *'Al-I-ttihad'* and *'Emirates'* he said, 'the established weapon states have sought to justify their retention of weapon on the basis of deterrence when none of them is threatened directly or indirectly in the post-Cold War era. He said, Pakistan is not focussing on Non-Proliferation issues 'which cannot be persuaded in a security void'. Pakistan's nuclear weapons were mainly to deter aggression against it whatever conventional or nuclear.[43]

Pakistan unlike India did not oppose the indefinite extension of the NPT. Pakistan endorsed the significance of the decision adopted by the NPT review conference to extend the treaty indefinitely. However Pakistan emphasized that indefinite extension of the NPT cannot imply the indefinite division of the world into two classes of states, nuclear and non-nuclear.

Pakistan believes that NPT is a factor of international stability. "We are happy that the treaty has been extended. This does not imply that we can overlook its discriminatory character, in view of our security concerns, which arises principally from threats within our region; Pakistan cannot accede to the NPT unilaterally.[44]

A Pakistani foreign analyst Shireen M. Mazari has enunciated that the NPT exemplifies the discriminatory approach to nuclear arms control and disarmament propagated by the US. The treaty has different sets of rights and obligations of nuclear and non-nuclear states. While the latter are forbidden to acquire nuclear weapon technology and weaponry, the former are simply required to pursue in good faith negotiations towards reduction and eventual elimination of their nuclear weapons under Article VI a non-binding commitment. The treaty also places compulsorily those facilities under IAEA safeguards that have imported components basically means the reactors of developing states. Again the treaty has a static definition of a nuclear weapon state. A state that tested a nuclear devise prior to 1 January, 1967 (Article IX) this clause makes the treaty redundant for new nuclear weapon states like Pakistan and India. However the two articles that do not impose the binding obligation on nuclear weapon states has never been operationalised. These are Articles IV and V which stress the rights of all parties to the treaty to fully exploit nuclear energy for peaceful purpose and parties to the treaty receive the benefits of peaceful nuclear explosion at low costs from the nuclear weapon states.[45]

The territorial conflicts along with the high probability of war between the two regional powers have created a situation where Pakistan was compelled to acquire nuclear deterrence. Mazari argues that territorial problem was central in Indo-Pak conflict. Pakistan's need for deterrence is so strong that it should never sign the NPT or the Comphrensive Test Ban Treaty, even if India does sign them. She continued that for deterrence Pakistan should never link its nuclear stance with India. This view was shared by others like Ross Masud Hussein who commented in a 1997 interview that even if India signed the NPT or the Comphrensive Test Ban Treaty, Pakistan would not do so for its security concerns. In 1996 Rasul Rais argued that Pakistan must consider its security options carefully to make decision on its own national security interests independent of what India does.[46]

Historical Development of Pakistan's Nuclear Programme

Pakistan was a late starter in recognizing the significance of atomic energy for its developmental purpose and security. It inherited a very rudimentary infrastructure for scientific and industrial research. Mohammad Ali Jinah and Liaquat Ali Khan did not have a scientific temper and vision of peace and security in the dawning nuclear age. Undoubtedly they were very much aware to Pakistan's security concern but nuclear factor did not enter into long-term calculations.[47] Pakistan's move to threshold has been more straightforward and more reactive to Indian developments. A look at the dominant strategic discourse of the 1960's will make clear that the nuclear factor was conspicuous by its absence in that decade and gradually became an integral part of strategic discourse in 1970's. The Indian threat and the construction of a Pakistani identity to counter it continued to the dominant political discourse.

By mid 1960's India had built a research reactor and reprocessing plant and the nuclear weapon issue had become a part of public debate at home. It is at relatively late juncture that Pakistan entered the nuclear field. Islamabad's nuclear preparations had a decidedly military orientation. Efforts began in earnest to produce indigenously or acquire clandestinely and illegally if necessary the essential components of such a programme.[48]

Ayub Khan ruled out utilizing nuclear weapon as a means to deter Indian threat despite of the fact that such weapon were in currency as effective deterrent in East-West rivalry. Ayub Khan inducted Zulfiquar Ali Bhutto into his cabinet in 1958. He was associated with Pakistan Atomic Energy Commission. It was Bhutto, the leader of a truncated Pakistan who methodically turned this dormant issue into a symbol of national identity.

Bhutto played a key role in bringing the nuclear issue into the political arena through his works and patronage of the Pakistan Atomic Energy Commission. Bhutto claimed in his writings[49] to be the political father of Pakistan nuclear weapon programme. In his speeches and writings as Foreign Minister, Bhutto argued in favour of Pakistan's nuclear option and a nuclear deterrent. During this period Pakistan's nuclear posture in relation to nuclear Non-Proliferation Treaty was not to join the regime. This posture signalled an intention to keep Pakistan's nuclear option open.[50] Pakistan's nuclear programme began in 1953 when Pakistan Atomic Energy Committee was upgraded to Pakistan's Atomic Energy Commission and soon made arrangements in training a large number of scientists in radioisotopes and research technology.[51]

Bhutto echoed for the first time in the public in 1965 that

Pakistan would acquire a nuclear weapon capability. His famous and often-quoted statement on the subject goes as follows "If India developed an atomic bomb, we too will develop one, even if we have to eat grass or to remain hungry because there is no conventional alternative to the atomic bomb".[52]

It was mainly due to Bhutto's persistent efforts that Pakistan institute for nuclear science and technology was set up and negotiations for the Karachi Nuclear Power Plant (KANUPP) started. PINSTECH is to Pakistan what Bhabha Atomic Research Centre (BARC) is to India. The two small research reactors are the Pakistan Atomic Research Reactor (PARR) at PINSTECH and they are the centrepiece of Pakistan's open nuclear research and development programme. PARR is a 10 MW pool type research reactor that was supplied by the US in 1965 and converted to a burn 20 per cent enriched uranium fuel.[53] PARR 2 is a Chinese supplied 27-kilowatt thermal pool type research reactor that is fuelled by one kg of HEU.[54]

Pakistan's first nuclear power plant KANUPP having a capability of 137 MW and located some 15 miles West of Karachi at paradise point on the Bulegi coast was built by Canadian General Electric Company and was inaugurated by Bhutto in November, 1972. This plant is under IAEA safeguards. Canada abrogated its nuclear cooperation agreement with Pakistan in December 1976 because of Pakistan's refusal to agree to full safeguards. Another plant was set up at Chasma Barrage in Minwali district, which was supposed to have the capacity of 500 MW. Pakistan had not been able to negotiate for new plants till then because countries, in a position to supply materials, insisted on adherence to full scope safeguards, which Pakistan had refused to do so. Pakistan continued with it's nuclear weapons programme by obtaining clandestine hardware and equipment for its plant located at Kahuta as well as other related installations from a number of western countries. Pakistan managed to procure equipment for it Kahuta plant from Vakkum Apparat technique and CORA engineering from Switzerland Emedson Electric of UK, Transussia of Netherlands and Leybald Haralow and Aluminium, Van Doorne Walzewala of West Germany.[55]

Pakistan during 1973-74 asked France for certain type of analyses, which were specifically relevant for the production of nuclear weapon. Though the aid was not given French did believe that Pakistan had an apparent interest in the development of nuclear arms.[56]

Pakistan under Zulfiquar Ali Bhutto and Mohammad Zia Ul Haq evaded the worlds export control restrictions and worked hard to develop the ability to enrich Uranium.[57] Adoption of nuclear Non-Proliferation measures by the US resulting in the discontinuance of nuclear aid to PAEC since the 1970's and the withdrawal of technical assistance, fuel and spare parts by Canada is supposed to have accelerated the pace of self-sufficiency in the nuclear field in Pakistan. Pakistan has faced numerous challenges in operating its Karachi Nuclear Power Reactor. However PAEC has over the years made efforts to create the technical infrastructure, the industrial resources and personal enterprise necessary to support station operation and to overcome the difficult inherent in use of nuclear technology, in a developing country.[58]

Pakistan's capability to produce fissile material rests on its ability to enrich Uranium. This is situated at the uranium enrichment facility in Kahuta. The facility in the hub of Islamabad's nuclear weapon programme and contains an unsafeguarded uranium enrichment plant using centrifuge technology based on Urenco U-1 and U-2 designs stolen by Dr. A.Q. Khan.[59]

In addition to Kahuta, Pakistan has two smaller centrifuge facilities at Golra and at Sinhala. Neither of these is subject to energy safeguard due to Pakistan's non-membership in the NPT. Western intelligence sources are reported to have claimed in 1987 that a uranium enrichment facility was being constructed at Golra.[60]

Pakistan began trying to enrich uranium in 1976. (A Pakistani national from European technology holder Urenco, the gas centrifuge enrichment constorium stole Gas Centrifuge designs.) Most reports identify the agent as A.Q. Khan a Pakistani metallurgist. The centrepiece of Pakistan's enrichment programme is Kahuta gas centrifuge plant near Islamabad. Pakistan turned to China for help. One 1989 report stated that China had supplied enough weapon, graded uranium to make two nuclear bombs.[61]

P. B. Sinha and R. R. Subramanium are of the view that Pakistan's effort to opt for the enrichment route had started as early as 1972. A significant step in this direction was Dr. A. Q. Khan returned to Pakistan in 1975 with a blue print of the ultracentrifuge plant. It would seem more appropriate to hold 'serious action' to acquire this technology and appropriate equipment and instrumentation started in 1977, when it was more or less clear that Pakistan ultimately might not be able to import a reprocessing plant from France.[62]

In February 1984, a report was published in the Times; London entitled 'Hint of Pakistan Atom Bomb'. This news was based on an interview by Dr. A. Q. Khan with the Urdu daily *Nawa-I-Waqt* in which Dr. Khan was purported to have said that 'Pakistan has broken the Western countries' monopoly in the enrichment of Uranium.[63]

It was believed that Dr. Khan had revealed Pakistan's successful mastery of the enrichment technology and resultant capability to produce nuclear weapons were based on highly enriched Uranium. Pakistan was estimated to have enriched Uranium up to 30 per cent in March 1986 and the January 1988 it was thought to have achieved a level up to 93 per cent.[64] Pakistan had thus crossed the 'red line' laid down by President Regan which was not supposed to be crossed by Pakistan as part of the understanding to exempt Pakistan from the application of the US Non-Proliferation Act, to allow the uninterrupted flow of economic and military aid Pakistan achieved a major breakthrough in nuclear reactor design technology in 1991 when in 5 November, Dr. Ashfaq Ahmad Khan who replaced Muir Ahmad Khan as Chairman of PAEC announced PARR— had been indigenously redesigned and upgraded from 5 November to 10 November by Pakistan nuclear scientists and technicians. Enriched Uranium fuel for the reactor would be provided by China under IAEA safeguards.[65]

After assuming power, Prime Minister Benazir Bhutto, tried to break the barriers created by the US and the Western powers aimed at curbing Pakistan's nuclear programme. She was particularly critical of US policy towards Pakistan's nuclear programme. She also held Washington responsible for Western attitude to Pakistan's peaceful intensions. The West in her view, always doubted its declarations about peaceful nature of its nuclear programme. She also tried to capitalize her international goodwill to break the nuclear blockade.[66]

Making his country's position clear on the issue of safeguards Munir Ahmad Khan stated, "Pakistan would not buy a nuclear power plant from any where without International Atomic Energy Safeguards. Pakistan will not accept so called full scope safeguards, i.e. putting its entire nuclear programme under International Atomic Energy Agency safeguards, nor will Pakistan sign the NPT which he characterised as a political issue".[67]

France after its decision to join the NPT and on persuasion from the US decided not to supply the agreed 900 MW reactors to Pakistan. The plant was expected to be supplied by the Framtome and was to be located in Chasma. The nuclear plant as assured by the then Prime Minister of Pakistan, Benazir Bhutto would be open to international safeguard and monitoring terms. However at the same time she stressed that Pakistan was not getting involved in a nuclear arms race and was ready to accept the NPT provided India did likewise.[68]

Now France was in a position to convey diplomatically to Pakistan to sign the NPT or take action that would guarantee sufficient safeguards. Pakistan however has been taking the position that it would submit its nuclear installations to IAEA safeguards if India does. Now with France's new status as Nuclear Weapons state party to the NPT, it would insist on all safeguards and Pakistan can get the reactor only by taking steps that do not depend on whether India takes them or not.[69]

Rationale for Going Nuclear

Pakistan's main efforts are directed towards achieving parity with India. If so far India has nuclear weapons capability then so must Pakistan. Pakistan's approach is based on real politic in the narrow sense of the term. Relative to India, Pakistani nuclear weapons programme, is more strictly national security oriented. Under different geographical circumstances, Pakistan would be a large and powerful country in its own right, but Pakistan had the misfortune to be born out of the shadow of a larger nuclear India that is transcendent fact of Pakistani geo-political life. The core aim of Pakistan's nuclear weapons is to prevent a repetition of 1971. In this context Pakistan's military rulers have emphasized, Pakistan's rationale for its nuclear weapons, which according to them would not only deter the threat of India's nuclear weapons but also to counter India's conventional military superiority. Even since the inception of its nuclear programme Pakistan's nuclear weapons have been in military custody and the country's rulers had no control over them.[70]

In the aftermath of loss of East Pakistan in 1971, Pakistan's sense of insecurity increased and the leaders became extremely worried about its survival and integrity. On 20 January, 1972, Zulfikar Ali Bhutto called a meeting of scientists in Multan and asked them how they could contribute to the security of the country to meet not only the conventional threat but also a looming nuclear challenge from India. At this meeting Mrs. Bhutto endorsed the idea of developing a nuclear capability for Pakistan and decided to completely reorganize the Atomic Energy in the country. He appointed Munir Ahmed Khan as the New Chairman of the Pakistan Energy Commission and created a new ministry of science and technology.[71]

Ever since its emergence as an independent nation Pakistan has tried to become a leader of the Islamic fraternity. For Pakistani leadership especially for Bhutto, the acquisition of nuclear technology and nuclear weapons would make Pakistan one of the most important and respected members of the Muslim bloc.[72] Declaring common cause with the Islamic countries Bhutto wrote from his death cell "we know that Israel and South Africa have full nuclear capability. The communist powers also possess it only the Islamic civilization is without it."[73] Bhutto called the nuclear capability as the 'Sword of Islam'. Francis Fukuyama has said "acquisition of nuclear weapons is very much bounded with Pakistan's self-conception as the leader of the Islamic world.[74]

The Indian nuclear explosion has been a major element in Pakistan threat perceptions. Pakistan does not subscribe to the Indian view that the 1974 Pokhran explosion was a peaceful one. There was a growing belief among Pakistani politicians and strategists that India possesses a small stockpile of nuclear weapons and hence proliferation across the border is an accomplished fact.[75]

Many analysts have argued that Pakistan's nuclear programme has emanated 'solely as a reaction to India's nuclear capabilities.' A Kroc institute study confirms the ethnocentric of basis of Pakistan's security. India is military mammoth with a blue water Navy. Pakistan's security and survival be in preparing as quickly as possible the weapons of ultimate destruction.[76]

Pervaiz Iqbal Cheema a Pakistan defence analyst has argued that "Pakistan's nuclear choices directly or indirectly linked with the developments in the region, more specially the Indian nuclear policy.[77] Akhtar Ali however blames the Indian 'bomb lobby' for popularising the view that Pakistan's nuclear effort antedate that of India, that it as an independent one and it was not a consequence of India's nuclear activities.[78]

The Indian nuclear explosion of 1974 proved to be a major blow to the Non-Proliferation regimes but it also changed the security climate in South Asia. Pakistan wanted the world community particularly the sponsors of the NPT to respond to this challenge to the Non-Proliferation regime. To Pakistan's dismay however the reaction was very muted at the government level. Pakistan also bought this matter up before the board of governors of the International Atomic Energy Agency on 8th June 1974. Pakistan warned the board that the underground explosion though called peaceful could not be distinguished from that of a nuclear weapon and would undersize the Non-Proliferation regime. Pakistan realized that the major powers were not ready to take serious action against the serious challenge to the Non-Proliferation regime by India. Instead they were barring Pakistan's access to nuclear technology and other facilities contracted under the International Atomic Energy Agency safeguards. All this added to Pakistan's disappointment but steeled its resolve and strengthened its determination to develop and acquire essential nuclear technology indigenously.

Another rationale for the bomb was based on the assumption that if Pakistan had the bomb, India would not so easily retaliate even if Pakistan started new adventures in Kashmir. Pakistan from its birth had been determined to wrest Kashmir from India and twice it tried to settle the issue by the force of arms. On such occasions, its efforts had been thwarted, partly by the people of Kashmir and due to superiority of Indian arms. Once Pakistan acquires the nuclear capability the strategic situation would change.[79]

Pakistan nuclear tests coming in response to India's nuclear explosions were triggered as a matter of fact by Bhartiya Janata Party's policy of using the nuclear options. Its proactive stand on Jammu and Kashmir asking Pakistan to vacate Azad Kashmir proved a key factor in Pakistan's decision to go nuclear. The Indian Home Minister L. K. Advani, right after the tests went to the extent of suggesting 'Islamabad should realize the change in the geo-strategic situation and roll back its anti-India policy especially with regard to Kashmir. India's bold and decisive decision to become a nuclear weapon state has brought a qualitative new stage in Indo-

Pak relations particularly finding a new solution to the Kashmir problem. It signifies India's resolve to deal firmly and strongly with Pakistan's hostile designs and activities on Kashmir.[80]

The arrogance on the part of the BJP leadership to seek a military solution to Kashmir dispute left Pakistan with little choice but show India that it would not hesitate to put to test it nuclear capability in order to have equitable resolution to the Kashmir problem. The nuclearisation of South Asia once again brought into focus the linkage between the Kashmir dispute and the proliferation of nuclear arms in South Asia.[81]

General Beg argues that Pakistan's nuclear weapons programme was a response to the "geo-political ambitions emanating from deeper recesses of the Hindu psyche". It was no act of choice but compulsion. Pakistan was forced to follow India. This involved "colossal hardships, but after having overcome this and attaining a nuclear capabilities there is no way it should give it up".[82]

In early October 1995, the Pakistan Senate called in several retired senior officials former Foreign Minister Agha Shai, Abdul Sattar, Zulfikar Ali Khan, Aziz Ahmed Khan and foreign policy analyst Shireen Mazari to express opinion about Pakistan's nuclear strategy. They reached a unanimous statement that nuclear deterrence is essential for national security". In mid December 1995 former Army Chief General Aslam Beg urged, Mrs. Bhutto to activate and accelerate Pakistan's nuclear programme in order to maintain, nuclear deterrence at a high pitch.[83]

Reaching for the Bomb

Pakistan's historical India-centric apprehensions led them to develop by 1984, the capability to produce low enriched Uranium. The leader of Pakistan's Uranium enrichment programme Dr. Abdul Qadeer Khan had periodic interviews boasting about Pakistan's nuclear prowess. It was in such an interview in February 1984, he first made the claim that Pakistan had achieved nuclear weapons capability. In July 1984, the *New York Times* reported that US intelligence had learned that the previous year China had supplied Pakistan with the design of an actual tested nuclear device, the design of China's fourth nuclear weapon tested in 1966 with a yield of 25 pt.[84]

The Pakistani Foreign Secretary Sharyar Kahn admitted in February 7, 1992, *Washington Post* interview that his country had the components to assemble at least one nuclear bomb.[85]

In 1991 Islamabad considered the new order advocated by the US and especially the call for Non-Proliferation a strategic threat to its independence. The new world order does not allow any country in the developing world except American surrogates to possess nuclear weapons. Fully aware that no single country can confront the US on its own, Islamabad stressed the growing significance of nuclear and military cooperation with other radicals as a profound issue, of cooperation with the US. If Pakistan surrendered before the Americans now in respect to its nuclear programme, there would be no limit for such surrender because the American, endeavour to demolish Pakistan's initiatory power and make her banana republic won't be lacking, so that the Muslim world should be enslaved by the US imposed world order.

It was in the context of this strategic perception that Pakistani nuclear capabilities were finally admitted officially. In a Karachi meeting Dr. Abdul Qadeer Khan, the father of the Pakistani bomb acknowledged that Pakistan was close to becoming a nuclear power. In the summer of 1995 despite western political pressing the Pakistani nuclear programme was accelerating. Dr. Abdul Qadeer Khan reaffirmed that Islamabad was not slowing down, let alone halting his various programme and projects. In the fall of 1995 Islamabad interpreted the partial lifting of the Pressler Amendment by passing the Brown Amendment in the US Senate as Washington's affirmation of Pakistani nuclear arsenal. In the aftermath of the US secrete vote, sources close to Mrs. Bhutto explained, "America now understands that our nuclear programme is not negotiable".

Pakistan's Nuclear Programme

Pakistan has continued with its nuclear programme through all possible means. It has also indulged in smuggling to obtain other elements needed for the manufacture of nuclear weapons. In 1984, Canadian authorities intercepted fifty nuclear triggers called Krytons intended for Pakistan. In 1988 the West German company Nuchem was caught shipping Tritium and Uranium hexaflouride to Pakistan.[86]

In fact Pakistani nuclear programme was heavily dependent on German assistance. Six on-going projects depended heavily on equipment and designs from the advanced nuclear states. These included original Kahuta enrichment plant, the Dera Ghazi Khan Uranium hexaflouride plant, a major expression in enrichment capability the designs of a reactor that could be used for the production of Tritium and Tritium purification plant. Pakistan also made several attempts to obtain beryllium from West Germany and United States, in some cases Pakistan has succeeded. China has assisted Pakistan in the construction of a 30 KW enriched Uranium fuelled reactor at Chasma. Pakistan is also reported to have sought China's help in obtaining ring magnets for its centrifuges. In 1996 it was reported that China supplied some 5000 ring magnets to Abdul Qadeer Khan research Laboratory at Kahuta, the site of Pakistan's main enrichment plant.[87]

Chagai Explosions

Chagai explosions mark a new era in the nuclear policy of Pakistan. After India's five nuclear explosions of May 11 and 13 May 1998, Pakistan was left with no choice but to give a corresponding response to India's nuclear tests.[88] Pakistan abandoned the show of atomic restraint by threatening an immediate response to India's nuclear tests. India's actions, which pose an immediate and grave threat to Pakistan security will not go unanswered stated Pakistan's Foreign Minister Gohar Ayub Khan. Pakistan's nuclear tests coming in response to India's nuclear explosions were triggered as a matter of fact by Bharitya Janata Party policy of using the nuclear option. Its pro-active stand on Jammu and Kashmir asking Pakistan to vacate Azad Kashmir proved to be a key factor in Pakistan's decision to go nuclear.[89] On May 28 Pakistan did the expected and simultaneously detonated five nuclear devices in a tunnel under the Ras Koh mountain range near Chagai in Baluchistan.The Mountain turned white. "Today we have settled a score", Nawaz Sharif declared over national television.[90]

The politically motivated nuclear explosion of Pokhran II put Pakistan in an inevitable 'no loss situation'. The consequent counter explosions on 28 and 30 May in Chagai have not only propelled Pakistan on the global and regional stage but also pulled out the country from all time low morale and disillusionment. Due to the

Vajpayee magic wand the post nuclear Pakistan is a new Pakistan that is nuclear.[91]

At the international level the rapid nuclearisation of the sub-continent has amassed four advantages for Pakistan. First Pakistan is no longer a clandestine nuclear state, having bombs in the basement. Nor is it a nuclear threshold state. It is a declared nuclear power.

Secondly the ultimate onus of triggering a nuclear arms race would always be squarely on India's shoulders. Thirdly the restrained reaction of Pakistan in counter exploding is being favourably viewed as a product of legitimate security concerns, mounting atomic pressure and the failure of the international community to effectively respond to India's adventure.

The Nuclear tests conducted out in July 1998 were the work of the Pakistan Atomic Energy Commission and National Development Council the rival group of the Khan Research Laboratory. The Prime Minister had first asked Dr. Khan if he could respond to the Indian tests and the time required to which Dr. Khan replied giving a schedule of one month. The Prime Minister was in a rush to get underway and it was then that the Pakistan Atomic Energy Commission offered to conduct the tests sooner. Six tests were undertaken within about 15 days of India's explosion. The head of the National Developmental Council, Dr. Samar Mubarik Mand hailed from the same province as Nawaz Sharif.[92]

On May 28 Sharif addressed the nation on television a few hours after testing five nuclear devices. Today we took a historic step for our security, he said 'we must stop India from nuclear domination'.[93] Pakistan Foreign Ministry spokesman Tariq Alatlaf, said "If we feel that strategic parity in the region is threatened we will take appropriate measures" to correct the strategic balance.[94]

The Pakistan Cabinet Defence Committee under the Chairmanship of Prime Minister Nawaz Sharif undertook a security and strategic review of the situation in the country. An official statement said Pakistan could not ignore India's grounding nuclear and conventional capabilities. Pakistan remains sensitive to international Non-Proliferation concerns. However Pakistan is opposed to an arms race on the introduction of weapons system, which could destabilise the security environment of the region.[95]

Benazir Bhutto blamed India for breaking the undeclared Non-Proliferation rule in South Asia and compelling Pakistan to declare its nuclear capability called for a full fledged diplomatic drive to convince the world that it had become inevitable for it to conduct nuclear tests because of security measure.[96]

One of the most significant gains of Pakistan in the aftermath of the successive nuclearisation is that India's military superiority in conventional forces vis-à-vis Pakistan has been effectively checkmated. The Indian design to become a regional power with even extending influence would suffer a setback. The six explosions at Chagai have all of a sudden firmly established moral and psychological ascendancy over India. The post nuclear strategy of Pakistan should be to draw continued attention to the explosive situation in the sub-continent thereby internationalising the Kashmir issue and thereby invoking third party mediation for its resolution. Because of India's sudden and reckless initiative Pakistan stands taller than ever as the seventh nuclear power in the world.[97]

Post-Chagai Reactions

The post-Chagai reactions from the major nuclear powers are significant and dampening for Pakistan. The United States and Russia have jointly urged India and Pakistan to sign the nuclear Non-Proliferation Treaty and back away from nuclear confrontation.[98] Secretary of State Madeline Albright said that the nuclear powers are in agreement that nuclear Non-Proliferation Treaty should not be amended to accommodate India and Pakistan as new nuclear weapons state "that would send a message that every nation is free to test to join the nuclear club."[99]

The Foreign Minister of China,. France, Russia, the United Kingdom and the United States met in Geneva on 4 June to coordinate their response to the grave situation created by the nuclear tests carried out in May by India and then Pakistan. The minister condemned the tests, expressed their deep concern about the danger to peace and stability in the region and pledged to cooperate closely in urgent efforts prevent a nuclear arms race in the sub-continent, to bolster Non-Proliferation Regime and to encourage reconciliation and peaceful resolution of differences between India and Pakistan.[100]

The US and Pakistan's Nuclear Proliferation

Pakistan's nuclear programme and its clash with Non-Proliferation policy was the main focus of US relations with Pakistan. In the mid 1970's new strains arose over Pakistan's apparent efforts to respond to India's 1974 underground test by seeking its own capability to build a nuclear bomb. Although limited US military aid to Islamabad was resumed in 1975, the Carter Administration suspended it again in April 1979 under section 669 of the foreign assistance act because of Pakistan's secret construction of a Uranium enrichment facility.[101]

The US Non-Proliferation goal in South Asia is to persuade India and Pakistan to first cap, them reduce and eventually eliminate their capabilities to produce nuclear weapons. The United States has important security interests in South Asia. For the US the consequences of a nuclear war between India and Pakistan would be catastrophic. The US Non-Proliferation concerns in the post-Cold War era may seem genuine but in reality it is nothing but sustaining the US leadership in the post-Cold War world.

As early as 1970s the US policy-makers have been endeavouring to halt nuclear proliferation in South Asia. According to Peter Galbraith a known nuclear expert, the United States resorted to a range of policy instruments to achieve this goal.[102] These policy instruments are viewed as under:

- An intensive effort to stop the acquisition by South Asian Countries of the technology, equipment and missile material for nuclear weapons.
- Threat of actual use of sanctions to discourage India and Pakistan from proceeding with nuclear weapons programme.
- The use of incentives to encourage India and Pakistan to remain non-nuclear.

The offer of reliable supplies of nuclear material equipment and technology of the recipient country would accept full scope IAEA safeguards.[103]

In the 1980's USA had a permissive attitude towards Pakistan's nuclear programme, America turned a blind eye to Pakistan's clandestine weapons programme. The reason behind the US soft line towards Pakistan nuclear programme was its pressing need during the Afghan crisis. Prof. Cohen opines, when Pakistan's role in countering the Soviet presence in Afghanistan became important, that issue tended to override proliferation concerns.[104]

In an article in the *Washington Post* Senator Jon Glenn accused former President Bush and Regan for having practiced nuclear Non-Proliferation policy "bordering on lawlessness" critiquing the administration he pointed out "nine years of US assistance had helped Pakistan release funds for its nuclear programme and had given it the means of delivering weapons".

In 1987 the US authorities arrested Pakistani born Canadian citizen Arshad Parvez, in Philadelphia on charge that he had tried to export to Pakistan a special steel alloy that could be used in the enrichment of weapons grade Uranium. In June 1984 another Pakistani Mr. Nazir Ahmad was arrested in Houston while trying to smuggle krytones electric switches that can trigger nuclear bombs to Pakistan.[105]

The United States expressed its serious concern over nuclear issue and said that Pakistan needed to take concrete steps to restore its credibility and further assurance that it was not trying to develop a nuclear weapon.

Pakistan was pursuing an aggressive nuclear weapons programme. The US therefore decided to manipulate the Pakistan nuclear agenda. United States also believed Pakistan was susceptible to a 'carrot and stick' approach in terms of US economic and military assistance and as a major provider of aid to Pakistan.

The Carter administration in April 1979 involved the Symington after it received intelligence assessments confirming Pakistan was building a secret Uranium enrichment facility.

The Pressler Amendment

The Pressler Amendment of 1985 is an effort to programme in Pakistan; Pressler offered a Non-Proliferation amendment to the US foreign assistance and authorization legislation. The provision is commonly known as the Pressler Amendment amended Section 620E, of the Foreign Assistance Act to read follows. "No assistance shall be furnished to Pakistan and no military equipment or technology shall be sold or transferred to Pakistan, unless the President would certify in writing to the Speaker of the House of Representatives and the Chairman of the Committee on Foreign Relations of the Senate during the fiscal year in which assistance is to be furnished or military equipment or technology is to be sold or transferred, that Pakistan does not possess a nuclear explosive device and that the proposed United States assistance on programme will reduce significantly the risk that Pakistan will possess a Nuclear Explosive Device."[106]

In 1985 Pakistan faced the threat of Soviet troops on its border and repeated cross border raids from Afghanistan. A draconian cut in US foreign assistance to Pakistan at that time would have undermined the security interests of both Pakistan and the United States. The Pressler Amendment was remembered in Pakistan as a sword of Damocles crafted specifically to hang over Pakistan's neck forming it to choose between US aids and pursuing nuclear development.[107]

In February 1992, reports emerged charging the US manufacturers of having continued private military sales to Pakistan despite the US assistance embargo mandated by the Pressler Amendment. The Bush administration had quietly permitted Pakistani armed forces to buy American made arms from commercial firms through the military items licensed for sale to Pakistan which were spare parts of American made F-16.[108]

The Secretary of State, James Barker appeared before the US Senate foreign relations committee in February 1992 and stated "we have indeed cut off all foreign assistance to Pakistan because we were unable to certify within the parameters of the Pressler Amendment. We have a legislative history and as legal matters we don't believe that it applies to commercial sales or exports controlled by the Department of Commerce so we look at munitions necessary to maintain the Pakistani military at the current level on a case by case basis.[109]

In 16 February, 1987 US ambassador to Islamabad Dean Hinton, delivered a speech at the Pakistan institute of strategic studies which sounded the first official public warning since President Carter had used the Sygmington Amendment in 1979. He declared that there were development in Pakistan's nuclear programme and there were indication's of Pakistan's efforts at seeking a weapons capabilitiy.[110]

His speech caused an immediate furore in the Pakistan's media as well as in the national assembly. Islamabad expressed strong objections to his statements. The forceful message emanating from Islamabad in the wake of Hinton speech was that Pakistan is not going to allow itself to be browbeaten and pressurized by the US in pursuit of the national objective and that its peaceful nuclear programme is in no way tied with US military and economic aid.[111] Pakistani Minister of State for Foreign Affairs Noorani on March 8th, 1987 stated in the National Assembly that Pakistan would go ahead with its nuclear programme and would not "accept unilateral restriction in our sovereignty". However he repeated Pakistan's claim that its nuclear programme was for peaceful purpose and added that it was prepared to accept any global or regional arrangement to keep the region free of nuclear weapons.[112]

The first move to wriggle itself out of the Pressler Amendment was made in June 1991 when the Chairman of Pakistani Senate Wasim Sajjad visited Washington with Prime Minister Nawaj Shariff's proposal for a five-nation meet on Non-Proliferation to deal with the nuclear question in the South Asia. He utilized his visit to impress upon the American policy makers the interest of Pakistan in Non-Proliferation and the Indian intransigence by carrying of a partial and narrow proposal to address the South Asian nuclear issue.[113]

In 1994 the US administration had insisted on these basic conditions for lifting the Pressler's Amendment against Pakistan firstly by ending the production of grade uranium, stopping the manufacture of additional nuclear weapons core. Michel Curry the US administration spokesman said on October 6, 1994 that we have offered Pakistan the opportunity to work with us to achieve our Non-Proliferation goal, which could lead to the waiver of sanction that have been imposed on Pakistan.[114] There were many in the American foreign policy establishment who accepted the Pakistani argument that Pressler Amendment punishes Pakistan unfairly without inducing India to change its behaviour in nuclear Non-Proliferation. In October 1995 the US Congress cleared the way for the resumption of American arms supply to Pakistan and soon provided an arms package worth $370 million under the provisions of the Hank Brown Amendment.

US Pressure Mounts after September 11

The terrorist attack on the World Trade Centre on September 11 2001 has transformed US policy towards South Asia. US is now reviewing its alliance with Pakistan in return for its cooperation in the war against terrorism. Secretary of States Colin Powell stresses nuclear Non-Proliferation will remain our important issue in US global policies as US embarks its campaign to eradicate terrorism. "We will not relax our standards and will continue to advance our fundamental interest in Non-Proliferation". Overlooking its past differences with Pakistan, the US has waived Glenn Amendment sanction on Pakistan and India.[115]

This post 9/11 phase marks the growing US concern about diffusion of Pakistan's nuclear technology to the terrorist organization like Al-Qaida. The former US government advisors and South Asian experts George Perkovich said that Pakistan's nuclear capability needs as much safeguarding as those of former Soviet Union. The real danger is the acquisition of nuclear weapons by developing states and their possible transfer to terrorist organisations who could not be easily deterred from using them against the US and its allies.[116]

The US has imposed sanction on Khan Research Laboratory at Kahuta for the export of nuclear technology. A March 21st Jane's Intelligence Digest Report says that a US contingency plan has been put in place to neutralize the threat of Pakistani nuclear assets and technology falling into the hands of Islamic fundamentalists. Headlined 'Musharraf in peril', the Jane's report says it is important for Washington to ensure that militant Islamic groups does not get access to Pakistan's nuclear assets and technology. The fear is that 'a dirty bomb' could be used to target America.[117] Concern about the safety of Pakistan's nuclear weapons the Bush administration is considering, providing Islamabad with perimeter security and other assistance to prevent unauthorized access to its nuclear facilities. In near turn, the US could assist Pakistan by providing it with blast proof doors at its nuclear facilities. Other safety measures under consideration are permissive action links high tech devices applied to warheads to prevent an outsider from detonating a nuclear weapon.

Washington has used a variety of economic and diplomatic levers to punish Pakistan for its nuclear test and refusal to sign the nuclear Non-Proliferation Treaty. Because Pakistan has not signed the NPT, the United States is prohibiting by law from participating in nuclear weapon related activities.[118]

The Pakistani Foreign Minister Khurshid Mehmood Kasuri ruled out any scope for joint US-PAK command and control system, "Our nuclear weapons are in comparatively safe hands and Pakistan has not transferred nuclear technology to any country". Pakistan ambassador to Washington Ashraf Jahangir Qazi has argued there is no 'smoking gun' to prove his country's complicity in North Korea's Uranium enrichment programme.[119]

Pakistan's alleged nuclear trade with North Korea in exchange for Nodong ballistic missiles shows clearly its determination to acquire an operational long-range nuclear strike force. The barter deal with Pyongyang raises troubling questions about nuclear decision-making in Islamabad. There is circumstantial and inferential evidence to suggest that Dr. A.Q. Khan and the Khan Research Laboratories were not acting independently in the matter, top military and civilian leaders were likely to have been privy to the decision.[120] Pakistan is not a signatory to the NPT therefore its nuclear trade with North Korea does not constitute a violation of any international treaty or agreement to which it is a party. However Islamabad has violated an assurance that it would abide by Non-Proliferation norms and export control regulations. The revelation that Pakistan is the source of North Korea's enrichment technology is a public disaster for the Pakistani government; it has undermined Islamabad's assertion that Pakistan is a responsible nuclear power. The public knowledge of Pakistan and North Korea's secret nuclear ties is likely to galvanize critics of the Bush administration engagement policy with Pakistan in Congress, the media as well as the think tanks that dot Washington's beltway.[121]

India and Pakistan crossed the nuclear rubicon by testing their nuclear weapons; the US policy of trying to roll back their nuclear and ballistic missiles programme have not met with success. Both sides have refused since 1998 to even countenance giving up their nuclear options. They have no incentive to behave differently. It is the most unlikely that future American economic pressure and political factoring will lead to the abandonment of nuclear weapons. The Indo-Pak dialogue has come to a standstill over the problem of cross border terrorism and Kashmir. The spiralling of the Indian and Pakistani programme cannot be addressed forthrightly without addressing both Pakistan sponsored terrorism and the Kashmir problem. Richard Armitage's visit to India in May 2003, was an effort to reach a solution to the problem of Non-Proliferation. The weakening of Kashmir deadlock will require an imaginative and bold shift in American Non-Proliferation strategy.[122]

The five Nuclear Weapon States have continued to use the NPT for two-fold purpose namely, to legitimise their own possession of nuclear arsenals and the right to retain them in perpetuity. Nuclear Non-Proliferation cannot be promoted in the absence of corresponding progress towards nuclear disarmament.[123]

Thus, Pakistan advocates a comprehensive approach to Arms Control and Non-Proliferation. Pakistan recognizes that international peace and stability are also threatened by the region's specific arms race caused primarily by ' rritorial and other disputes in the region. This perspective is partly shaped by Pakistan's own security predicament, which is regionally situated in the neighbourhood of a bigger military power namely India. Pakistan feels that a powerful state with regional ambitions can cause insecurity to smaller neighbour thereby triggering a regional arm race. It has been observed in this chapter that Pakistan emphasises that the two countries should agree to simultaneous accession to the Non-Proliferation Treaty, concurrent acceptance of safeguards prescribed by the IAEA, mutual inspection of each other's nuclear installation and a regional nuclear weapon free Zone in South Asia. It has been noted that India's response on these proposals has been negative. It refuses to accept any restriction on its nuclear programme under bilateral or regional arrangements. A Non-Proliferation policy has minimal chance of success in South Asia, unless it applies equally to Pakistan and India and it addresses the security predicament of the smaller and militarily weaker of the two states.

NOTES

1. Rajesh Kumar Mishra, "Nuclear Pakistan Implication for National and International Security," *South Asian Analysis Group,* Paper No. 429, <http://www.saag.org.papers 5/papers429.html>
2. Ashok, Kapur *Pakistan's Nuclear Development,* (New York: Croom Helm Ltd., 1987), p. 84.
3. "Boundaries of Pakistan", <http://www.upinfo.com/countryguidestudy/Pakistan/pakistan34.html>.
4. Ron Ben Yishai, *'Iran is the Next in Line'*, <www.mfa.go.il/mpa/go.asp? MFAHU8m90>
5. Amir Sajedi " Iran's Relation with Saudi Arabia", *Strategic Analysis,* Vol. XVI, No.6, Sept. 1993, pp. 763-77.
6. "Iran says All its Nuclear Plants are Open to Inspection ", *Dow Jones Newswire,* 13 December, 2003, <http://www.fpc.state.govt/documents/organisation/ 16597.pdf>
7. Mirza Aslam, Beg, "*Development and Security Thought and Reflection*", (Rawlpindi: Friends, 1994), p. 211.
8. Zulfiquar Ali Bhutto, "Reshaping Foreign Policy, A Collection of Articles, Statements and Speeches", Hamid Jalal and Khalid Hassan, *Politics of the People Series,* (Rawalpindi: Pakistan Publication), p. 222.
9. Munir Akram, "Statement of Permanent Representative of Pakistan to The United Nation Conference on Disarmament on India and Pakistan Nuclear Tests", *Plenary Second Session on the Conference on Disarmament,* Geneva, 14th May1998 <http:cns.miis.edu/research/India/statement.htm>.
10. Maleeha Lodhi, "Security Challenges in South Asia", *The Non-Proliferation Review,* Summer 2001, p. 119.
11. Dr. Rodney Jones, " Pakistan's Nuclear Posture, Quest for Assured Nuclear Deterrence, a Conjecture" *Regional Studies,* Vol. XVIII, No. 2, Institute of Regional Studies, Islamabad, p. 6.
12. Mirza Aslam Beg, "Nuclear Programme and Political Rumbling", *Defence Journal,* Vol. 19, No. 11-12, 1993, p. 21.
13. Chris Smith, " Security Sovereignty and Nuclear Weapons in South Asia", Faraday Discussion, paper no. 20, University of London, P-14, in Mirza, Aslam, Beg, *Development and Security. Thought and Reflection,* (Rawalpindi: Friends, 1994), p. 210-17.
14. Munir Ahmed Khan, "Understanding Pakistan's Nuclear Plan", *The News,* Islamabad, 8 March, 1995.
15. Smruti S. Pattanaik, "Ensuring Nuclear Peace and Stability in India-Pakistan Relations", *A Journal of International Affairs,* India Council of World Affairs, p. 46.
16. *Ibid.*
17. Kanti Bajpai, "The Military Utility of Nuclear Weapons and the Case

for Disarmament", 25-22 March 2001, <http://www.pughwash.org/ reports/nw/nw13 crhtml>.

18. Rafi Raza, *Pakistan in Perspective 1994-1997*, (Oxford University Press, 1997), p. 116.
19. Samina Ahmed, "Pakistan the Crisis Within in Muthiah Alayappa", *Asian Security Practice*, (Calfornia: Stanford University Press, 1998), p. 355.
20. Dr. Maqbool Ahmed Bhatty, "Pakistan China Relation in the 21st Century", *Regional Studies*, Vol. XVIII, No. 1, Institute of Regional Studies Islamabad, Winter 1999-2000, p. 344.
21. Gaurav Kampani, "India's Compliance Strategy Calling Pakistan's Nuclear Buff Over Kashmir", *Monterey Institute of International Studies*, <www. cnsdate?action=18.concept=09mime=19collection= cns+wen+s4/15/03>.
22. *Chinese Embassy*, 6 June, 1998.
23. Agha Shai, Statement to the First Committee of the General Assembly, "Non-Proliferation of Nuclear Weapon on Disarmament", US Government, Washington, 10 September, 1969, p. 317.
24. UN Document, AC I /1.206
25. UN Document, A/ PV 113326, September 1962, p. 150.
26. GAOR, 20m Sessions, First Committee, 1369 meeting, 29 October, 1965.
27. Brig. Mohan Kaushik, O. M. Mehrotra, *Pakistan's Nuclear Bomb*, (New Delhi: Sopan Publication House, 1980), pp. 50-51
28. Dawn Karachi, 5 June, 1968 Cited in Khalizad, Goldbllat, *Non-Proliferation The Why and Wherefore*, (Great Britain: Taylor and Francis), pp. 133-34.
29. Ashok Kapur, *Pakistan's Nuclear Development*, (London: Croom Helm Ltd., 1987), p. 126.
30. "The Near Nuclear Countries and the NPT", *SIPRI*, (New York: Humanities Press, 1972), p. 25.
31. Dr. Usmani, "Pakistan to Review Policy if India Refuses to Sign the Treaty", *Pakistan Times*, 17 July, 1968.
32. *Defence Journal*, Karachi, Vol. X, No. 4, April 1984.
33. Mohammad, B. Alam, *"Essays on Nuclear Proliferation"*, (Vikas Publishing House, 1995), pp. 28.
34. UN Document ENDC, IPU 429.
35. GAOR, 37 First Committee Mtg. 18, pp. 41-45
36. Hindu, 2 May, 1981, pp. 8.
37. SIPRI, 1972, *Op cit.*, p. 27.
38. *Ibid*, p. 26.
39. Prof. Khurshid Ahmed, 'CTBT and Pakistan's Nuclear Capability' <http://www.jamaat.org/isharat/2000/isho22000html>.

40. Ghulam R. Malik, "*Nuclear Non-Proliferation and the NPT Review Conference: The Pakistani Perspective*" <http://www.Kas.org.za/publications/seminarreports/nuclea %20DDisarmament/pakistan.pdf>
41. Haider K. Nizami, *The Roots of Rhetoric, Politics of Weapons in India and Pakistan*, (New Delhi: India Research Press, 2001), p. 78.
42. Sartaz Aziz, " Signing of NPT is Not Under Debate", *Associated Press of Pakistan, News Summary*, 25 February, 1999.
43. "NPT is Discriminatory, Nawaj Sharif laments of Double Standards" <http://www.fas.org/news/pakistan/1998/06/980608-app.htm>
44. Statement and the Speeches at the UN, <http://www.fas.org/ news/pakistan /1997/13971120htm>
45. Shireen M. Mazari, "From Non-Proliferation to Stability, The Case of South Asia", <http://www.defencejournal.com/2000/mar/southasia.htm>
46. Saira Khan, "*Nuclear Non-Proliferation Dynamics in Protracted Conflict Prone Region": A Comprehensive Study of South Asia and Middle East*, (England: Ashgate Publishing Ltd, 1988), p. 136.
47. P. L. Bhola, "*Pakistan Nuclear Policy*", (New Delhi: Sterling Publishers Pvt. Ltd.), p. 19.
48. Steve Wiseman and H. Krosney, *The Islamic Bomb*, (New Delhi: Vision Books), 1983, p. 89-90.
49. Bhutto, "*If I am Assassinated*", (Ghaziabad: Vikas Publishing House), 1979, pp. 117-18.
50. Ashok Kapur, *Op. cit.*, p. 78.
51. Major General D.K. Palit and P. K. S. Namboodri, *Pakistan's Islamic Bomb*, (Ghaziabad: Vikas Publishing House Pvt. Ltd.), p. 18.
52. Z. A. Bhutto, "*Awaking the People*", Speeches of Zulfikar Ali Bhutto, 1966-69, (Rawalpindi: Pakistan Publications, 1970), p. 21.
53. "PARR's New Lease of Life", *Nuclear Engineering International*, 36, December, 1991, p. 3.
54. "China and Pakistan Collaboration on PARR—2", *Nuclear Engineering International*, 35 December, 1990, pp. 46-47.
55. Leonard S. Spector, *Nuclear Proliferation Today*, Ballinger Publishing Co., 1984, p. 62 and Weiseman, pp. 182-217.
56. Steve Weiseman, *Op. cit.*, p. 90.
57. George H. Quester, "Nuclear Pakistan and Nuclear India, Stable Deterrent or Proliferation Challenge", *Strategic Studies*, Institute, 1992.
58. Gregg M. Taylor, "Pakistan: Going it Alones at KANUPP", *Nuclear News*, March 1990, p. 42.
59. Andrew Koch Jennifer, Topping "Pakistan's Nuclear Weapons Programme's A Status Report", *The Non-Proliferation Review*, Spring, Summer 1997, <http:// cns.miis.edu/pubs/npr/vol 04/43/koctop 43.pdf>

60. R. R. Subramanium, Time to Call Pakistan Rebuff, *The Hindustan Times*, 18 December, 1987, p. 11.
61. David Albright Mark, Hibbis "Pakistan's Bomb: Out of the Closet, *The Bulletin of the Atomic Scientist*, 48, July-August 1992, pp. 38-43.
62. Sinha, Subramanium, *Nuclear Pakistan, Atomic Threat to South Asia*, New Delhi, 1980, p. 49.
63. "Scientist Affirms Pakistan Capable of Uranium Enrichment Weapons Production", *Naw-I-Waqt*, (Lahore, 10 February 1984), p. 1 (Translated from Under).
64. Leonard S. Spector, *Nuclear Ambitions*, (Colorado: West View Presses Boulder, 1990), pp. 91-96.
65. General Mirza Aslam Beg, "Pakistan-Nuclear Programme, A National Security Perspective", *The Nation*, Lahore 22-22, June, 1993.
66. K. D. Kapur, *Nuclear Non-Proliferation Diplomacy, Nuclear Power Programme in the Third World*, (New Delhi: Lancer Books, 1993), pp. 264-265.
67. "Nuclear Proliferation in South, Containing the Threat," *A Staff Report to The Committee on Foreign Relation, US Senate*, Washington DC, USGPO, p. 17.
68. *Nuclear News*, Vol. 33, No. 5, April 1990, pp. 74-75.
69. "Reactor Deal with France Stalled by NPT Status", *Nuclear News*, August 1999, pp. 95-96.
70. Gurmeet Kanwal, *Nuclear Defence Shaping the Arsenal*, (New Delhi: Knowledge World, Institute for Defence Studies and Analysis, April 2001), p. 57.
71. Munir Ahmad Khan, "Nuclearisation of South Asia, and its Regional and Global Implication," *Focus on Regional Issues*, Vol. XVII, No. 1, (Institute of Regional Studies, Islamabad, 1998) p. 11.
72. Pervaiz Iqbal Cheema, *"Pakistan's Quest for Nuclear Technology"*, ANU, Working Paper 19, Canberra 1980, p. 10.
73. Bhutto, *Op. cit.*, p. 138.
74. K. Subranmanyam, "Pakistan's Nuclear Capability and India Response", V. D. Chopra (Ed.), *Studies in Indo-Pak Relations*, (New Delhi: Patriot Publisher's, 1984), p. 134.
75. Shirin Tahir Kheli, *The United States and Pakistan, The Evolution of an Influence Relationship*, (New York: Prager, 1982), p. 120.
76. Samina Ahmed, David Cortright, *Pakistan and the Bomb, Public Opinion and Nuclear Options*, (Norte Dame Indiana: Norte Dame Press, 1998), p. 70.
77. Pervaiz Iqbal Cheema, *Strategic Digest*, IDSA, New Delhi, April, 1991, pp. 196-97.
78. Akhtar Ali, "A Framework for Nuclear Agreement and Verification", Stephen Philip Cohen (Ed.), *Nuclear Proliferation in South Asia*, (New Delhi: Lancer International, 1991), p. 312.

79. Amitava Mukherjee, *India's Policy Towards Pakistan*, (New Delhi: Associated Book Centre, 1983), pp. 93-95.
80. *The Nation*, Lahore, 19 May, 1998.
81. Mehrunnisa Ali, *Readings in Pakistan's Foreign Policy*, (1971-1998) (Oxford: Oxford University Press, 2001), pp. 454-55.
82. Zia Mian, *Pakistan's Atomic Bomb & Search for Security*, (Lahore: Gautam Publisher's, 1995), p. 74.
83. Yossef Bodansky, *"Pakistan's Nuclear Brinkmanship"*, January 1998, <http:// www.freeman.org/in-online.bodansky/Pakistan.htm>.
84. Carey Sublette, *"Pakistan's Nuclear Weapon Programme Development"*, <http:// nuke testing. environ web.org/news/Pakistan/Pak Develop.htm>.
85. David Albright and Mark Hibbs, *Op. cit.*, pp. 38-43.
86. S. Gupta, "Nawaz Sharrif's Bombshell", *India Today*, September 15, 1994, p. 28.
87. Dr. Sanjay Badri Maharaj, *The Armagedelon Factor Nuclear Weapons in India Pakistan Context*, (New Delhi: Lancer Publishers and Distributors, 2000), p. 88.
88. Ishtiaq Ahmad, *"Why Pakistan Went Nuclear"*, <http://www.fas.org/ news/ Pakistan/1998/06/www.tiger03.html>.
89. Farzana, Shakoor, Nuclearisation of South Asia and the Kashmir Dispute in Mehrunnisa Ali, (Ed.), *Readings in Pakistan Foreign Policy (1971-1998)*, (Oxford: Oxford University Press, 2001), p. 454.
90. John Ward Anderson, Kamran Khan, "Pakistan Sets Off Nuclear Blasts", *Washington Post*, 29 May, 1998, p. 1.
91. Faiz Mukhtar, "Post Nuclear Pakistan", *Defence Journal*, September 1998, <http://www.defence journal.com/ Sept. 98/Poster Pakistan. htm>.
92. Siddiqa Agha Ayesha, pp. 187-88.
93. Ayesha, Khan, "Pakistan Joins the Club", *The Bulletin of Atomic Scientist*, July/August,1998, Vol. 54, No. 4 <http://www.thebulletin.org/ issues/1998/ja98/ja 98khan.html>.
94. "Pakistan to Keep Option Open on Test has Treaty", <http:// www.rediff.com/ news/1998/July/04homit3.htm>.
95. Abdul Stattar's, Statement on The Sixth Review Conference of the NPT, New York, 24 April to 20 May, <http://mission.itu.int/ Pakistan/Disarm-NPT-FM>.
96. *Nation*, 29 May, 1998.
97. *Nation*, 3 June, 1998.
98. Masood Haider, "Fear of Nuclear Conflict Expressed: US, Russia Ask India, Pakistan to Sign The nPT", *Dawn*, 6 June 2000, <http:// www.dawn.com/2000 /06/06/topl.htm>.
99. *Ibid.*

100. Joint Commique on India and Pakistan Nuclear Tests by Five Permanent Members of the Security Council", <http: www.org/ news/India/1998/06/ 19980605 SC6527.htm>.
101. Peter R. Blood, "Pakistan US Relations", CRS Issue Brief for Congress, Foreign Affairs, Defence and Trade Division, February 12, 2002, <http://usembassy. state.gov/Karachi/wwwh02feb.html>.
102. Peter Galbraith, "Nuclear Proliferation in South Asia: Whose Business", in Sulochana Raghvan (Ed.) *Conflicting Image: India and The United States*, (Riverdale: Maryland, 1990), p. 70.
103. *Ibid.*
104. Aftab, Alam, *US Policy Towards South Asia*, (Delhi: Raj Publications, 1998), pp. 91-92.
105. *Ibid*, p. 125.
106. "Nuclear Proliferation in Pakistan: Reaffirming the Intent of the Pressler Amendment", Senate, August 5, 1994, <http: // www.fas.org/news/Pakistan/ 1994/940705.htm>.
107. Teresita C. Schaffer, "US Influence in Pakistan, Can Partners have Divergent Priorities", *The Washington Quarterly*, Winter, 26, 2003, pp. 169-183.
108. Murray Waas and Douglas Frantz, "Despite Ban US Arms Sold to Pakistan", *Los Angeles Times*, 6 March, 1992, p. 1.
109. James Baker, "Hearing on Foreign Policy Overview", Senate Foreign Relations Committee, 5 February, 1992.
110. Dilip Bobb, Raminder Singh, "Pakistan's Nuclear Bombshell", *India Today*, 31 March, 1987, p. 73.
111. Jaswinder Kumar, "*Irritants in Indo Pak Relations*", (New Delhi: Deep and Deep Publication, 1989), p. 108.
112. *The Tribune*, Chandigarh, 9 March, 1987.
113. "The US Pressure on Pakistan Wassim's Mission to Washington", *Strategic Analysis*, Vol. XIV, No. 6, September 1991, pp. 644-45.
114. *The Times of India*, New Delhi, 7 October, 1994, p. 15.
115. Samina Ahmed, "Countering Nuclear Risks in South Asia", Council for a Liveable World Education Fund, December, 2001, <http:// www.clw.org/control/ countering nuclear risks.pdf>
116. Marvin Miller and Lawrence Scheinman, "Israel, India and Pakistan: Engaging the Non-NPT States in the Non-Proliferation Regime", *Arms Control Today*, Arms Control Association, December 2003, <http://www.armscontrol.org/act/ 2003-12/miler and scheinman.asp>.
117. Shisir Gupta, "Pakistan Nukes Come Under US Scanner", <http:// www. Pakistan-facts.com/index.pnp? Topic=word.proliferation>.
118. Bryan Bender, "US Considers Helping Pakistan", *Boston Globe*, 20/ 9/2001, <http://www.global security.org/org/news/2001/010920- attck 01.htm>.

119. Ashraf Jehangir, Qazi, "An Unwanted Attack on Pakistan", *Washington Post*, 29 October, 2002, p. 20.
120. Gaurav Kampani, "Second Tier Proliferation: The Case of Pakistan and North Korea", *The Non-Proliferation Review*, Vol. 9, No. 3, Centre for Non-Proliferation Studies, Monterey Institute of International Studies, Fall Winter, 2002, p. 114.
121. "US Reactions Very Severe if Pakistan-North Korea Links Proved", *Daily Times*, Islamabad, 26 November, 2002, <http: www.dailytimes .com.ph>.
122. Jim Fisher Thompson, "Indian Professor Calls India/Pakistan Confrontation Dangerous", *Journal of Aero Space and Defence Industry News*, March 28, 2000, <http://www.aerospacetech.news.com/starc/ 2000/032800/IndiaPakistan. html>.
123. Statement Issued by the Permanent Representative to the United Nation in Response to Security Council Resolution, 1172, 6, June 1998, in K.R. Gupta's, *Select Documents on Nuclear Disarmament*, No. 111, (New Delhi: Atlantic Publishers, 2001), p. 198.

4

The North Korean Case

North Korea's recent admission that it has continued to pursue a nuclear weapons programme in violation of the Non-Proliferation Treaty has startled the international community.[1] In December 1985 North Korea joined the NPT as a non-nuclear weapon state and announced its final withdrawal from the NPT in January, 2003.[2] North Korea is one of the most closed societies of the world, ruled by a dictatorial military regime.[3] It has an authoritarian political system based on the distinctively Korean type of socialism, known as Juche. North Korea is the first country to withdraw from the NPT and restart its Plutonium related nuclear facilities, that represents a roll back of the agreed framework promises.[4] North Korea's threat to withdraw from the NPT in January 2003, is not the first crisis concerning North Korea's development of nuclear weapons. In 1993, amidst demands for the IAEA special inspectors, North Korea announced its intention to withdraw from the NPT, but refrained from doing so at the last moment. The revelation of Pyongyang's second violation hardens negative Western impression of North Korea as an unreliable and unpredictable "Rogue State".[5] In this chapter an attempt is made to examine North Korea's fluctuating attitude towards the NPT within the context of the geo-political environment and its political and security compulsions. There is considerable literature on this subject from the Western perspective. It is felt, however that it would be very difficult for a Western observer to understand the complex security concerns that shape the North Korean leaderships decision on nuclear and strategic issues. This chapter deals with North Korea's security dilemma and attempts to study North Korea's hostile relations with South Korea, Japan, China and the US.

GEO-POLITICAL ENVIRONMENT AND SECURITY PERCEPTIONS

South Korea

North Korea's security has been conditioned by its hostile relationship with South Korea. A cornerstone of the hostile South Korean policy towards North Korea since 1948, has been its claim that the Republic of Korea is the legitimate government on the Korean Peninsula and the regime in Pyongyang's is illegitimate and unworthy of diplomatic recognition. From the inception of their respective systems the two regimes evolved politically along different paths. In South Korea, American educated Syngman Rhee assumed power with the blessing of the US setting the stage for democratic institutionalisation. Conversely, North Korea was consolidated under the leadership of a young Soviet officer Kim II Sung. In fact North Korean communism had always been predicated upon the premises and ideals of nationalism.[7] The Korean War of 1950-53 left the legacy of armed truce and most militarised border in the world euphemistically known as the demilitarised zone.[8] The UN Security Council on the instruction of the US condemned North Korea for its invasion of South Korea. Pyongyang's grievous misconduct earned it the label of an international outlaw. North Korea continued its nationalist struggle against foreign domination against US and its surrogate powers. One of the most important factors affecting the strategic and military balance of the Korean peninsula has been the US-ROK Alliance system, which was formed with the signing of the mutual defence treaty and was designed to contain expansion of communism in the region. Under the treaty signed on 1 October, 1953, the US and South Korea each recognize that an attack on either would be dangerous to its own peace and safety. They would act to meet the common danger in accordance with its constitutional process. South Korea works closely with the US, Japan, China to block suspected North Korean efforts to use the nuclear card to gain unilateral, military, political and economic concessions from the US.[9].

The dominant North Korean emotion was underlying its fear of encirclement and invasion. North Korea views South Korea as a vital threat to its existence. The annual US-ROK team spirit military exercises that have been accompanied by offensive operations are seen as destabilising the North Koreans.[10] North Korea has been trying to persuade South Korea to abandon its dependency oriented foreign policy, remove the US troops from the Korean peninsula, put a permanent end to joint military exercises and disassociate itself from the US nuclear umbrella.[11] During the 1970 South Korea actively attempted to procure nuclear weapons which prompted strong reaction from North Korea.[12]

The US deployed 36,000 troops in South Korea with additional missiles and nuclear warheads at sea. North Korea was threatened with nuclear weapons during the Korean War and afterwards the US nuclear weapons like atomic demolition mutions, Nike Hercules missiles were stationed in South Korea. This heightened North Korea's security dilemma and led to the quest for nuclear weapons even while remaining a party to the NPT. South Korea's objective in dealing with the North Korean nuclear problem is to prevent North Korea from developing nuclear weapons and to secure a nuclear free Korean peninsula.[13] South Koreans have failed to understand that North Korean nuclear crisis cannot be delinked from the presence of US troops in South Korea threatening North Korea's very existence. The new Roh government has put fourth three principles in dealing with North Korean nuclear problem; zero tolerance for North Korea's nuclear development, a peaceful resolution of the situation through dialogue and South Koreas active role in solving it.[14]

Disintegration of Soviet Union and its Impact in North Korea's Security

The rapidly changing security environment in the post-Cold War period with the demise of Soviet Union and the normalisation of relationship with North Korea's former allies like Russia and China with South Korea have posed a great danger to North Korea's security and survival. North Korea began to develop its nuclear programme with the assistance of Soviet Union. In 1956, Pyongyang and Moscow concluded two agreements concerning nuclear research. They signed additional protocols in 1959. North Korea security arrangement with Moscow and Beijing provided adequate nuclear umbrella for it and reduced any desire it might have had in the direction of military application.[15] In mid 1980's,

North Korea was seeking Soviet assistance to build its major nuclear programme. Accession to the NPT was part of the price that Pyongyang had to pay for Soviet assistance to its power reactor programme.[16] The 1990's has seen a radical change in the North's alliance relationship. While the US alliance with ROK remains firm, North Korea relationship with Russia has suffered a setback. The Soviet Union stunned North Korea in September 1990 when it established diplomatic relationship with South Korea. In 1990, DPRK Foreign Minister Kim Yong Nam released a memorandum stating that if diplomatic relations were established with the South, the USSR-DPRK alliance would effectively cease to exist and North Korea would not have any choice but to take measures to make its own nuclear weapons.[17] The DPRK found itself virtually abandoned in 1992 when Yelstin publicly declared that the guarantee of military assistance to North Korea in the event of war was laid down in their 1961 mutual friendship treaty which no longer applied. In addition, the Russian foreign secretary Anderi Kozyrev has said that Russia would support any collective measure against Democratic Peoples Republic of Korea if it continued with its refusal to comply with the IAEA inspections.[18] The DPRK in 1992 was spending around 22 per cent of its GNP on defence, yet in absolute terms it was only half the amount spent by South Korea. Russians refused to supply arms to North Korea though it said that it would continue to supply spare parts.

China's Deteriorating Relations with North Korea

China's overriding national interest in maintaining regional stability, especially near Chinese border informs China's policy towards the Korean peninsula. China's relations with North Korea have deteriorated significantly since China established a diplomatic tie with South Korea in August 1992. Though China had longstanding personal and ideological ties with North Korea even then it refused to sell military equipment to it. The Chinese after having signed the NPT were not in a position to support the North Korean stand on the nuclear issue. The Chinese obviously wanted to avoid a situation in which nuclear-armed neighbours may ring it if South Korea and Japan would follow the North Korean's in a pursuit for nuclear weapon.[19] China shares a common cause with the US on the North Korean nuclear issue and the implementation of the 1994 agreed framework aimed at halting and eliminating Pyongyang's nuclear weapons.[20] The North Koreans realized that they no longer had economic, political and military backing from its cold war allies. North Korea needed a new strategy to ensure its survival in the face of shifting military', economic and diplomatic balance in favour of South Korea. North Korea realized that its nuclear weapon programme provided a strong card to play against the US to achieve its political, economic and security benefits for the post-Cold War environment.[21]

United States and North Korean Insecurity

The US enemy image of North Korea have blinded the military strategists in North Korea and heightened its perception of its own legitimate natural security interests.[22] The Clinton Administration had formally labelled North Korea as a "Rogue State". President Clinton had threatened to wipe out North Korea from the face of the earth if the latter dared to make and use a nuclear device and not subject it to international inspections.[23] The Clinton administration's 1995 US Security strategy for East Asia Pacific Region affirmed that US had a permanent interest in the Asia Pacific region. The US would continue essential forward deployment of 100,000 troops in the region to strengthen its alliance with South Korea and to implement the "agreed framework", to dismantle North Korea's nuclear weapons infrastructure.[24]

When President Bush named Iraq, Iran and North Korea as the 'Axis of Evil' [25], he created a terror among these developing states. North Korea has been alarmed by the Bush administration harsh 'Axis of Evil' rhetoric and the new US doctrine of pre-emption. This doctrine asserts the right to use military force against rogue regimes seeking Weapons of Mass Destruction before those regimes can harm the United States. North Korea interprets it as a threat of US nuclear 'first use' on the Korean peninsula.[26] The former US National Security Advisor Anthony Lake identified Rogues as nations that exhibit a chronic inability to engage constructively with the outside world.[27] The more hardline members of Bush's foreign policy team Dick Cheney and Defence Secretary Donald Rumsfeld have demanded the curtailment of Weapons of Mass Destruction including missile and nuclear weapons.[28] They emphasized the need for continued presence of the US military forces in Korea. A report of the US Institute of Peace, headed by Richard Solmon, former Assistant Secretary of State for East Asia has expressed serious concern about North Korea's nuclear programme. The USIP working group noted that North Korea's efforts to develop nuclear weapons threatened security of South Korea and the US troops stationed there, the credibility of the US defence commitment to Japan and the integrity of the global nuclear Non-Proliferation regime.[29] The September, 11 attack on the twin towers diminished the tolerance risk of the US. North Korea has apprehension that the US is bent on confrontation rather than engagement with it.

Japan-US Alliance Threatens North Korea

The deepening of the US-Japanese alliance reinforces the hierarchy of Asia Pacific power. In 1996 the US-Japan mutual security treaty was redefined to revitalize the strategic alliance, which the two countries have considered the keystone of Asia Pacific hegemony since 1951. Japan's interest is not identical to that of the US but they strongly overlap. In bilateral talks with Japan, the DPRK representatives exacerbate historic animosities by repeatedly referring to Japan's occupation of Korea earlier this century. Japan has been playing an important role together with the US and the Republic of Korea in ensuring the implementation of the agreed framework. The Japanese government fully shares American concerns about a nuclear-armed North Korea, but have been very reluctant to go along with the US to impose economic sanctions on the North.[30]

The fact that Japan had piled up huge quantities of Plutonium which in future could be easily diverted for bomb making was a matter of grave security concern for North Korea.[31] Though Japan's atomic industry was subject to international monitoring and was meant for peaceful purposes, the objective fact was that it had ample military potential. There has been growing concern in North Korea over the transparency of Japan's Plutonium management.[32] Japan is a *de facto* nuclear weapons state with all capabilities to build nuclear weapons. The Japanese former Prime Minister Tsutomu Hata had acknowledged before the Upper House Budget Committee that Japan had the capability to build nuclear bombs but had not made them because of its adherence to the NPT.[33] The

Japanese efforts to develop theatre missile defence, has enhanced North Korean fears about its security.

The rise of Japanese economic and military power, the South's stunning growth and the cold relations with Soviet Union and China have combined to make North Korea consistently feel that it is truly alone in a dangerous world.[34] North Korea has serious security interests out of proportion of its size. A state's decision to build nuclear weapons is the result of security equation it faces. North Korea's effort to acquire nuclear weapons is derived from a deep sense of insecurity and even paranoia as well as long standing ambition of unifying the peninsula. This logic unites many developing nation's strategists. The liberal opposition to proliferation consists at best imperialistic arrogance reflecting Yellow Peril and White man's burden psychology. The problem of this school is that undue confidence that Pax Atomica of stable US-Soviet deference can be replicated in other regions.[35]

Isolated by the transformation of its cold war patrons and facing a Southern neighbour with its growing economic power and global stature, North Korea began to bring its offer it to acquire nuclear weapon to its fulfillment.[36]

The most important rationale behind North Koreas nuclear programme is to offset Pyongyang's vulnerabilities in the face of robust Republic of Korea, Japan and the US deterrence systems. For the North Korean regime, its military and nuclear prowess is a symbol of the country nationhood and an important guarantee for its regime survival.[37]

North Korea and the NPT

North Korea signed the NPT under Soviet pressure in 12 December 1985. North Korea's hopes to establish a nuclear weapon free zone in the Korean peninsula could not materialize due to the US deployment of tactical nuclear weapons in South Korea. Even though North Korea subscribed to the NPT it had a negative perception of the treaty. As a signatory to the NPT, North Korea derived little benefit from the treaty, for the NPT did not provide any security benefit to North Korea. In accordance with Article IV in the NPT where non-nuclear weapon states had agreed to give up then nuclear options in return for fullest possible exchange of equipments, materials, scientific and technological information for peaceful uses of nuclear energy. As years progressed, North Koreans realized that the nuclear weapons states would not provide any assistance for they were bent upon halting horizontal proliferation.

North Korean experience showed that although it was clearly provided for in the NPT under Article V, benefits of peaceful uses of nuclear energy have not been generously shared with non-nuclear weapon signatories. The sharing of nuclear technology was done on a selective basis and was subject to political conditions. North Koreans have complained that the nuclear weapon states have not up held their promises in nuclear disarmament. The nuclear weapon states should try to lessen their dependence on nuclear weapons in the military strategies in order to set and example to prevent other nations from going nuclear. North Korea expressed deep concern that the IAEA had not been fair or just regarding the inequity between the 'nuclear weapon have nots' and 'nuclear weapon haves'.[38]

The unjust international order, that protects and guarantees the interest of only nuclear powers is the fundamental cause of the conflict. The moral authority of the NPT has been destroyed by the nuclear powers that promised to dismantle their own nuclear weapons arsenals and try to stop the proliferation of nuclear weapons to non-nuclear states but on the contrary developed and produced large number of nuclear weapons.

The North Korean nuclear programme seemed paradoxical. It joined the NPT in 1985 to assuage Western suspicion that it was building nuclear weapons at the same time continued with its clandestine nuclear programme. This was precisely the path Iraq, also a NPT signatory had followed. The NPT cannot prohibit the signatory states from converting spent reactor into Plutonium in a reprocessing plant. Plutonium is critically important fissionable material. There was nothing in the NPT Charter to prevent North Korea quite legally stockpiling large amounts of Plutonium and equally legally quitting the NPT provision with three months notice. North Korea was regarded as a prime threat to the Non-Proliferation regime. It certainly had a nuclear weapon programme and it undoubtedly reprocessed more Plutonium than it was willing to acknowledge to the IAEA. Although North Korea had signed the treaty in 1985, it did not ratify its safeguards agreement with the IAEA, until April 1992 nearly five years latter than the deadline stipulated in the treaty.[39]

North Korea Refuses to Sign the Safeguards Agreement

According to Article III of the NPT, the IAEA states that signatories of the NPT must sign the nuclear safeguards agreements within 18 months.[40] The end of the negotiating period that can last up to 180 days. Therefore NPT can function in its originally tended risk only after its members sign a safeguards agreement that non-nuclear armed member states of the treaty, are obliged to sign.

North Korea failed to conclude the safeguards agreement with the IAEA during the first 18 months period after signing the NPT and with their consistent refusal until 16 July 1991. At an IAEA meeting the Japanese and Australian delegates pressurized North Korea to sign the IAEA safeguard agreement.[41] In return for signing the safeguard agreement, North Korea has always sought the elimination of nuclear weapons in the peninsula, at least some reduction in US nuclear threat. North Korea also demanded that two amendments be introduced into standing INFCIRC—TYPE—153 IAEA safeguards agreement. The first Pyongyang wanted, as a rider to the preamble was that nuclear-armed signatory nations should not threaten non-nuclear armed signatories. Here, North Korea claimed that the US was threatening it that such a threat violates UN Security Council resolution. The US claims that UN resolutions refer not to nuclear threat *per se* but to nuclear aggression as well. The US will not use nuclear weapons against any non-nuclear weapons state except in case of an attack on the US or its allies by such a state allied to a nuclear weapon state or associated with a nuclear weapon state in carrying out or sustaining the attack.[42] North Korean representative to the IAEA Yun-Ho-Jin listed conditions for signing the IAEA safeguard agreement. North Korea should be allowed to declare the safeguard agreement 'null and void' depending on its evaluation of the attitudes of nuclear weapon states. The United States rejected this demand due to North Korea's larger conventional forces on the peninsula.[43] According to a North Korean Foreign Ministry statement released by the North Korean permanent observer mission to the United Nations, North Korea can sign a nuclear safeguards agreement only on the condition that the USA gives legal assurance that it would not resort to threats of nuclear use.[44] The South Korean Defence Minister Lae Jong said that it could bomb the nuclear facilities at Yongbyon if it does not sign the IAEA safeguards agreement. North Korean President Kim Il Sung reiterated that the announcement was a "virtual declaration of war".[45] Finally North Korea concluded the safeguards agreement with the IAEA on 16th July, 1991.[46]

Since South Korea had an alliance with the US and North Korea with the nuclear-armed USSR and China, the US would not exclude nuclear retaliation should North Korea attack the South. This stand was described concretely in the US presidential directive manifested in the UN on 17 November, 1978 and was proclaimed once more at the meeting of the Committee on Disarmament held in Geneva on 13 March, 1990. In response to the US, North Korea contended that the very existence of Nuclear Weapons on the Korean Peninsula poses a nuclear threat to North Korea and goes against the fundamental spirit of the NPT as well. North Korea also warned that it might secede from the NPT if the demands are not fulfilled.

The possibility of nuclear weapons capability plays a deterrent against any security threat from the US and South Korea. This same logic is used by the US, when it deploys nuclear weapons in South Korea to prevent North Korea from initiating an aggression. The governments of ROK, US, Russia, China and Japan were pressurizing the DPRK to sign the safeguards agreement and North Korea was holding as the last and only resort to gain diplomatic points. Postponing their conclusion of the agreement has played a meaningful card to solicit a diplomatic relation with USA and Japan and strengthens its ties with China and the USSR.

On June 7, North Korea's special envoy Chin Chung Guk arrived in Vienna and promised that the DPRK would send negotiating team to Vienna in mid July to settle the substance of the standard agreement and begin working level negotiations.[47] If a final agreement were settled with the IAEA approval, the DPRK would sign the agreement in September.

At the IAEA Board of Governors meeting held at Vienna on 10 June, 1991 North Korea withdrew its two previous conditions that American nuclear weapons be removed from South Korea and the US guarantee not to pose a nuclear threat. On July 16, however North Korea agreed with the IAEA to the standard INFCRIC TYPE 153 safeguards agreement draft with preconditions.[48]

Firstly, the decision represents North Korea's realistic reaction to the pressure of the international community. It was made in order to escape international isolation and to establish a footing to overcome economic difficulties. North Korea's unrealistic intransigence is probably one of the greatest elements causing tension in the North East Asia particularly its refusal to allow IAEA inspections.

Secondly, Pyongyang concluded the safeguards agreement to establish relation with the US. Thirdly the desire to improve relations with Japan also influenced the decision. In September 1990 the Pyongyang meeting between Kim II Sung and former Prime Minister Kanemara Shin and the third round of DPRK—Japan tolls took place in 20 May, 1991.[49] Since the third meeting, however the condition reversed and North Koreans decided to accept Japanese preconditions, resumption of North-South Korean dialogue, simultaneous entrance of North Korea and South Korea into the UN, conclusion of a safeguards agreement.[50]

Evolution of North Korean Nuclear Programme

The process of developing nuclear weapons involves three stages, research, development and armament. Following a decision to establish a research institute for nuclear Physics made during the second plenary meeting of the North Korean Academy of Sciences in April 1955, North Korea entered to the initial research stages. This was followed by an agreement with the Soviet Union Dubna Nuclear Research Institute on March 16, 1956, under which North Korean scientists were dispatched for training at this institute.[51]

North Korea signed protocols on peaceful uses of nuclear energy with Soviet Union and China. This marked the beginning of a relationship between North Korea, Soviet Union and China in the field of nuclear technology. Under the North Korean Soviet agreement, the Soviet Union promised to assist North Korean Academy of Sciences in building nuclear research facility.[52] North Korea established a nuclear research facility at Yongbyon in 1969[53]. North Korea received a 2MW nuclear research reactor and a small 0.1MW critical assembly from Soviet Union. Both the reactor and critical assembly was installed at Yongbyon and placed under the IAEA safeguards.[54]

North Korea began an active programme of weapons development in 1980's when the construction of a small natural

Uranium graphite power reactor began in Yongbyon. The reactor was best on 1950 Magnox technology, which is very good for producing weapon grade plutonium as a bye-product.[55] After start up problems it was operating at 20-30MW 1990. A large 50MW Magnox type reactor was under construction at Yongbyon with completion date in 1995. A 200MW of the same was under construction at Taechon, 60 miles North of Pyongyang and a 600-800 MW in Taechon to be completed by 1997.

The South Korean 1996, defence white paper asserts that North Korea conducted more than 70 tests in high explosive devices during the 1983-88 period. Lae Chung Guk who defected from North Korea in March 8, 1994, while serving in the Nuclear and Chemical Defence Bureau of the Army general staff shocked the South Koreans by presenting evidence that North Korea has a nuclear capability. Lee Chung Guk emphasized that he personally participated in test on nuclear explosion detonating devices conducted on a hill in Sogramri Pyongnnamdo province in October 20, 1993. US satellite photos also showed that such tests were conducted about eighty times. He also informed that he was involved in preparing a report on nuclear test results to be submitted to Kim II Sung, which showed that one test conducted in Russia and two others in Ukraine in July 1992 of 0.5 yield were successful.[56]

In 1980's North Korea planned the expansion of its nuclear infrastructure by the construction of an indigenous designed 5MW gas cooled reactor. According to a Southern report, Kyong Won Ha, a former US nuclear engineer at Los Alamos National Laboratory in New Mexico and a former professor at Mc Gill University in Canada repeatedly gave North Korea design information on a condition heavy water research reactor. This data may have been helpful in constructing the 5MW reactor.[57] A US Surveillance photographed what appeared to be a nuclear reactor vessel under construction is Yongbyon in April 1982.[58]

In 26 December 1985 North Korean workers party secretary Kang Song Sam signed a science and technology agreement with Soviet Union. The agreement was made in exchange of North Korea acceding to the NPT.[59] Under the agreement the Soviet Union would construct a nuclear power plant in North Korea as well as commit to a long-term agreement on trade and economic cooperation from 1986-1990. The power plant would be built near

Sinp'o and would consist of four 444-MW reactors.[60] In 1986 North Korea completed its experimental 5-MW reactor. It installed the 5 MW reactors. It installed the 5 MW reactors at Yongbyon. The North Korean Ministry of Atomic Power Industry was established under the leadership of Choe-Hak-Kun. The purpose of the ministry was to assist North Korea in acquiring a Nuclear power generating capability.[61] A German intelligence agency determined that North Korea might have obtained Uranium melting information from Pakistan. It is suspected that the information was stolen from Urenco, a western European consortium in 1984.[62]

On 12 December, 1985 North Korea informed the IAEA of the existence of the Yongbyon facility. On 5th April 1992, North Korea made its initial declaration of holding nuclear material. The key facilities at Yongbyon include an operational 5MW experimental nuclear power reactor and partially completed large-scale re-processing plant for Plutonium extraction.[63] During an inspection by the IAEA soon after to verify its declaration, North Korea revealed that it had separated 100 gram of Plutonium in March 1990's. US intelligence agencies judged that North Korea had extracted Plutonium at the Yongbyon reprocessing plant and possibly a nuclear of hot cells using irradiated fuel rods from 5 MW reactors which is thought to have been partially or fully refuelled in 1989. Technically North Korea could have manufactured one or two nuclear weapons. North Korean has accused the IAEA of acting at the behest of USA, having Western bias during the inspections.

In mid-December, 1991, North Korea decided not to manufacture, test, posses acquire, store and use nuclear weapons and not to enrich Uranium or reprocess Plutonium. At that time, North Korea and South Korea signed a treaty of reconciliation and non-aggression followed by a joint declaration for a non-nuclear Korean peninsula where they agreed to establish a joint nuclear commission to work out procedures for bilateral inspections capping these agreements. Pyongyang finally signed the safeguards agreement with the IAEA on 30 January, 1992.[64] But this relief at Pyongyang's decision to stay in the NPT is tinged with concern about what it will do next. Pyongyang did not come any closer in accepting special inspection of its suspected nuclear facilities, nor it has ruled eventual withdrawal from the NPT.[65]

For its part the DPRK had emerged with the bulk of its national security interest intact despite ongoing military stand off and level of tension unparallel anywhere. More significantly DPRK's objective to be taken seriously is, to be dealt as an independent and sovereign nation-stable and to be negotiated as on equal across the table.[66]

In May 1992, the DPRK supplied a list of her nuclear facilities and fuel to the IAEA inspectorate. Six inspections took place between June 1992 and February 1993, these inspections confirmed that the processing of Plutonium had taken place between 1989 and 1991.[67] On 4 May, 1992, North Korea gave the IAEA its initial declaration a statement of all its nuclear material subject to safeguard. The IAEA began inspection to verify the initial disclosure and to access its completeness. Soon after Hans Blix, the IAEA Director General visited North Korea for the first time. The North Korean official told the IAEA that they had used then facility to separate 100 grams of Plutonium in spring of 1990's. They said that Plutonium came when initial cladding has damaged during reactor operations. The IAEA officials also toured the North's graphite reactors, only one of which was in operation. At Yongbyon, the IAEA delegation visited a small operational reactor as well as 200 MW thermal reactor. During its initial inspection of summer of 1992, the IAEA collected sample of material cost in various processing steps as well as different types of a nuclear waste generated during those separation process. The samples were analysed at the IAEA laboratory in Seisbersdorf Australia and affiliated laboratories there Europe and USA. These analysis uncovered discrepancies that led the IAEA to suspect that the North had separated more Plutonium than it had admitted.[68]

One set of analysis called into question the claim that Plutonium had been separated only in March, 1990. The IAEA took smear or swipe samples from the inside of the glove boxes at the end of the separation process where freshly purified Plutonium is handled. The decay product test suggested that North Korea had infact separated Plutonium in 1989, 1990 and 1991.[69]

In another test, the IAEA tried to verify that the Plutonium declared by the North and the Plutonium found in the waste came from same source. The irradiated full rods which North Korean officials said had been damaged. The IAEA compared the ratio of Plutonium isotopes in several waste and glove box samples to the ratio in the separated Plutonium. Both the Plutonium and trace quantities of Plutonium remaining in the waste would have the same amount of Plutonium isotopes 239, 240, 241. Instead, the IAEA felt that the ratio of Plutonium 240 in the waste sample differed from that in the separated material.[70]

A third inconsistency involved the degree of irradiation of fuel, which North Korea seemed to have processed during its single reprocessing campaign. The isotopic ratio of separated Plutonium recovered from the waste were not consistent with the North's report of fuel irradiation history. Meanwhile, the IAEA began to receive disquieting intelligence reports that the North Korea had hidden that of its nuclear waste sites. A US official said that they had been camouflaged just before the start of IAEA inspection. The IAEA therefore asked to inspect the sites to see if it contained any radioactive waste that had been generated during reprocessing campaign as 1/5 satellite photos there over many years show what appear to be two nuclear waste sites near the radio chemical laboratory. The sites are large enough to hold large quantities of both liquid and solid nuclear waste. One set of photos shows a uninspected outdoor waste site willing to be associated with an earlier Russian supplied IRT megawatt thermal nuclear reactor that would have been under the IAEA safeguards since 1977.

In 1989, the satellite reconnaissance system sighted a long narrow structure at Yongbyon. The structure looked like a Plutonium reprocessing plant. If true it would allow North Koreans to execute the crucial steps towards building a nuclear bomb by separating Plutonium from other elements. Reports soon followed that North was also building a large gas graphite reactor that produced large quantities of weapons grade Plutonium.[72] This second hidden waste site is said to be a building about 50m long that could be connected to the Radio Chemical laboratory by underground pipes. The building was about 150m East of the radio chemical laboratory and was separated from it by a small hill. The photos show a two-story building with two trenches connecting it to the radio-chemical laboratory. In more recent photos however the building appeared to be one story because dirt has been pushed up around it cancelling the lower floor but could only conduct a visual inspection. But in late 1992 and early 1993, agency inspectors asked specifically for access to this building. North Korean officials refused to allow them to visit at the site claiming that they were both exempted from non-nuclear military facilities.

However disagreement between the IAEA and North Korea rose in large part from North's demand for inspection of US bases, in the South where nuclear weapons were known to have been stored. The IAEA for its part demanded special inspections as permitted under the terms of the treaty of the NPT of two undeclared sites of the North Korea's nuclear programme.[74] On February 10, 1993, North Korea refused to permit the IAEA to conduct special inspections, as permitted under the terms of the NPT of two nuclear sites to clarify discrepancies of North Korea nuclear programme. On March 12, 1993, North Korea announced its intention to withdraw from the NPT effective on June 12, 1993 due to the insistence of the IAEA on exercising inspection rights under the NPT.

On April 1993, the IAEA declared North Korea to be in non-compliance with the NPT. On April 2, 1993, the IAEA voted to refer North Korean violations of the treaty to the UN Security Council and on April 17, 1993, the IAEA consigned a formal censure on North Korea for non-compliance with the NPT, the first censure in the history of the IAEA.[75] On May 11, 1993, the UN Security Council passed a resolution asking North Korea to allow the IAEA inspectors under the NPT and on May 12, 1993, North Korea rejected the request of UN Security Council and subsequently impeded on refused access to any of its sites by the IAEA inspectors. When North Korea withdrew from the NPT in March 1993, the US intelligence community debated the capabilities and implications of its nuclear programme. Some viewed North Korean actions as a blatant threat to US interests, while other saw essentially a defensive move by Pyongyang, playing the nuclear card to strengthen the regimes hand in dealing with the loss of Soviet support.[76]

North Korea's attempt to withdraw from the NPT threatened US regional interests containing nuclear proliferation in Japan and South Korea. North Korea's action also threatened the global US non-proliferation policy. If North Korea pulled out of the NPT, it could affect the outcome of the 1995 NPT extension conference. For a small isolated and a relatively weak state likes North Korea, it was an important step. It followed the typical North Korean negotiating style to go to the brink and retrieve the situation only in the last minute.[77]

The American Senate condemned North Korea for its stated

intention to withdraw from the NPT. It emphasized that the US had withdrawn all tactical weapons from the Korean peninsula in 1991 and annual team spirit excesses were conducted for defensive purpose were not a provocative act of war.[78]

The North Korean threat to withdraw from the NPT brought North-South progress to an abrupt halt. Tensions ran high on the Korean peninsula as the conformation on North Korea and the US deepened.

On June 2, 1993, the US and North Korea initiated a series of meeting in New York to discuss the impasse over the nuclear site inspections, which continued until January 4, 1994, when under secretary of state Lynn Davis announced that North Korea had agreed to inspections of several declared nuclear related sites. North Korea explained that what it had agreed to was an inspection aimed at continuity of safeguards and limited purpose inspection dictated by its special status. It was not required to fulfil all obligations under the NPT including safeguards agreement with the IAEA. North Korea was during March 19, Panmunjon meeting that North Korean negotiators walked out of the conference room, after making some influential remarks against South Korean delegates.[79]

Several months latter North Korea suspended its NPT withdrawal clause, by claiming that it had a unique status with regards to the treaty. On April 8, 1994 it shut down the small reactor for the purpose of unloading the core in early May. In spite of the IAEA insistence that it must view the unloading process to ensure that nonc of them was diverted for a weapon programme, the North began to unload the reactor without safeguard measures the IAEA had demanded.[80]

The IAEA informed North Korea that it must allow the IAEA to sample and segregate the fuel rods to pressure the evidence of part-Plutonium production. Again North Korea refused but offered to allow two inspectors to watch the fuel removal process. On May 12, North Korea offered to allow IAEA access to spent fuel if US would agree to open new round of talks during illicit fuelling operation. The tensions escalated as the United States prodded the UN Security Council to evict sanctions against the North Korea if it continued to deny the IAEA full access to its nuclear facilities. The Security Council has authorization to call for sanctions under action with respect to threats to peace under chapter 7, Article 41.[81]

In June 1994 former President Carter reached an agreement with President Kim Il Sung that the North Korea would freeze its programme temporarily and return to negotiation in Geneva.[82]

The Agreed Framework of 1994

North Korea's acceptance of the agreed framework culminated in a decade of ups and downs in the relationship between North Korea and the international Non-Proliferation regime. Under the terms of the US-North Korea agreed framework concluded on October 21, 1994, North Korea pledged to:

- Freeze operations at or cease construction of graphite-moderated reactors and cease operating Yongbyon reprocessing plant units, the freeze to be verified by the IAEA.
- Not to separate Plutonium from spent fuel removed from 5-MW reactor in May 1994, the status of the fuel to be monitored by the IAEA.
- Ship the opened fuel out of North Korea.
- Thereafter dismantle all facilities of nuclear proliferation concern. In exchange North Korea will be provided with two less proliferated prove light water reactors and a nuclear of another energy related inducements as well as security assurances.[83]
- The formation of an international consortium to provide two proliferation resistant light water reactors to replace the current graphite moderated facilities. The ROK and Japan would provide the bulk of funding. The US would organize under its leadership an international consortium to finance and supply the LWR project to be provided to the DPRK within six months of the date of this document for the provision of the LWR project with a total generating capacity of approximately 2000 MW by a target date of 2003. The US representing the consortium would make best effort to ensure the conclusion of a supply contract with the DPRK within 6 months of the date of this document for the provision of the light water project. As necessary the US and the DPRK would conclude a bilateral agreement for cooperation in the field of peaceful uses of

> nuclear energy. Delivery of heavy oil would begin within three months of the date of this document and would reach the rate of 500,000 tonnes annually in accordance with an agreement of deliveries.[84]

The most important example of engagement with North Korea was negotiation with the agreed framework of October 1994. This agreement remains controversial largely because of the provision to build two nuclear power reactors in North Korea in return for the dismantling of North Korea's existing reactors. The immediate strategic consequence of the agreed framework negotiated with the DPRK is that the US would have a special responsibility and serve as a mediator between North and South Korea. The way in which Washington carries out its responsibilities will influence the credibility of the NPT regime.[85]

The October 1994, agreed framework with the US provides incentives for North Korea to accept necessary inspection and clarify the critical issues. North Korea has already frozen it nuclear weapon programme and stopped producing Plutonium. It has also committed to dismantle its current nuclear facilities. In exchange South Korea and Japan are financing and building two light water reactors for Pyongyang.[86]

On the other hand the agreed framework is controversial. First by postponing the IAEA inspections of two undeclared sites for an extended period, four to six years the accord delays attaining full compliance with IAEA safeguards and creates an unprecedented status for North Korea. It introduces a double standard and a troubling precedence. Moreover, critics stress the agreement preserves for somewhat longer period, North Korea's ability to acquire additional nuclear weapons. A final criticism is that the agreement sets a precedent for others to toy with the NPT. On balance it seems clear that the agreed framework provides a credible means of keeping North Korea in the Regime and of blocking nuclear weapons manufacture. Critics of the agreed framework have raised serious concerns. North Korea has a poor history of adhering to agreements would be looked upon as rewarding a country for flagrant violations of obligations it undertook in the past. If Pyongyang fails to comply in, it would be difficult for the US or any regional partner to exercise a strict option without being accused of abrogating the agreement. Also, the agreement's vagueness allows North Korea plenty of opportunities to rationalize non-compliance.[87]

US support for the 1999 agreed framework has been inconsistent. Washington has delayed shipment of heavy oil and made only token moves towards normalizing relations with North Korea. The US has contributed to North Korean worries by pursuing a theatre missile defence system and by encouraging Japan to expand its military role in the region. The problem began with Washington half-hearted commitment to the 1994 agreed framework. When US signed the agreed framework many in the administration expected the North Korean government to collapse before the promised light water reactors should be operational in 2003. The agreement functioned as a stopgap measure rather than a step towards normalization. There has been serious Congress criticism of the agreed framework. Congressional pressure is already being bought to bear on various aspects of the pact slowing required funding for the purchase of heavy fuel oil for North Korea.

North Korea too had a list of grievances. It charged the US of violating the agreed framework by not delivering the heavy fuel oil according to schedule and not by moving forward as planned with the light water reactors. It also accused the Clinton administration of backtracking on its premise to normalize relations and to lift economic sanctions.

China recognized the limitation of the agreed framework. A senior PLA analyst commented that the US North Korea accord "doesn't signify a relaxation of mood nor of adverserial sentiments", of the two sides and predicted "North Korea will never give up its military preparedness". North Korea was very sensitive about US intentions and feared interference in its internal affairs. China predicted that North Korea may change its attitude and may not fulfil the agreement if it thinks that US is still hostile towards it. The Chinese feel that North Korea used the nuclear programme as a balancing chip to get economic aid and diplomatic relations with the US. North Korea may ask for more aid from the outside world.[88]

According to Hwang Jang Yop, a former secretary of International Affairs of the North Korean Workers Party the main reason why North Korea insisted upon light water reactors as opposed to thermonuclear unit is that North Korea possess huge Uranium ore but lacks the ability to secure Plutonium needed for operating thermoelectric plants. The agreed framework of 1994 with the US gave North Korea everything it wanted though the fact remains that Pyongyang still retains its nuclear option. North Korea wanted to show to the world that it was supporting a peace process and also cover it up for nuclear development North Korea signed the agreed framework accord with the US in October 1994 as a part of its strategy to buy time to develop its nuclear arms.[89]

The agreed framework was a necessary but not sufficient response posed by North Korea to the US. Some senior administration officials like Frank S. Jannuzi, minority staff of the of the Senate Foreign Relations Committee, Robert Manning member Council on Foreign Relations, assumed that the agreed framework had ended North Korea's nuclear programme. They felt that the agreed framework would induce North Korea to open up to the outside world and institute a gradual process of North South reconciliation.[90] The discovery of a suspect North Korean nuclear site in 1998 and the launch of a Taepo Dong missile on 31 August, 1998 raised questions about Pyongyang's intentions, its commitment to the agreement. There is a strong presumption in the intelligence community that North Korea may possess one or two nuclear bombs containing Plutonium produced before 1994 agreed framework froze Pyongyang's Plutonium programme.[91]

Kumchangri Controversy

Kumchangri is an underground site located North West of Yongbyon, North Korea's foreign nuclear complex. It has been suspected that the site had or was intended to have a nuclear reaction.[92] North Korea continued to deny that site was nuclear related, rather it emphasized that Kumchangri's was a civilian site.[93] A 15 member team inspected Kumchangri from 18-24 May 1999. James Rupin US Department of State spokesman denounced the Kumchangri does not contain a Plutonium production reactor on a reprocessing plant.

According to Kenneth Quninones, former Director of North Korean Affairs at the US Department of State, it is false to assume that the agreed framework gives the United States the right to inspect any facility at Kumchangri or elsewhere. According to the agreed framework the only inspections that North Korea must adhere to are inspection at specified facilities at the Yongbyan nuclear complex. North Korea is not obliged to permit inspections of Kumchangri and is not a violation of the agreement.[94]

North Korea Vice Foreign Minister Kim Gye Gwan and US envoy came in 16-18 November 1998, to discuss the suspected nuclear related site at Kumchangri. Kartman demanded that the IAEA be given access to the site, if access is denied, North Korea would be breaking the agreed framework. Kim agreed to grant access to the site in return for $300 million in monetary compensation. The talks ended in a stalemate. North Korea threatened to abandon the agreed framework if the United States does.[95]

In mid-February 1992, a meeting between the North Korean Vice Foreign Minister Kim Gye Gwan and US envoy for Korean Nuclear Affairs Charles Kartman met in New York to discuss the suspected nuclear site at Kumchangri. Kim Gye Gwan demanded 1 million tones of foodgrains in return for the access to the site. Charles Kartmen offered to denote 700,000 tons of food assistance and support a series of bilateral food programme with North Korea in return for access to the entire site.[96]

The Korean Peninsular Energy Development Organization

On 9 March, 1995, the United States, Japan and South Korea formed a multinational consortium called the Korean Peninsular Energy Development Organization (KEDO) to supply North Korea with two promised light water reactors. Besides being the agency for implementing the reactor deal, KEDO has taken over the responsibility for raising funds to pay for oil deliveries. One of the initial stumbling blocks in carrying out the reactor related portion of the agreed framework was North Korea's refusal to accept South Korea reactors. On 13 June, 1995, North Korea and the US issued a joint statement, which resolved some of the more contentious issues that has been stalling implementation of the agreed framework.

Both sides agreed that the KEDO would select a reactor model based on a US origin design and would also select a prime contractor for the project. The programme coordinated would be an American firm chosen by the KEDO. On the same day, the KEDO announced that 1000 more Korean standard nuclear power plant based on the system 80-reactor design of US firm Asea Brown Boveri Combustion Engineering would be modelling for reactors to be supplied to North Korea.

After months of further negotiations, North Korea and KEDO concluded a supply agreement on December 15, 1995, for actual financing and supply for reactors. The supply agreement has three main component, setting out the scope for two light water reactors outlining the terms of repayment of North Korea for the cost of the reactors and outlining the general terms and conditions under which KEDO will operate at a project site.[97]

Attention surrounding North Korea's nuclear programme arose as the US and North Korea hammered to yet another agreement in Kualalmpur, Malaysia in 13 June, 1995. In the talks between Thomas Hubbard Deputy Assistant Secretary of State for Asian and Pacific Affairs and North Korea's Chief negotiator Kim Kye Kwan, the resolution of the North Korean nuclear issue seemed at least on surface to be translated into action between the US and North Korea. A US working level delegation visited Pyongyang to study conditions to providing heavy oil to North Korea.[98] In addition the inspection team visited North Korea to access the conditions of proposed sites of planned construction of light water reactors.

North Korea has become more of an international pariah as Russia and China, its two most powerful friends moved gradually to distance themselves from it. That may have spurned Pyongyang to adopt a new garbling tactics, when it announced that it would no longer honour the NPT.[99] The more was widely interpreted that North Korea would proceed with its long suspected programme to develop nuclear weapons. The blackmail worked. North Korea negotiated an accord with USA under which it would get two nuclear power plants in exchange for scrapping its atomic arms plan.

A North Korea policy review team led by William Perry and working inter agency by Wendy R. Sherman was sent on November 1998 by President Clinton and his national security advisor to conduct extensive review of US policy towards DPRK. The policy review team determined that a fundamental review of US policy was needed since much has charged in the security situation in the Korean peninsula since 1994 have witnessed development testing deployment and export by DPRK of ballistic missiles of increasing range including those potentially capable of reaching the US.[100]

South Korean President Kim Dal Jung's Sunshine policy advocated humanitarian aid and economic engagement with North

Korea. North Korean Special Envoy General Jo Myong-Rok visited the US in October 2000 and Madeline Albright made a return visit latter that month. In March 2001, the Bush administration publicity cast doubt on Sunshine policy. In January 2002, President Bush labelled North Korea as a part of an 'Axis of Evil'. The frequency of US condemnation of North Korea increased after the state of union address. The nuclear posture review leaked in March indicated that North Korea would be targeted by the US nuclear weapons. In April the administration did not certify North Korea being in compliance with the agreed framework.[101]

The US has to move beyond the agreed framework and seek to negotiate on engagement on Pyongyang. This will not happen unless Washington abandons its belief that the way to get states give up their nuclear ambitions is to denounce them at outlines and force to disarm the crime and punishment approach to non-proliferation. Such an approach is not likely to succeed especially with Pyongyang.[102]

While North Korea had held open its nuclear option as leverage for cooperation, it has been punctious in observing the letter of the agreed framework as demonstrated for instance, in coming of spent fuel rods in Yongbyon. After talks in New York in early September, Pyongyang allowed the conning of spent fuel rods to resume and is in near agreement with Washington on access to underground sets. In return the North wanted progress in engagement in the form of further relaxation of the US sanctions which Washington held up when the renewed activity at Kumchangri was discovered. In short North Korea had been threatening to break the October accord without actually violating it. It looks like tit for tat behaviour by Pyongyang to cooperate when US cooperates and retaliate to get Washington to negotiate.[103] On March 15, 2001, North Korea threatened to take revenge on the US and its intention to torpedo the dialogue between North and South Korea. The statement issued by state run Korean central news agency called Washington's new policy hostile and noted that Pyongyang remains fully prepared for both dialogue and war. Following Bush's demand for verification in dealings with North Korea, Republican leaders in the House and the Senate urged the administration to recognized the terms of the agreed framework under which North Korea is to be provided with two light water reactors. On March 9, 2001, Chairman of the Soviet foreign relation committee Jesse Helms along with senator make of wine and Bow Smith sent a letter to Bush calling for the administration to abandon the reactor project in favour of several clean burning cold field power plant to meet North Korea's civilian needs. The letter called into question Pyongyang tract record and said that North Korea's regime can hardly be trusted with light water technology or with Fissile material.[104]

The DPRK delegate in a speech to the first committee meeting of the 57 UN General Assembly session in October stressed to ensure peace and security in the Korean Peninsula. The US hostile policy towards the DPRK should be terminated in order to achieve durable and lasting peace.

North Korea Withdraws from the NPT

On 10 January, 2003, North Korea announced that it would withdraw from the nuclear Non-Proliferation Treaty. Its withdrawal from the NPT would leave it free from the binding force of its safeguards agreement with the IAEA. Article X paragraph of the NPT provides "Each party shall in exercising its National sovereignty have the right to withdraw from the treaty if it decides that extraordinary events, related to the subject-matter of the treaty have jeopardized its supreme interest."[105]

North Korea stated reasons for withdrawing from the NPT. It accused the United States jeopardizing its security by its hostile policy towards it.[106] According to North Korea the United States had singled it out as the target of preemptive nuclear strike and threatened it with blockade and military punishment.[107] Although Article X of the NPT requires that a country needs three months notice in advance of withdrawing. North Korea argued that it had satisfied this requirement because it originally announced its decision to withdraw in 12 March, 1993 and suspended one day before it was to become legally binding.

The IAEA Board of Governor adopted a resolution on the implementation of the IAEA safeguards in the Democratic Peoples Republic of Korea at its meeting in Vienna 21 November, 2002. It noted with extreme concern the DPRK statement of 25 October, 2002 that it is entitled to possess not only nuclear weapons but also any type of weapons more powerful than that.[108]

When US officials confronted North Korea in October 2002 with allegation of its clandestine programme to enrich Uranium for nuclear weapons, North Korea expelled the International Atomic Energy inspectors, removed IAEA cameras and seals on nuclear facilities. It suspended activity under the 1994 agreed framework and announced its withdrawal from the 1968, Non-Proliferation Treaty.[109] On 12 December, 2002, the IAEA received a letter from Mr. Ri Je Son, Director General of the Department of Atomic Energy of the Democratic People's Republic of Korea, informing the IAEA of the DPRK's decision to 'lift the freeze' on its nuclear facilities according to the DPRK-US agreed framework and to resume operations of these facilities for power generation. The IAEA Director General Dr. Mohammed El Baradei called upon the DPRK to act with restraint and not to take any steps unilaterally to remove or impede the functioning of such seals or cameras.[110]

The US has threatened to suspend the construction of light-water reactors in North Korea unless the communist country accepts an international inspection of its nuclear related activities. In a testimony before the hearing of Asia Pacific sub-committee of the House International Relations Committee, Jack Pritchard special envoy for Korea peace talks said "The light water reactor project will stop until the North Korean are in full compliance with their obligation."[111]

North Korea surprised the entire international community by admitting that it had a Uranium enrichment programme in violation of the agreed framework signed in October 1999.[112] The revelation was made when a senior North Korean diplomat Kang Suk Joo, a Chief architect of the agreed framework met the US Presidential envoy James A. Kelley in Pyongyang on 4 October, 2002. The North Korea's first denied but with Kelly insistence they confessed the existence of enrichment programme.[113]

North Korea's announcement that it intended to restart 5 Megawatt Plutonium reactor frozen under the agreed framework was a calculated act of diplomatic brinkmanship designed to bring Washington to the negotiating table.[114] North Korea attempted to develop nuclear weapons to attract the attention of the US to force it to negotiate according to Sah Jae Jean, Director of the Korean Institute for National Unification. By enriching Uranium for use in weapons, North Korea violated Article II of the NPT requiring non-nuclear weapon states, "not to manufacture or otherwise acquire nuclear weapons or other explosive devices." If North Korea has received assistance from Pakistan or any other country it also has violated Article II of the Non-Proliferation Treaty.[115] By producing enriched Uranium without safeguards North Korea would be violating Article III of the NPT which requires non-nuclear weapon states to accept safeguards monitored by the IAEA.[116] North Korea decided to disclose the existence of its nuclear programme in an effort to come clean about the violation of its international non-proliferation commitment. This is an apparent manifestation of "confessional diplomacy".[117] Pyongyang's official Korean central news agency said that the country was pulling out of the Non-Proliferation Treaty, but its nuclear activities would be confined to peaceful purposes such as production of electricity.

North Korea rejected a resolution by the IAEA to readmit its monitors who were expelled from the country. The DPRK government vehemently rejected the January 6 resolution of the IAEA considering it as a grave encroachment upon the sovereignty of the Democratic People's Republic of Korea and the dignity of the Korean nation. The IAEA is used as a tool for executing the US hostile policy towards the DPRK therefore North Korea could no longer remain bound to the NPT, allowing the country's security and dignity to be infringed upon.[118]

North Korean Foreign Ministry accused the US of breaking the 1994 agreed framework and said that if wanted the removal of the threat to its existence, an apparent reference to the US forces in South Korea.[119]

International Response to North Korea's Withdrawal

North Korea had to face international criticism after it announced its intention to withdraw from the NPT. President Bush dispatched Under Secretary of State John Bolton and Assistant Secretary Kelly to China, Russia, South Korea and Japan to coordinate an international response. These nations expressed concerns over North Korea's nuclear programme. They demanded that North Korea must completely dismantle its nuclear weapons programme as well as all weapons of mass destruction in its possession. North Korea must allow the IAEA weapons inspector's complete and unrestricted access to all nuclear facilities so that disarmament can be monitored and verified. North Korea must promise not to export or transfer weapons of mass destruction, delivery systems, related technologies and material to any country group or individual.[120]

In a trilateral statement, the United States, Japan and South Korea used similar language demanding North Korea to dismantle its nuclear programme in a 'prompt and verifiable manners'. US proposed to suspend economic assistance and political contacts with North Korea until it makes visible progress on the above demands. Secretary of State Colin Powell stated that North Korea regards the agreement as nullified and therefore the United States in not obliged to continue construction on promised light water reactors or provide regular heavy fuel oil deliveries to Pyongyang.[121]

Ari Fleischer, White House press secretary stated that North Korea's plan to resume the operation and construction of its nuclear facilities were regrettable. The international community had made it clean that North Korea's relations with the outside world triggered on the elimination of its nuclear weapons programme. They insisted that North Korea should dismantle its nuclear weapons programme in a visible and verifiable manner.[122]

Alexander Yakovenko, the official spokesman of the Russian Ministry of Foreign Affairs said that the Russians were for the strict observance of the treaty on Non-Proliferation of nuclear weapons implementation of the IAEA safeguards agreement and the denuclearisation of the Korean Peninsula.[123]

United Nation Secretary General, Kofi Annan, expressed regret about Pyongyang's withdrawal from the nuclear Non-Proliferation Treaty and strongly urged Pyongyang to reconsider the decision. He emphasized that the NPT was the linchpin of nuclear Non-Proliferation and disarmament regime with 188 state parties and as no state party to the NPT has ever withdrawn from the treaty in the 33 years since its entry into force.[124]

The US intelligence community concluded that North Korea had enrichment project based on Pakistan technology. The CIA publicly estimated that North Korea was contracting a plant that could produce enough weapons grade Uranium for two or more nuclear weapons per year when fully operational.[125] Pakistan may have provided North Korea with nuclear weapons design assistance and even supplies of weapons grade Uranium. Pakistan's acquisition of Nodong Ballistic missiles from North

Korea also raises inevitable questions about what North Korea gained from transferring complete ballistic missile systems and technologies to Pakistan.[126]

Washington's basic approach seems to ignore and downplay the North Korean threat, while focussing its energies on Iraq. Washington seems determined to resist being 'blackmailed' by North Korea into direct negotiations, even though North Korea might agree to halt its reprocessing campaign as a condition for pursuing talks with United States. Although North Korea claims that it only seeks security assurances from the US to resolve the nuclear issue, its real demands are likely to be much more extensive. North Korea would resist any arrangement requiring sacrifice of its nuclear edge in process leading to full normalization of political and economic relations with North Korea.[127]

It is again witnessed that the nuclear Non-Proliferation Treaty has become a flawed institution that requires considerable tending to include constant efforts to obtain a consensus of its parties concerning evolving interpretation of its provision in order to be effective as a Non-Proliferation tool. The North Korean case points to the fact that there is nothing in the treaty that prohibits a non-nuclear weapons state that is party to the NPT from assisting another non-weapon state from manufacturing or otherwise acquiring the bomb. The treaty does not define a point at which we can say the construction of a nuclear explosive device has begun. The treaty has no provision of sanctions for violation or withdrawal from the treaty.

The Non-Proliferation Treaty divides the world along nuclear lines concentrating nuclear weapons in the hands of powerful states while subjecting third world nations to intensive inspections. It seems odd that a treaty aimed at achieving nuclear disarmament should focus its opening Article I on keeping weapons away from certain states that do not possess nuclear weapons instead of those states that already have them. The Non-Proliferation Treaty does not attempt to put an end to nuclear weapons capability but determines who can have it and who cannot. The NPT killer clause comes in Article III, which opens the world up to intrusive inspections in the name of nuclear transperancy.[128] North Korea, was very reluctant to accept unjust IAEA inspections based on US manipulated "intelligence data". North Koreas security would be threatened by open its bases to its enemies when it was constantly under the US nuclear threat.[129]

North Korea had been repeatedly at odds with its treaty obligations ever since it became a member of the Non-Proliferation Treaty in 1985. North Korea took its confrontations with the international community a significant step further by announcing its immediate withdrawal from the key global non-proliferation regime on 10 January, 2003. On April, 2003, North Korea declared that its bilateral "denuclearisation agreement" with Seoul was no longer valid. Since then North Korea's alleged effort to acquire a nuclear weapons capability has served as a potent catalyst of renewed global attention in Korea. The reassessment of its long-term security calculations vis-à-vis the US, led North Korea to defy the NPT and finally withdraw from it. North Korea had always been apprehensive of the US nuclear threat. The US pre-emption doctrine, which was drafted largely in response to the terrorist attack of 11 September, 2001, and which was used in justifying the recent invasion of Iraq, had a serious negative effect on the NPT regime. The lessons that North Korea learned from Iraq was that it had to accelerate its nuclear weapons programme in order to avoid the fate of the Bath regime.[130]

This chapter thus, examined North Korea's perception towards the Non-Proliferation Treaty, in the context of its geo-political environment. It was observed that North Korea's final withdrawal from the NPT and its apparent efforts to accelerate its nuclear programme was largely a response to adverse changes in the external environment. North Korea's hostile relations with South Korea, Japan, China and the US were the main factors behind its need to develop nuclear weapons as a deterrent. The US has been manipulating the IAEA and using it to advance its own interests by trying to build a highly discriminatory Non-Proliferation regime. That the IAEA had increasingly degenerated into a servile organ and a mouthpiece of the US was no doubt noted by North Korea. The IAEA resolutions have turned a blind eye to the abandonment of the agreed framework by the US. North Korea was unwilling to be tied to the NPT or to allow it to encroach its national security or sovereignty. Thus, it is argued that as Nuclear weapons states moved further away from their obligations under the treaty, they simultaneously weakened incentives for non-nuclear weapon states to remain as parties within the NPT regime.

NOTES

1. Steve La Montagne, "North Korea's Nuclear Programme: An Assessment of US Options", *Non-Proliferation Project Issue Brief*, Vol. 2, No. 10, (Washington DC: Center for Arms Center and Non-Proliferation), p. 1 <http: www.arms control center/org/prolit project/nk nuclear.html>
2. "Past North Korean Non-Proliferation Agreements", *Arms Control Today*, Vol. 33, No. 4, (Washington DC: The Arms Control Association, May, 2003), p. 11.
3. Choi Byoung Woon, "Prospect of Social Reform and Disarmament in North Korea", *Korea Focus*, Vol. 9, No. 3, (Seoul: Korea Foundation, May-June, 2001), p. 101.
4. "Nuclear Weapons on the Korean Peninsula", *Arms Control Today*, Vol. 33, No. 4, (Washington DC: Arms Control Association, May 2003), p. 3.
5. Seongwhum Cheon, "North Koreas Nuclear Programme Heading Towards the End", *Korea and World Affairs*, Vol. XXVI, No. 4, (Seoul: Research Center for Peace and Unification of Korea, Winter 2000), p. 475.
6. "Geographical Location", <http://nk.chosun.com/English/factbook/factbook.html>.
7. Kyung A.C. Park, Dalchoong Kim (*Eds.*)", *Korean Security Dynamics in Transition*", (New York: Palgrave, New Publishers Ltd., 2001), p. 7.
8. Barry K. Gills, "Prospects for Peace and Stability in North East Asia, the Korean Conflict", *Conflict Studies*, 278, (Research Institute for the Study of Conflict and Terrorism, February 1995).
9. Richard P. Cronin, "North Korea's Nuclear Weapons Programme, US Policy Options", CRS, *Report for Congress*, CRS 94-470F, June 1, 1994, <http:www. fas.org/spp/star wars/crs/94-47 of.htm>.
10. William Tow, "Reassessing Deterrence on the Korean Peninsula", *Korean Journal of Defence Analysis*, 3: 1, Summer 1991, pp. 179-218.
11. Yong Byung Kie, "Changes in North Korea's Military Policy and East Asian Security", *Korea Focus*, January-February, 2003, p. 52.
12. Leonard Spector, *Nuclear Proliferation Today*, (Ballinger Publishers, Cambridge, 1984), pp. 241-42.
13. Haksoon Paik, "Steering Between Red Basis: A South Korean View", *Arms Control Today*, Vol. 33, No. 4, (Washington DC: Arms Control Association, May, 2003), p. 15.
14. "Explanation of the Peace and Propensity Policy", *Ministry of Unification*, Republic of Korea, 10 March, 2003.
15. Jamesclay Moltz Alexander, Y. Mansourov, *The North Korean Nuclear Programme, Security, Strategy and New Perspectives from Russia*, (New York and London Routledge, 2000), pp. 130-31.

16. Andrew Mack, "The Nuclear Crisis in the Korean Peninsula", *Asian Survey*, Vol. XXXIII, No. 4, April, 1993, p. 345.
17. Leonard S. Spector, Jacqueline R. Smith, "North Korea: The Next Nuclear Nightmare?", *Arms Control Today*, 21:2, March 1991, p. 13.
18. "Russia Backs Sanctions Against North Korea", *International Herald Tribune*, June 1994, pp. 11-12.
19. ."China's North Korean Test", *The Economist*, June 11-17, 1999, p. 12.
20. Banning Garrett Bonnie, Glaser, "Looking Across the Yalu, Chinese Assessment of North Korea", *Asian Survey*, Vol. XXXV, No. 6, June 1995, p. 528-529.
21. *Ibid.*
22. Hazel Smith, Chris Rhodes, Diana Pritcard, Kevin Magill, *North Korea in the New World Order*, (St. Martins Press Inc.), 1996, p. 30.
23. K. D. Kapur, *Nuclear Diplomacy in East Asia, US and The Korean Nuclear Crisis Management*, (New Delhi: Lancers Books, 1995), p. 343.
24. Joseph Gerson, "Key Problems", *Asia Pacific and Security Issues*, Vol. 2, No. 10, January 1997, <http: //www.foip.org/brief/vol.2.v2n asi-body.html>
25. Alex Wagner, "Bush Labels North Korea, Iran, Iraq as Axis of Evil", *Arms Control Today*, (Washington DC: Arms Control Association, March. 2002).
26. Steve La Montagne, *Op cit.*, p. 2.
27. Meghan L. O. Sullivan, "Replacing The Rogue Rhetoric, A New Label Opens the Way to a Better Policy", *Brooking Review*, Vol. 18, No. 4, (The Brooking Institution, Washington DC, February 2000), pp. 38-40.
28. Chung Oknim, "Outlook for Bush Administer North Korea Policy", *Korea Focus*, Vol. 9, No. 2, March-April 2001, p. 67.
29. Lee Shun Ho, "North Korea's Development of Weapons of Mass Destruction", *Korean Focus*, Vol. 4, No. 2, March-April 1996, p. 41.
30. David E. Sanger, "US Delay Urged on Korea Sanctions, *New York Times*, November 1993, p. A-9.
31. K. D. Kapur, *"Nuclear Diplomacy in East Asia"*, (New Delhi: Lancer Books, 1995), p. 334.
32. *Ibid.*
33. "Japan has the Ability to Make Nuclear Bombs, Hata Admits", *The Japan Times*, Tokyo, June 18, 1994, p. 1.
34. David C. Kang, "Rethinking North Korea", *Asian Survey*, Vol. XXXV, No. 3, March 1995, p. 262.
35. Richard K. Betts, "Paranoids, Pygmies, Pariahs, and Non-Proliferation Resisted" In Zachary S. Davis and Benjamin Frankel (eds.), *The Non-Proliferation Puzzle, Why Nuclear Weapons Spread and What Results*, (London: Frank Class, 1993), p. 110.
36. Rush Deming, "Testimony before the Senate Foreign Relations

Committee, *Subcommittee on East Asian and Pacific Affairs,* (Washington DC, July 14, 1998).

37. Prakash Nanda, *Nuclearisation of Divided Nations,* (New Delhi: Manas Publication, 2001), p. 81.
38. "Korean Nuclear Crisis: Statement of Peace and Reunification of the Korean Peninsula", *Bulletin of Concerned Asian Scholars,* Vol. 26, No. 1, January-June 1994, <http://csf.colorado.edu/bcas/sample/doc3-ch.htm>.
39. Leon V. Sigal, "The North Korean Nuclear Crises: Understanding the Failure of Crime and Punishment Strategy", *Arms Control Today,* (The Arms Control Association, May 1997)., <http:www.armcontrol.org/act/1997-05/s.gal.asp>.
40. Don Oberdorfer, *"Two Koreas: A Contemporary History"*, (Reading MA: Addison Wesley, 1997), p. 254.
41. Michael R. Gordon, *New York Times,* 25 October, 1989, p. A4.
42. The UN Disarmament Yearbook, Vol. 12, 1987, (New York: Department of Disarmament Affairs, UN), p. 186.
43. Andrew Mack, *Far Eastern Economic Review,* 31 May, 1990, p. 24.
44. Leonard S. Spector, Jacqueline R. Smith, *Op cit,* p. 10.
45. Carles, Lane, *News,* August 1991, p. 116.
46. *Nuclear News,* August 1991, p. 116.
47. *Chosum Ilbo,* 9 June, 1991.
48. Young Sum Song, "The Korean Nuclear Issue, *Korea and World Affairs,* Fall 1991, p. 483.
49. At the Mt. Myonyang Meeting Between Kim II Sung and Kanemaru Shin, a Joint Declaration was made by North Korea and Japan. The Ist Meeting was held in January 30, 31, 1991 another in Tokyo on March 11 & 12, 1991.
50. Young Sun Song, *Op cit.,* p. 484.
51. Yang Byung Kie, "Changes in North Korea's Military Policy and East Asian Security", *Korea Focus,* Vol. 9, No. 5, January-February 2003.
52. Joseph S. Bermudas Jr, *Jane's Intelligence Review,* September 1991, pp. 405-06.
53. Leonard S. Spector, *Op cit.,* p. 9.
54. Leonard, S. Spector *"Nuclear Ambitions: The Spread of Nuclear Weapons 1989- 1990"*(Boulder: West View Press 1990), p. 139.
55. Lee Wna Rang, "North Korean Nuclear Arsenal" 27 April, 1996 <http://www.kinsoft.com/Korea nk-nukes.html>
56. Lee Shun To, *Op cit.,* pp. 44-45.
57. Chao Kap-che, *Wolgan Coson,* Seoul, April 1990, pp. 220-25.
58. Don Oberdorfer, *Op cit.,* p. 250.
59. *Ashai Simbum,* Tokyo, 19 May, 1992, p. 20.
60. Joseph S. Bermudas Jr. *Op cit.,* p. 40.

61. Song Yong Song, *Singdong A*, Seoul, August 1990, pp. 206-15.
62. Mark Hibbis, *Nucleonics Week*, 28 November, 1991, pp. 1, 7-8.
63. "Tracking Nuclear Proliferation", *Carnegie Endowments*, 1998 < http://www.ceip.org/files publication Tracking North Korea asp? P = 8!@from = publication data).
64. Hazel Smith, Chris Rhodes, Diana Pritchard, Kevin Magill, *North Korea in a New World Order*, St. Martins Press Ltd., 1996, pp. 33-34.
65. "North Korea Pyongyang Pulls Back", *Far Eastern Economic Review*, June 1993, p. 15.
66. D. Blackwill, Albert, Carnesale, "*New Nuclear Nations, Consequence for US Policy*" (USA Council of Foreign Relations, 1993), p. 26.
67. Hazel Smith, Chris Rhodes, Diana Pritchard, Kevin Magill, *Op cit.*, p. 59.
68. David Albright, "How Much Plutonium does North Korea Have", *Bulletin of Atomic Scientist*, September/October 1994, Educational Foundation for Nuclear Science, pp. 46-53.
69. *Ibid.*
70. *Ibid.*
71. *Ibid.*
72. Bruce Cummings, "A Monstrous Idea", *The Bulletin of Atomic Scientists*, Educational Foundation for Nuclear Science, September/October 1994, p. 4.
73. David Albright, *Op cit*, pp. 46-53.
74. Catherine B. Wrenn, "The Korean Nuclear Crisis, the Nuclear Non-Proliferation Treaty in Retrospect, the Case of North Korea", *Bulletin of Concerned Asian Scholars,* Vol. 26, No. 1-2, January-June 1994, Philadelphia: Routledge, <http://csf. colorado.edu/bcas/sample/doc 2-w.htm)>.
75. "North Korea Nuclear Crises", <http://www. global security.org/military/ops/prknite. html>.
76. "Interim Arrangements for North Korea. Are They Secure," *The Atlantic Council of United States*, Vol. V, No. 12, 30 Dec., 1994, <http://www.acus.org/publication/bulletins/internationals...../Korea.html>
77. Peter Hayes, "What North Korea Wants," *The Bulletin of Atomic Scientist Educational Foundation for Nuclear Science*, <http://www.the bulletin.org/issues/ 1993/d93/d93 Hayes.html>
78. "North Koreas Proposed Withdrawal from the Treaty on Non-Proliferation Nuclear Weapons", *Senate,* 2 April, 1993, p. 54433.
79. Jim Hoagland, "Thinking About Korean War II", *Washington Post,* 12 May, 1994, p. 24.
80. John, C.H. and Ruth, M. Gubel, "The North Korean Nuclear Weapon Crisis The US and Its Policy Options", *Korean Observer*, Institute of Korean Studies, Vol XXVI, No. 1, spring 1995, p. 104.

81. Catherine B. Wrenn, *Op cit.*, <http://csf.Colorado.edu/pcas/sample/ doc 2cur.html>.
82. Walter B. Slocombe, "The Agreed Framework and the Democratic People Republic of Korea", *Strategic Forum*, No. 23, March 1995, p. 2.
83. Tracking Nuclear Proliferation, 1998s, <http:/www.ceip.org/files/ publication/ Tracking North Korea. Asp? p = 8 &from = pub date>.
84. David Albright and Kevin O. Neill, *Solving the North Korean Nuclear Puzzle*, (Washington DC: Institute of Science and International Security, 2000).
85. Thomas L. Wilborn, "*Strategic Implications of the US-DPRK Framework Agreement*", <http://www.milet.com/milenet/Korea/US/dprk. 3.html>
86. John Feller "*US-North Korea Relations*", Vol. 4, No. 15, May 1999, <http:/www. Fpix.org/brief/vol 14/v 4n 15 kor-body.html>.
87. David Albright, Jon Wolfsthal, "Back to the Future in North Korea", *Proliferation Brief*, Vol. 3, No. 36, Carnegie Endowments., 13 December, 2000.
88. Prakash Nanda, *Op cit.*, pp. 92-93.
89. Banning Garrett and Bonnie Glaser, *Op cit.*, pp. 536-37.
90. Prakash Nanda, *Op cit.*, pp. 92-93.
91. Richard L. Armitage, "A Comprehensive Approach to North Korea," *Strategic Forum, Institute for National Strategic Studies*, No. 159, March 1999, pp. 1-2.
92. *Ibid.*
93. Dana Priest, "US Warns North Korea on Nuclear Facility", *Washington Post*, 26 August, 1998, p. 16.
94. Selig S. Harrison, "The Korea Show Down that Shouldn't happen", *Washington Post*, 22 November, 1998, p. 62.
95. *Korean Central News Agency*, Pyongyang 23 November, 1998, <http:/ /www.//knca. coijp)>.
96. *Korea Times*, Seoul, 2 March 1999.
97. Tracking Nuclear Proliferation, *Op cit*.
98. Lee Dang Bok, "The States of North Korean Nuclear Programme", *Korea Focus*, Vol. 3, No. 6, November-December, 1995, p. 48.
99. "Playing with Fire, North Korea May be More Dangerous Than Ever", <http://www.asia week/96/0426/ed/html>.
100. William J. Perry, "Review of US Policy Towards North Korea Funding and Recommendations", *Unclassified Report US Department of State Washington*, October 12, 1999, <http://www.state.govt/www/ regions/eap/991012-North Korea-rpt. html>.
101. "*US Policy Towards North Korea*", July 2002, Washington DC <http: / /www.fcnl. org/issues/int/sup/nkor-overlaw.html>.
102. Leon V. Sigal, "Averting a Train Wreck in North Korea", *Arms Control Today*, November-December, 1998, Washington DC: The Arms

Control Association, <http://www. armscontrol.org/act/1998-11+2/ sgnd 98.asp>.

103. Leon V. Sigal, *"Disarming Strangers, Nuclear Diplomacy with North Korea,"* Princeton, Princeton University Press, 1998, Chap-5.
104. Alex Wagner, "Bush Puts North Korea Negotiation on Hold, Stress Verification", *Arms Control Today,* The Arms Control Association, April 2001, <http:www. arms.control.org/act/2001-04/korea.asp>.
105. Frederic L. Kirgis, "North Korea's Withdrawal from the Nuclear Non-Proliferation Treaty", *The American Society of International Law,* January 2003, <http: www.asil. Org/insights/insignt 96.htm>.
106. "Text of North Korea's Statement on NPT Withdrawal," *Monterey Institute of International Studies,* <http: //cns.miis.edu/research/ Korea/nptstate. html>.
107. Frederic, L. Kirgis, *Op cit.*
108. "IAEA Board of Governors Adopts a Resolution on Safeguards in the DPRK", <http://www.iaea.org/worldaton/press/p-releas.... Med-advise - 033.html>.
109. Issues for the 108 Congress, <http:/www.arms control center.org/ 2003 issues. html>.
110. "IAEA Director General Calls for DPRK Restraint", *IAEA Press Release,* PR 2002/21, December 12, <http://www.acronym.org.uk/ docs/0212/doc 08.html>.
111. "US Threatens to Stop Reactor Work if North Korea Insists Inspections", *The Korean Herald Times,* May 27, 2003 <http:// www.koreaherald.com>.
112. Seongwhun, Cheon, *Op cit.*, p. 475.
113. *Ibid.*
114. Steve La Montagne, *"North Korean Brinkmanship Continues"*, December 12, 2002, p. 4 <http://www.arms control center.org/ prolifproject/nk 1212.html>.
115. John Burroughs, "Press Statement on North Korea, The United States and Non-Proliferation," *IEER,* 24 January, 2003, <http:// www.ieer.org/reports/treates/nkoreal.html>.
116. *Ibid.*
117. Steve La Montagne, *Op cit.*, p. 3.
118. "Nations Condemn North Korea Over Nuclear Treaty", <http: www.abic.net.aa/news/2003/01/item 200301101436121.html>.
119. Sebastian Moffitt, "North Korea Calls for a New Pact with US on Nuclear Weapons", *Wall Street Journal,* 23 October, 2002.
120. Steve La Montagne, *Op cit.*, p. 6.
121. *Ibid.*
122. Ari Fleischer, "Remarks by White House Press Secretary", *White House Press Briefing,* 12 December, 2002, <http://www.acronym.org.uk/ docs/02/2/doc 08 html>.

123. Alexander Yakovenko, "The DPRK Decision to Unfreeze Its Nuclear Programme", Russian Foreign Ministry, <http://www.mid.ru>.
124. "UN Chief Urges Pyongyang to Reconsider Decision on NPT", *People's Daily,* January, 2003, <http:english.peopledaily.com.cn/2003……eng20030111109956. 5html>.
125. Garry Samore, "The Korean Nuclear Crisis", *Survival,* Vol. 45, No. 1, The Indian Institute for Strategic Studies, London, Spring 2003, p. 12.
126. Gaurav Kampani, "Second Tier Proliferation: The Case of Pakistan and North Korea," *The Non-Proliferation Review,* Vol. 9, No. 3, Fall/winter 2002, p. 109.
127. *Ibid,* pp. 22-23.
128. Brendan O. Neill, *"NPT: A Destructive Agreement"*, 17 February, 2003, <http://wwww. spitsed.online.com/article/00000006DBFI. html>.
129. "North Korea Explains Withdrawal for the NPT", *Korean Central News Agency,* Pyongyang, 22 January, 2003, <http://www.fas.org/nuke/guide/dprk/nuke/dprk01 2203.html>.
130. David Krieger, Devon Chaffee, *"Facing the Failures of the Nuclear NPT Regime"*, April 23, 2003, <http://wagining peace.org/articles/

5

Iraq—A Prisoner of the Non-Proliferation Treaty

Iraq presents yet another distinct case of a non-nuclear weapon state, signatory to the NPT since 1969, which has been subject to aggression on two occasions on charges of perceived violation of the treaty. This chapter attempts to locate the roots of the insecurity of Iraq that led it to pursue a clandestine nuclear programme, in defiance of the NPT, a treaty that it pertained to uphold. In this chapter an attempt has been made to delve into the geo-political environment of Iraq, the historical background of Iraq's nuclear programme, its confrontations with the UN inspection teams, its tussle with the US finally leading to "Operation Freedom Iraq". This chapter outlines the considerations, which led the Americans to forcibly disarm Iraq. An attempt will be made to evaluate the western views critically in order to understand Iraq's position towards the NPT from the point of view of its national security. This would bring out the double standards in US policy in trying to punish Iraq for the crime it did not commit and bring out the fallacies of the iniquitous Non-Proliferation Regime, which allows nuclear weapon states to retain their own arsenals and go to the extent of attacking a non-nuclear weapon state on the basis of suspicion that the state possesses Weapons of Mass Destruction i.e. Nuclear, Chemical and Biological Weapons. The five Nuclear Weapon states were permitted to retain their nuclear weapons as parties to the NPT. Any other state that became a party joined as a non-nuclear weapon state and thereby received a pledge 'not to receive the transfer of nuclear weapons or nuclear explosive devices or control over such weapons directly or indirectly, not to seek or receive any assistance in the manufacture of nuclear weapons or other explosive devices'.

Iraq is presently singled out as pre-eminent villain of the proliferation discourse and identified as a pragmatic "Rogue State."[1] Iraq was a prototype threat to the contemporary world created through proliferation of strategic nuclear weapons. Iraq was a small state that was trying to retain its sovereignty and independence amidst pressure from the US to force it to conform with the Non-Proliferation norms. The particularity and contingency of state identity are apparent in the aftermath of Iraq's transformation into a "Rogue State". Iraq was identified with Saddam Hussain who in turn was constructed through his assertion into a discourse recalling Hitler's Nazi Regime.

Iraq is situated in South West Asia and is bounded on the East by Iran, on the South by Kuwait, Saudi Arabia, on the West by Jordan and Syria and on the North by Turkey. The Iraqi strategy is thus determined to a large measure by its geographical position being landlocked and surrounded by six states. Iraq has only a small outlet to the sea, a short stretch in the extreme South of the Northern Sector of the Gulf.[2] Iraq tried to develop a high technology weapons capability as a vital element in self-defence under the overwhelming stress of war with Iran. Peace with its neighbours and with the US was a prerequisite for the development of progress and prosperity of Iraq. The regime for the control of the spread of nuclear technology was believed to be quite effective at the time of the Gulf war. The regime was sustained by the Non-Proliferation Treaty, which aimed to prevent the acquisition of nuclear weapons by states other than those that had tested nuclear weapon by the year 1968.[3]

The Geo-political Environment and Iraq's Insecurity

Iraq's geo-strategic predicament created both insecurity and ambitions in the regional relations. The Iraqi nation state created by a victorious Britain after World War I, suffered a combination of domestic and foreign impediments making it an unstable regime while giving it, perennial urge to change the regional *status quo*. It has a long and partly disputed border with two more powerful states Turkey and Iran. The quest for Iraqi regional hegemony from the Mediterranean to Kuwait thus served also a domestic political purpose.[4]

Iran's Nuclear Programme and Iraqi Apprehensions

Iraq is surrounded on the East by Iran with which it went to war during the 1980. During the eight-year war, Iraq failed to bring down the regime of Islamic Republic of Iran. The relationship between Iran and Iraq have been confrontationist, the main bone of contention being Shatt-al-Arab.[5] Iraq has accused Iran of providing support to Shia revolutionaries in the South. Iran is also suspected of seeking to develop nuclear weapons. Although Iran is a member of the NPT, according to the Pentagon, China is the principal supplier of nuclear technology to Iran. China and Iran signed a ten years nuclear cooperation agreement in 1990. A research reactor capable of producing Plutonium and Caultron technology that could be used to enrich Uranium was provided by China. The China-Iran nexus poses a grave security threat to Iraq.

Turkey-US Nexus Poses a Grave Threat

Iraq's relations with Turkey have been characterized by extreme contradictions. Since 1991 Turkey has allowed an Anglo-American air force to use its Incerlik airbase to monitor the Northern "No Fly Zone" and occasionally even to attack Iraqi target outside the no fly zones. The US had tried to draw Turkey into aggression and offered $30 billion in US aid against Iraq during Operation Iraqi Freedom.[6] Turkey yielded to the US pressure and gave America airspace to fight against Iraq. This has placed Iraq in a disadvantageous position, for the US is using Iraq's neighbour to obtain its own objectives to maintain dominance in the gulf.

Saudi Arabia as a Threat

Iraq-Saudi hostility did not originate with the 1968 Ba'th coup in Baghdad. Some of its ingredients are geo-political and go back to the ancient symbiotic relations between fertile Mesopotamia and arid Arabian Peninsula. The Hashmites ruled modern Iraq in 1920's. Saudi-Iraq relations were dominated by historic hostility between the house of Saudi and the Hashmite family. The essence of Gulf politics was strategic triangle between stronger powers of Iran and Iraq and weaker Gulf monarchies. Saudi Arabia supported Iran against Iraq considering a US backed Saudi Iranian Gulf security arrangement as a threat to its vital lifeline. Iraq began ideological competition with Saudi Arabia and Gulf States and sought Soviet support.[7]

American Presence in Kuwait and Iraqi Insecurity

Kuwait is located towards the South of Iraq. In 1988 the boundary with Kuwait became another outstanding problem when Iraqi Government laid a claim to various parts of Kuwait. The relations between the two nations have been hostile ever since Iraq invaded Kuwait on August 2, 1990. The UN Security Council condemned the invasion. Iraq overran Kuwait in 1990s but was forced to relinquish it by a coalition of Western and Arab countries in the Persian Gulf War. Kuwait has been demanding that Iraq must prove its peaceful intentions towards its neighbours and admit that invasion of Kuwait was a violation of Arab and international legitimacy as well as Arabic league charter. Kuwait has embarked upon negotiating a military cooperation agreement with UK, France and US since its liberation in 1991. The idea behind the move was to have military ties with countries, which have the capability to speedily and effectively intervene to protect Kuwait in a future conflict.[8] Since, then there has been American presence in the region. This poses a grave security threat to Iraq. This threat became real when Kuwait became a base during the 2003 American war against Iraq to oust Saddam.

Jordan-Iraq Cordial Relations

Jordan and Iraq have a more or less cordial relationship. Jordan's economy has been heavily dependent on trade with Iraq and it cannot afford to criticize Baghdad. Jordan therefore has become an ardent spokesman of Arab solidarity. Therefore its friendship with Iraq has assumed more importance.

Syria-Iraq Cordial Relations

Syria has a softer policy towards Iraq since 1991. It has begun to call for an end to the international sanctions. Iraq has cordial relations with Syria.

Israel Confrontationist Approach Towards Iraq

Although geographically distant and lacking a common border with Israel, Iraq has always featured in Israeli thinking as an active formidable confrontationist state. Israel always had suspicions about Iraq's development of nuclear programme. They therefore destroyed the OSIRAQ in June 7, 1981[9] so that the Iraqis could pose no threat to them. Israel is not a party to the NPT[10] and has a nuclear weapons programme. It is also supported by the United States. These two factors have led to insecurity in Iraq. Iraq was one of the strong states in the Middle East but it has been considerably weakened by the bombings, that have led to economic and humanitarian suffering of the Iraqi people. The involvement of extra regional power the US in the politics of the Gulf has continued to pose problems in Iraq's national security.

US Policy on Iraq

In the 1980's the US supported Iraq in order to contain Iran's rising power, and kept silent when Iraq used chemical weapons against Iran. The US effectively coddled Saddam's dictatorial regime in 1980's with economic and military supplies and likely emboldened the invasion of Kuwait.[11] However this policy underwent a change after Iraq's invasion of Kuwait. Camouflaging its basic and abiding interest in the energy resources in the region, the US posed itself as the peacekeeper and upholder of state's sovereignty and territorial integrity.[12] Iraq's invasion of Kuwait encouraged the US to assert its own perceived position as international policeman. The US provides a security guarantee to small states in the Middle East. Saudi Arabia depends on America to counter the balance of power of Iran and Iraq.

US strategic policy in the region has operated on the basis of these facts. Firstly the need for access to reasonably priced oil, secondly the need to ensure that no hostile forces control the region and its oil supplies. It was committed to use force if necessary to protect and further these interests. With the fall of Shah in 1979 and Islamic Revolution in Iran the US found itself without a regional security strategy. The dual pillars of Iran and Saudi Arabia had essentially been reduced to one, the house of Saudi. With the eruption of Iran-Iraq war in 1980's the US gradually acceded to the idea that a strong and viable Iraq should be a primary component of the region's security structure.[13]

As early as August 1990 conservative war hawks such as Frank Gabbrey, Henry Kissinger, Richard Perle claimed that smashing Iraq's military potential and destroying its capacity to develop nuclear weapons was America's coveted objective in the Gulf. Liberal supporters of Bush policy also felt that the potential Iraqi nuclear threat to the United States was the real reason for war against Iraq. Nuclear Proliferation should not be encouraged and the international community should attempt to stop the spread of nuclear weapons related technology. But when proliferation does occur it is essential to disseminate command and control technology to ensure that nuclear weapons are not used accidentally. The results of the first and second inspection conducted by the IAEA in Iraq were issued as a joint report. The first was carried out on 15 to 21st May by a team of 34 inspectors. The second inspection occurred from 22nd June to 3rd July and was carried out by 18 Personals from 8 countries. The first inspection team inspected only two sites at Al Tuwaitha and Al Tarmiya. During the second inspection the team visited Abu Ghraile, Al Hammat, Al Musayyib, Al Fallujat and Al Zaafaraniya the site latter targeted in January 1993 attack by the US using 40 to 50 Cruise Missiles. Maurizio Ziffereno the head of the first inspection team said that the site had been rearranged for peaceful purposes after the Persian Gulf war.[14] There was a need to keep Saddam Hussain's finger off the nuclear trigger. The US Secretary of State James Baker warned Tariq Aziz, the Deputy Prime Minister of Iraq in Geneva in 1991 that Iraq would be bombed back into the stone age.[15]

After Soviet Union had withered and disintegrated, Iraq and Islamic fundamentalism were projected as new sources of threat. Paradoxically although Iraq was militarily paralysed and castrated, the potential fear about Iraq's resurrection was made the pretext for new security structure. The American support to Kuwait, Saudi Arabia, states bordering Iraq were naturally considered by Iraq as grave threat to its national security. Saudi Arabia and Kuwait demanded Iraqi compliance with most important UN resolution, total relinquishment of its WMD and the return of Kuwaiti prisoner's property.[16]

The Historical Background of Iraq's Nuclear Programme

Iraq's nuclear programme was established under Iraqi Atomic Energy Commission in the 1950's. Under a nuclear cooperation agreement signed with Soviet Union in 1959, a nuclear research centre equipped with a research reactor was built at Tuwaitha, the main Iraqi nuclear research centre. The research reactor worked up to 1991. On May 18, 1974, Saddam Hussain was chairing the meeting of the revolutionary command council and he was informed of India's nuclear test. "If the Hindus can do it, why can't we", he asked there at the table. The Baath Party had been trying to recruit nuclear experts from all across the Arab world.[17] The surge in Iraqi oil revenue supported the expansion of the research programme. By the end of 1984 Iraq was self-sufficient in Uranium ore. One of the reactors was destroyed by Israel air attack in June 1981 shortly before it was to become operational the other was never completed.[18] Just days after Israeli attack on Iraq's nuclear reactor on 7th June 1981 President Saddam Hussain declared that Iraq would not be discouraged by the attack but rather transform lessons into programmes.[19]

By the mid 1980's the deterioration of Iraq's position in the war with Iran prompted renewed Iraqi interest in military use of nuclear technology. Iraq followed a parallel programme to produce Highly Enriched Uranium (HEU), Electromagnetic Isotope Separation (EMIS) and gas centrifuge enrichment. By 1991 one EMIS enrichment faculty was near completion and another under construction. However Iraq never succeeded in the EMIS technology and the programme had been dropped by 1991. Iraq decided to concentrate on gas centrifuges. In August 1990 Iraq instigated a crash programme to develop a nuclear weapon within a few years. This programme envisaged the rapid development of a small 50 MW centrifuge cascades to produce weapons grade HEU using fuel from Soviet reactor, which was already substantially enriched.[20]

Following the June 1981 Israeli raid on Tamuz reactors those efforts entered a hectic phase that involved medium range missiles. Foreign Minister Tariq Aziz declared that Iraq needed missiles because it was still threatened by Iran.[21] In February 1990, Iraq secretly inaugurated its first Uranium enrichment site at Tarmiyah.

One of the questions before Iraqi rulers was about continued membership in the Non-Proliferation Treaty. The diplomats were of the view that Iraq should stay in the NPT and go ahead with a clandestine programme. They said that it would just draw too much attention to the programme if Iraq got out. The scientists differed and said, "no get out of the NPT, it did not protect us anyway when the Israeli's attacked our reactor. Let us go ahead with our clandestine programme as in our right."[22]

The Persian Gulf War and Iraq's Nuclear Programme

When Iraq invaded Kuwait, it was only a few years away from possessing atomic weapons.[23] It had assembled a complex nuclear establishment dedicated to producing fissile materials and operational warheads at an estimated cost of $8-11 billion. Some 15,000 to 20,000 scientists and engineers took part in an enterprise that was exemplary not only for its technical ingenuity but also for its successful concealment. Iraq has misled the US, Israeli and all other interested intelligence communities. The sixth inspection was held on 22nd–30th September 1991. Thousands of pages of documents including computer printouts and blueprints[24] dealing with nuclear programme were discovered. The CIA estimated that Iraq could produce enough fissile material for an atom bomb in five to seven years. Access to fissile material obtained illicitly overseas could shorten the time frame to less than one year.[25]

Gulf War Set Back to Iraq's Nuclear Programme

The 1991 Gulf War gave a set back to Iraq's nuclear programme by many years. Many of the installations involved in the efforts were destroyed by the US bombing raids during the conflict, although in some cases key equipment had been previously removed. Many facilities however had been unknown to the US and its coalition partners were revealed by Iraq itself after the war.[26]

Because of repeated violations of its international Non-Proliferation obligations Iraq is a special case. It is the only country forbidden to possess separated plutonium and HEU commonly called "Fissile Materials". Soon after the inspection began in 1991 the IAEA inspectors estimated Al Tarmiya's output at 12-15 kg of weapons grade Uranium a year.[27]

The IAEA, Non-Proliferation and Verification Responsibilities

There have been startling discourses about Iraq's effort to develop nuclear weapons since the end of the Persian Gulf War. The fact that Iraq was able to engage in an ambitious nuclear programme without being discovered or deterred by IAEA safeguards. The international framework to restrain and deter the spread of nuclear weapon capabilities called the nuclear Non-Proliferation regime comprises five distinct elements:

- Undertakings by states not to make nuclear weapons.
- Measures that deter dissemination of the means to make nuclear weapons.
- Verification to ascertain adherence to undertaking and effectiveness of restrictive measures.
- Restrictive measures
- Enforcement of the sanctions imposed by IAEA.

The IAEA was created to carry out verification activities. The predominant verification activity of the IAEA is the implementation of comprehensive safeguard of all nuclear materials in all-peaceful nuclear activities in non-nuclear weapon states party to the NPT. The IAEA safeguards are applied to ascertain that initial declarations made by the states are complete and correct. The IAEA safeguards are applied to verify that declared materials are not diverted to the manufacture of nuclear weapons or other nuclear explosives. The IAEA safeguards are also required to verify that all nuclear operations are declared and no clandestine nuclear operation takes place.[28]

On July 18 and August 1991, the IAEA formally declared Iraq to be non-compliant with its safeguards agreement with the agency (INFCIRC/172) for undeclared possession of fissile materials and operations on those fissile materials. Iraq was also engaged in nuclear weapons research and development activities in violation of Article II of the nuclear Non-Proliferation Treaty prohibiting the manufacture of such weapons. While the research activities did not constitute a violation specifically of the IAEA safeguard agreement, the comprehensive inspection mandated by Security Council Resolution 687 that uncovered the nuclear weapon activities, enabled the United States to determine in its annual report on compliance with arms control treaties that Iraq's nuclear activities were indeed a violation of its obligation under NPT Article II.[29]

The Gulf war had revealed several flaws in the existing NPT Regime, which largely depended upon NPT signatories to act in good faith. Signatories were supposed to declare to the IAEA all activities that could assist nuclear proliferation if misused. All declared activities were to be made subject to a safeguards agreement and to semi-annual IAEA inspections. It is significant to note that Iraq got most items from members of nuclear supplier groups.[30]

UN Resolution 687 and Curtailment of Iraq's Nuclear Programme

Iraq's potential to develop nuclear weapon has been curtailed by implementation of UN Security Council Resolution 687 adopted in April 1991 following Iraq's defeat in the 1991 Persian Gulf War. The UN Security Council Resolution 687 has added a new punch and reinforced the coercive diplomacy of the Non-Proliferation Regime now being practiced by five permanent members of the Security Council.[31] The post Gulf war inspections of Iraq under UN Security Council Resolution 687 revealed that Iraq was pursuing its own Mini-Manhattan Project.[32]

Iraq's destruction of nuclear weapons capabilities firstly during the Gulf war and subsequently under the overall supervision of UN Security Council as per its Resolution 687 and the use of IAEA, by the UN to enforce the removal of Iraq's nuclear capabilities are indicative of major structural changes in the nuclear Non-Proliferation Regime. The UN Security Council seems to be emerging as the new instrument to strengthen Non-Proliferation and enforce its norms through collective actions. The existing Non-Proliferation Regime of control and denials is now being supplemented by a more vigorous intrusive mechanism resorting to coercive diplomacy of threats and even actual punishment both political and economic with a view to bringing around the defiant states. The Iraqi incident is supposed to have conveyed the impression that in future as well the "Council would act decisively against political proliferators." The resolution also opened the way for more intrusive inspection in future in the suspect states. It also laid the foundation for creation of mechanism for providing "IAEA inspection team with intelligence information to guide then activate".[33] Iraq protested at the US bombing of its research reactors and apparently the denial through Resolution 687 of the UN Security Council of its rights under Article IV of the NPT to an 'unconstrained peaceful nuclear energy programme.'

Mr. Hans Blix IAEA-Director General to Iraq, said that in view of the situation created by Iraq's clandestine pursuit of nuclear weapons capability and the action taken by the US, there had been a change in the situation. Now IAEA would obtain mandatory access to any facilities about which there were misgivings on the basis of information provided by member countries gathered through satellites even though the country under suspicion may not have signed the NPT. The NPT based inspection's regime of minimum intrusion was to be replaced by a system of special inspections (Challenge inspections) based on intelligence collected by 'National Technical Means'.

Blix pointed out that despite IAEA's inspection visits twice a year to Baghdad for many years they did not find any violations of the safeguards agreement. However the recent more intensive inspections performed by the IAEA under the authorization of the United Nations Security Council have uncovered major efforts of Iraq to enrich Uranium by different methods. Iraq according to his information has been using a small reactor under the IAEA Safeguards for secretly irradiating natural uranium to produce plutonium. It subsequently separated three grams of plutonium by chemical means. There could be ascertaining the purposes for these programmes.[34] That may not be concerned with development of Nuclear Weapons.

In October 1991 the inspectors started to destroy enrichment related equipment, as well as equipment related to the separation of plutonium from spent reactor fuel which they discovered in earlier inspections. On September 19, 1994, the IAEA Director General Hans Blix stated that his agency had completed the destruction, removal and rendering harmless of all known nuclear weapons usable material.

Iraq's nuclear potential has often been exaggerated sometimes to justify military action and other to bolster UN inspection efforts. The Gulf War did unmask a determined well-funded nuclear programme that largely escaped detection. If the war, had not led to the destruction of the programme, Iraq might soon have had its first nuclear weapons. It is obvious the NPT, Nuclear Suppliers Control and the IAEA safeguard system failed to detect Iraqi nuclear programme or to stop it. But 'Bombing to stop the bombs' is not the way to end proliferation. Better national and international monitoring is needed for the verification of the existing agreement particularly the NPT.

Iraq is not the only country to have tried to develop nuclear weapons in violation of International Law. Israel has developed a nuclear arsenal in violation of the Non-Proliferation Treaty. It has not been subject to intrusive inspections. The NPT also requires the US and other nuclear nations to work to abolish their own nuclear weapons. The US has openly defied the treaty.

Shortly after the Gulf War ended and after the failure of the NPT-IAEA regime had been revealed, the UN Security Council approved a resolution establishing a special commission to oversee the onsite inspections and destruction of Iraq's nuclear weapon related installations. The cost of inspection and nuclear installation was to be paid by Iraq. In October 1991, the IAEA Iraq programme was $ 60 million in debt. The 8th inspection was cancelled because of the lack of funds.

In its Resolution 687 (1991) the Security Council laid down the obligation that Iraq should unconditionally accept the destruction removal or rendering harmless, under international supervision of its prohibited weapons. That resolution also set forth the steps that need to be taken by Iraq in each of the prescribed areas, ballistic missiles and chemical and biological weapons[35] in fulfillment of its disarmament obligations. Throughout the period of crises, Iraq has claimed that it no longer has prohibited weapons, either 'in the control of the Government of Iraq, or in the territory of Iraq'. It has stated, further that it has made available to the commission all that is necessary to enable the commission to verify the claim and that nothing further of substance will be made available by Iraq. Iraq's claim that it has no more prohibited weapons, which it has not been possible for the commission to verify, doesn't in itself satisfy the three steps system the council established in order to enable Iraq to fulfil its obligation under Resolution 687 (1991). Those three steps are full declaration by Iraq, verification by commission and destruction, removal or rendering harmless under International Supervision. These three steps form the integrity of the whole programme. The Security

Council requires Iraq, to unconditionally accept the destruction, removal or rendering harmless under international supervision of all ballistic missiles with a range greater than 130 km. Iraq was required to submit to the Secretary General within 15 days of the Resolution 687 (1991) a declaration of the locations, amounts and types of all items mentioned in the missile area.[36] The Resolution bans Iraq from possessing separated Plutonium or Highly Enriched Uranium (HEU) or obtaining technology for producing separated Plutonium or for enriching Uranium.[37]

In October 1991, the inspectors recommended to destroy enrichment related equipment as well as equipment related to the separation of Plutonium from spent reactor fuel, which they discovered in earlier inspections. On September 19, 1994 IAEA Director General Hans Blix stated that his agency completed destruction, removal or rendering harmless of all known nuclear weapons usable material facilities and equipment in Iraq that might have potential to contribute to the development of nuclear weapons.

The defection of Lt. General Hussein Kamel former Iraqi Minister of Industry and Military Industrialization to Jordan on August 8, 1995, prompted the Iraqi government to invite UNSCOM Chairman Ekeus and an IAEA delegation to Baghdad so, that it could disclose new information about past non-conventional activities that had allegedly been withheld by General Kamel. During these discussions and in subsequent inspections it was revealed that following the invasion of Kuwait in August 1990, Iraq embarked on a Crash Programme to develop a nuclear device by extracting weapons grade material from safeguards, research reactor fuel. The scope and magnitude of Iraq's WMD capabilities just prior to the 1991 Gulf War was one element of its discourse. In the nuclear realm, Saddam Hussain ordered for the development of an accelerated device as soon as possible.[38]

In a report on January 27, Dr. Khidir Hamza the former head of Iraqi nuclear bomb design programme, until his defection in 1994 provides a compelling testimony that if Iraq were to acquire Plutonium or Highly Enriched Uranium it could have nuclear bombs in a short order. An IAEA inspector said that Iraq was believed capable of producing Uranium metal 18 to 24 months before the invasion of Kuwait.[39] Dr. Hamza said that Iraq was two to six months from completing a bomb when the Gulf War interrupted the programme and that Iraq had added five thousand more employees into the nuclear weapons programme since the war.[40] At the time of defection Lt. General Hussain Kamel, Saddam Hussain's Son-in-law and official-in-charge of Iraq's WMD programme, disclosed to UNSCOM in August 1995, that following the August 1990 invasion of Kuwait, it had embarked on a Crash Programme in parallel with its long-term efforts to develop nuclear weapons grade material from safeguarded research reactor fuel.

After Iraq's defeat in the 1991 Gulf War, the IAEA discovered that Iraq had violated its NPT obligations by secretly pursing a multi billion-dollar nuclear programme code named "Petrochemical 3" with thousands of workers in numerous facilities. During the course of the Sixth inspection the IAEA located thousands of pages of documents that revealed the extent of Iraqi nuclear programme forcing the Iraqi authorities to finally acknowledge its existence. The IAEA investigations revealed details of Baghdad's efforts to design an implosion type nuclear explosive device and to test its non-nuclear components. The plans to produce large quantities of Lithium 6, a material used usually for production of "boosted" Atomic Bombs and Hydrogen Bombs were also found disarmed. In addition the inspectors found that Iraq was pursuing a parallel programme to develop missile delivery system for its nuclear arms. The IAEA officials estimated that Iraq could have to, had the war not intervened, manufacture its first atomic weapons using indigenously produced weapons grade Uranium as early as the fall of 1993.[41]

Dismantlement of Iraq's Nuclear Weapons

During the Seventh IAEA inspections in October 1991, the inspectors started to destroy enrichment related equipment as well as equipment for separation of Plutonium, which they discovered in earlier inspections. In April 1992, during the eleventh inspection, inspectors destroyed buildings and equipment at Al Atheer and Al Hateem sites, Iraq's key complex for designing of fabricating and assembling and cold testing nuclear weapons.

In October 1996 assessment, the IAEA stated that the industrial infrastructure, which Iraq had set up to produce and weaponise special nuclear material, had been destroyed. However the agency was aware that the know-how and expertise acquired by the Iraqi scientists and Engineers could provide an adequate base for reconstituting a nuclear weapon oriented programme.

This raises the question of whether Iraq has made enough progress in the weaponisation process to clandestinely produce a weapon if it were to acquire nuclear materials through illicit sources. According to Konrad Porzer, Head of Germany's BND secret service, Iraq has been seeking to purchase nuclear materials in the black market through third parties.

In the aftermath of the Gulf War, revelations about Iraq's programme provoked intense criticism of the NPT and the IAEA safeguards. In public debate about Iraq's nuclear programme many have asserted that the old Non-Proliferation order defined by the NPT has shown to be ineffective and no longer credible. In the view of one of the critics of the NPT, the allied raid on Iraq's nuclear facilities and infrastructure not only set back the Iraqi programme but destroyed once for all the fiction, created in the public mind over many years by artful propaganda and obstruction, that the safeguards regime and the current international export controls provide an effective barrier to proliferation. The NPT regime itself provides no early red flag indicating that one of its members has begun marching down the road towards weapons production even if no treaty violations have yet occurred.[42]

Revelations concerning the scope and success of Iraq's nuclear programme were startling and threatened the NPT and the IAEA safeguards. It was apparently damaging the International Non-Proliferation regime that none of the paths pursued by Iraq to develop nuclear weapons would have been detectable by the IAEA inspectors even though they were violations of the NPT and Iraq's safeguards agreement with the IAEA pursuant to the NPT.[43]

After the ceasefire on 28th February and following the formal conditional termination of the war by the UN Security Council Resolution 687 (1991) was extremely delimitating as *inter alia* as it laid down the guidelines for imposing a guided development on Iraq under the regime of sanctions, reparation and a machinery to enforce and verify destruction or rendering harmless the country's weapon system. Subsequent UN Resolutions severely circumscribed the sovereignty of the government in the domestic field, for example, imposition of no fly Zones north of the 36th and South of 32nd parallels. Saddam Hussain tightened his grip over the nation. He initiated a three-pronged strategy to pull the nation together. Firstly special care was taken to provide subsistence nutrition to the masses. Secondly the task of reconstruction was undertaken on a war footing. Thirdly, Saddam sought to cement support in the Arab and the developing world at mass level. He touched the vital chord of the Iraqi people, the majority of whom did not desert him in the midst of misery and suffering.[44]

Iraq's clandestine enrichment programme in violation of the safeguards agreement with the IAEA has brought about dramatically both the strength and the weakness of the IAEA safeguards system and prompted efforts to strengthen it. The fact that for its weaponisation programme Iraq did not use nuclear material, which was under safeguards inspection, was probably due to the effectiveness of the safeguards system. On the other hand the ability of Iraq to construct and operate undeclared Uranium enrichment facilities without detection highlighted the weakness of the system. The system has worked well in providing assurances with regard to no diversion or other misuse of material or facilities declared by the state, but it was not designed to detect possible undeclared material and facilities.

The situation in Iraq raised a number of issues. The IAEA safeguards, spelt out in the information circular and established in accordance with Article III of the NPT, are intended to deter proliferation by imposing a considerable risk on detection of the diversion of significant quantities of nuclear material. In Iraq the international community confronted a state party to the NPT, which was not deterred by probability, with statement of diversion and which in the end had to be physically stopped from carrying out weapons oriented programme.

Iraq is one of the original signatories of the NPT and has been under the IAEA safeguards from the beginning. It has not yet manufactured nuclear weapons or other explosive devices. Article III of the NPT states that safeguard agreements should be applied to all sources or special fissionable material on all peaceful nuclear activities.

Iraqi Perceptions on NPT

Iraq celebrated the twentieth anniversary of its ratification of the Treaty on the Non-Proliferation of Nuclear Weapons (NPT)—of which Iraq was among the first signatories, thus expressing its profound belief in the Treaty's objectives and its principles in the field of international relations through sincere and serious participation in the efforts of the international community to establish a new world free from weapons of destruction and annihilation and to strengthen the foundations of peace and security for mankind.

Iraq realized early as a developing country that, atomic energy can play a significant role in the scientific and developmental programmes of various social and economic sectors, serving the interests of all States and in particular those of the developing countries. In 1987, in his message to the United Nations Conference for the Promotion of International Co-operation in the Peaceful uses of Nuclear Energy, President Saddam Hussain emphasized the right of all States "to acquire and use nuclear technology for such purposes according to their priorities, interests and needs under appropriate, agreed international safeguards to prevent all kinds of nuclear proliferation, without any discrimination" and urged the Conference participants "to create a positive atmosphere for the promotion and development of international co-operation, eschewing attempts to hinder the transfer of peaceful nuclear technology and to apply pressure on developing countries to prevent them from proceeding with their peaceful nuclear programme".

In a statement by the foreign ministry, Iraq pointed out that on 7 June 1981, its nuclear research centre was subjected to heinous armed aggression carried out by Israeli fighter aircraft. This aggression constituted a dangerous precedent and was considered by the Security Council, in Resolution 487 (1981), to be "a serious threat to the entire IAEA safeguards regime which is the foundation of the Non-Proliferation Treaty". Moreover, the Agency, in many resolutions, described this aggression as an attack on the Agency itself and its safeguards system.

The NPT in letter and spirit reflects the belief, of the states party to it, that the destruction caused by nuclear war must be avoided and that nuclear proliferation would lead to a serious increase in the danger of nuclear war and weaken the security of all states; thus, the question of the proliferation of nuclear weapons should be taken seriously by all states. The introduction of nuclear weapons into the Middle East by Israel is not only a severe blow to the international Non-Proliferation efforts being made since the inception of NPT, it also reflects an irresponsible policy harmful to the continuing efforts to protect the region from the dangers of the arms race in all its forms and to make it a nuclear-free Zone. This policy is exposing the region to serious perils and consequences, for international peace and security are unknown.[45]

The US Role in UN Moves Against Iraq

Since 1991, the United States and United Kingdom have regularly violated the sovereignty, independence and territorial integrity of Iraq in the illegally imposed No Fly Zones. They have committed military acts of aggression on daily basis since the end of 1998. They launched five large-scale military attacks against Iraq in 1993, 1996, 1998 and 2001. They apply an official policy of interference in internal affairs of Iraq and one attempting by every means to invade Iraq with a view to installing a puppet regime there, in flagrant violation of international law, the charter of the United Nations and relevant resolutions of the Security Council.[46]

The Iraqi's feel that they have been subjected to inspections time and again and their scientists have been psychologically tortured to reveal information about Iraq's supposed nuclear weapons programme. An important and revealing fact that needs to be stated when it returned to Iraq, the inspection team carried out 427 inspections between mid-November and mid-December 1998 and Chairman of UNSCOM Richard Butler noted that Iraq had failed to cooperate in 5 or 10 per cent of these inspections. This means that even in the opinion of intransigent and suspicious persons like Richard Bulter, Iraq cooperated with certain questions in 90 per cent of the cases.[47] Yet between 16th to 20th December 1998 Iraq was rewarded for this very high level of cooperation with the launching by the United States and the United Kingdom of 460 Cruise missile and thousands of Ariel bombs and missiles.

The Iraqi Foreign Minister presented his opinion to the UN Secretary General in a session of talks on 7th March 2002. Iraq's Foreign Minister asked the Secretary General how he could explain the stance of a permanent member of a Security Council which officially calls for the invasion of Iraq and the imposition of an agent regime on its people by force, is clear violation of Security

Council resolution itself, which clearly state that Iraq's sovereignty, independence and territorial integrity and rules of International Law and the UN Charter must be respected.

He also questioned how would inspectors from states, which are declaring their intention to threaten Iraq's national security, invade it and change its regime, apply their international and biased mandate on Iraq or respect the Security Council Resolutions and their duties under the charter. The presence of United States and British inspectors on the special committee and the IAEA helped the US and UK to collect intelligence data and specify locations that were targeted in their aggression. All locations, which have been visited by the inspection teams, were thus easily attacked during the 1998 aggression including the presidential sites, despite the inspector's statement that there were no weapons of mass destruction. The United States and United Kingdom also bombed all industrial sites.[48]

The permanent representative of Iraq to the United Nations in a statement, in consultation of an IAEA representative, said that the statements by the US were merely rubber stamped by the agency. The statement contravenes the objectives and principles of the NPT, the statute of the agency and its safeguard.[49]

The statement of the IAEA representative says "The IAEA carried out in January 22nd-25th, 2000 a physical inventory verification of the nuclear material subject to safeguards in Iraq with the limited objective of verifying the presence of declared material in question."[50] This is a wrongful description of the inspection which took place in Iraq in January 2000, in accordance with the safeguards agreement between the agency and Iraq". All nuclear facilities in Iraq have been destroyed. The nuclear fuel has been transferred out of Iraq. All peaceful nuclear activities including those referred to in operative paragraph 3/vi of the Resolution 707 have come to halt.

Iraq's Cooperation with the IAEA Safeguards Agreement and the NPT

A five person Atomic Energy Agency inspection team visited Iraq during the period 22nd to 25th January 2000. The inspection team carried out a physical inventory verification of nuclear material in Iraq under the terms of the safeguards agreement between Iraq and the IAEA in connection with the treaty of Non-Proliferation of nuclear weapons. The Agency Inspectors were able to verify the nuclear material subject to safeguards, which consists of low enriched, natural and depleted uranium. The IAEA stated that Iraqi's provided the necessary cooperation for the inspection team to perform its activities effectively.[51]

In Iraq as a part of the UN effort to determine the extent of Baghdad's weapons of mass destruction programme, inspectors were looking at facilities that have been or may be associated with nuclear weapons development. The puzzle, facing El Baradei Director of International atomic energy agency, and the world, is as to why US seems to be bent on a war with Iraq where inspectors have virtually free reign to act. According to El Baradei no smoking gun has been found. The real reason to target Iraq is about reliable access to cheap oil for United States and its allies.[52]

On 11 November, Vice President Taha Yassin Ramadan stated, "They are all spies and they collect security data. We will not deal with any resolution that doesn't lift the embargo completely and clearly condemn the December aggression and the end of so called No Fly Zones. Throughout 1999, US and British planes had been attacking Iraqi anti-aircraft installation in the no fly Zones in the North and South of Iraq.[53] In June 1996, after the dispute between the Iraqi government and UNSCOM over the inspection of sensitive sites, the then head of the UNSCOM, Rolf Ekeus, negotiated a set of special procedures with Baghdad, for the inspection of sites which the Iraqi considered sensitive in terms of their national security, dignity and sovereignty. According to former UNSCOM inspector, Scott Ritter, sensitive sites included various ministries, Republican guards and intelligence of agencies. It was agreed that during the inspection of sensitive sites only four inspectors would be permitted to enter the suspect property.[54]

The UN Special Commission on Iraq (UNSCOM) was established by the Security Council and accepted by Iraq following the Second Gulf War to verify the destruction of Iraqi WMD. There have been many clashes between UNSCOM and the Iraqi government most famous of which took place in 1998 and led to air strike launched by the UK and US against Iraq. Iraq accused the head of UNSCOM then, Richard Butler of being a US spy. Recently the UN itself declared the fact that Butler might have been spying on Iraq to gain US favour and this was one of the reason why Scott Ritter another former inspector resigned from his job in UNSCOM. Scott Ritter, the former UN weapon inspector alleged that Clinton's advisors had deliberately provoked a showdown with the Iraq by manipulating Mr. Butler and UNSCOM. Mr. Butler wrote the final UNSCOM report for Security Council on 14 December 1998. Mr. Butler is said to have given the first draft of his report to senior US diplomats at the UN on Sunday 13, December. They transmitted it instantly to President Clinton who apparently found it too weak. US officials thereafter played a direct role in shaping Butler's text during multiple conversations with him at the secure facilities at the missions to the United Nations.[55] Although Iraq was supported by China and Russia in the request for changing the head of the command, the United States and Britain insisted that Butler should head the UN special committee. In his report to the Security Council in September 1998 Butler accused Iraq of possessing the capacity to produce weapons of mass destructions, this very report led to Anglo-American air strikes on Iraq in 1998. Butler believed that if Iraq acquired enough highly enriched Uranium, it could fabricate an Atomic Bomb.[56]

UNSCOM in Iraq has apparently been a pawn in the hands of the American's imposing unreasonable demands aimed at provoking Iraqi intransigence. The Americans have used a pliant Australian Richard Butler, head of UNSCOM as their patsy. Madeline Albright in gobbelsian terms, justifies the murderous attack on Iraq as necessary for "world peace".[57]

Iraq has been wrongly accused of 'defying' UN Security Council Resolution. In reality it has cooperated with them in particular the all pervasive Resolution 687 which mandates the destruction of weapons of mass destruction under international supervision yet the ultra hawkish US Vice President Dick Cheney claims with confidence, there is no doubt that Saddam Hussain now has WMD's. He is able to use against our friends, against our allies and against us. The risks of war are far greater than the risks of action.

In December 1996, the National Security Council advisor designate Samuel Berger described US policy towards Iraq in his first foreign policy statement as "A little bit like a Whack-a-Mole game at the circus. They pop up and you whack them down. Such attitudes do not encourage confidence that the White House has thought seriously about deterrence vis-a-vis Iraq.[58]

Moreover there is also a potential nuclear problem in regard to Iraq. Following Hussain Kamel's defection, it was learnt that Iraq has been much further along in developing an Atomic Bomb than anyone had imagined.[59] Quite possibly all Iraq lacks is the fissile material. With present Russian economic decrepitude the material might well be for sale. Recent Israeli estimates are that Iraq would probably have a bomb within a year if sanctions were to end and UNSCOM monitoring to cease to be rendered ineffectual. The UN inspectors believed that Saddam might have several dozen Scud missiles along with warheads and bombs filled with Chemical and Biological agents.[60]

In West Asia Iraq was caught cheating the NPT after the 1991 war. If Iraq is permitted to keep its weapons of mass destruction, it will fuel on arms race in the region. The spread of nuclear weapon occurs when one state fears that its neighbours might have them. At least that is one primary motive... and that is Iran's, increased nuclear activity... they fear if they fought a war with Iraq it would use chemical weapons against them. They have no illusions that an Iraq with nuclear weapons would pose a grave threat to Teheran."[61] Scott Sagan said that the nuclear progress of the North Korea, Iraq and Iran constitute violations of a treaty they have signed and therefore have a far worse impact in terms of setting a precedent for others. In 1995 when the NPT was extended in perpetuity, the US government agreed that the Comprehensive Test Ban Treaty would be a legitimate piece of evidence that nuclear states were working towards the eventual elimination of all nuclear weapons. Unfortunately the Senate didn't ratify the agreement that the executive arms of the administration had passed. Sagan noted, "we set a standard for the goal but we have not kept our side of the bargain". He warned that if the US indeed resume nuclear testing it would violate the sprit of the NPT and encourage a number of the states to start their testing programmes."

US Game Plan in Iraq

The US strategic and resource priorities especially securing access to the region's oil reserves is one key factor in the US attitude towards Saddam's regime. Iraq was one of the countries named in President Bush's nuclear hit list, those states that the US should consider attacking with nuclear weapons.[62] The countries like the

US and Britain should not criticize others for breaking these treaties when they themselves do the same. It is an ironical situation where US a country with more nuclear weapons then any other, wants to stop another country from having any at all.

At the NPT preparatory committee meeting in May 2002, Iraq informed that the inspectors would be allowed back in if a timeframe was agreed. Proposal from the UN wanted inspectors to go wherever they liked, when they liked and to stay as long as they liked. In November 2002 a resolution put by US and UN Security Council was finally agreed by UK. It was decided that the inspectors would be back in Iraq by December 2002, reporting back about a month later.

A former UN weapons inspector, Scott Ritter dismissed the allegations that Iraq could have re-established its weapons programme since the inspectors withdrew in 1998. He explained that the manufacture of Chemical and Biological weapons emits rented gases that would have been detected by now if they existed and nuclear weapons emit gamma rays that would have been detected. Truly alarmed by the way Iraq had managed to play game with the NPT system, the 40 member National Supplier Group was formed to control dual use of items as well. In effect the National Supplier Group has become an export 'enforcer' and the IAEA import 'enforcer' for preventing weapon proliferation. The UN Security Council can impose sanctions for NPT violations and may authorise the use of force.[63]

UN Security Council Resolution 1441 and Iraq

On November 8, the United Nation Security Council unanimously adopted a resolution 1441, setting out the terms and conditions of a final international effort to completely disarm Iraq by peaceful means. The resolution, was the result of eight weeks of intense deliberations among a frequently divided council, places a fundamental, two fold onus on Iraq substantive cooperation, most importantly to fully account for any past or present programme to acquire or deliver weapons of mass destruction and functional cooperation acting in full support of the inspection process itself. Ironically enough, perhaps the two main drafters and champions of 1441, the United States and United Kingdom were ready to declare Baghdad in comprehensive material breach of the resolution, and urge the council to adopt a second resolution calling for serious consequence of Iraqi non-compliances strength predicted in 1441 to duly materials. Under the November 8, 2002, UN resolution, threatening Iraq, the inspectors could demand the Iraqi officials to turn over government documents for examination and account for any equipment or material that may have something to do with unconventional weapons. UN Resolution 1441 also ordered, Iraq to provide a list of military scientists and allow the inspectors to interrogate those scientists outside the presence of Iraqi government observers.[64] According to Resolution 1441 passed on 8 November, 2002, Iraq must give UNMOVIC and IAEA a currently accurate, full and complete declaration of all aspects, its Chemical, Biological and Nuclear Weapons programme and ballistic missile systems as well as information on all Chemical Biological and Nuclear programme by December 8.[65] The US and Britain cannot unilaterally declare that Iraq is in material breach of it's disarmament obligation. There was no legal justification for a war against Iraq.[66] Under the November 8th 2002 UN resolution threatening Iraq, the inspectors could demand the Iraqi officials to turnover Government documents for examination and account for any equipment that may have something to do with unconventional weapons.

In December 19, 2002 the Security Council heard an initial closed door assessment of the Iraqi dossier from Dr. Blix and El Baradaei which said "Iraq is cooperating well in terms of process. We need much cooperation from Iraq in terms of substance, in terms of coming up with evidence to exonerate them and prove that they are clean from Weapons of Mass Destruction."

US Ambassador Negroponte stated bluntly Iraq has again defied the Council demand and chosen deception and concealment over full disclosure. President Bush said "on or before December 8, Iraq must provide full and accurate declaration of its weapons of mass destruction and ballistic missile programmes". The declaration must be credible and complete.

On December 4 speaking on ABC television in America, Iraqi Deputy Prime Minister Tariq Aziz repeated the invariable position of his government that Iraq's imminent weapons of mass destruction cannot be expected to contain resolution of non-existent programmes. "We don't have chemical, biological or nuclear weaponry but we do have equipment which was defined as dual use".[67]

Iraq submitted a currently accurate and complete declaration to UNMOVIC officials. The submission was delivered a day in advance of the deadline set in 1441, runs some 12,000 pages. Senior Iraqi official Major General Hussan Muhammad Amim summarized the contents in a single sentence "We declare that Iraq is empty of any weapons of mass destruction".[68]

Iraq submitted the nuclear portion of its declaration running to some 2,400 pages, 300 in Arabic to IAEA officials in Baghdad. A Russian Foreign Ministry statement suggests that the timely presentation of both parts of the declaration, "together with the continued, normally running cooperation in carrying out international inspection activities, confirms Baghdad's positive line with regard to compliances with the provisions of Resolution 1441".[69]

Blix and El Baradei provided an interim report prior to full scale update scheduled for January 27, 60 days after the first inspections to the Security Council. Blix told the reporters before the meeting "In course of these inspections we have not found any smoking gun..." The White House Press Secretary Ari Fleischer stated "The heart of the problem is Iraq is very good at hiding things... Iraq has failed to comply with the United Nations resolution.... The problem with Guns that are hidden is that you cannot see their smoke". US Ambassador Negroponte argues that it is now clear that Iraq's non-compliance "constitutes a further material breach" of its international obligations.[70]

Then El Baradei the IAEA chief stated "We have till date found no evidence that Iraq has revived its nuclear weapons programme since the elimination of the programming of 1990's. With our verification system now in place barring few exceptional circumstances, and provided these are sustained active cooperation by Iraq, we should be able within the next few months to provide credible assurances that Iraq has no nuclear weapons programme. These few months would be valuable investment in peace because they could help us avoid a war"[71]. The IAEA Chief Mohamed Baradei told the Security Council that several documents supporting US, and British allegations about Iraq's nuclear programme were fake.[72]

Providing Washington's immediate response Ambassador Negroponte told the council that there is nothing in either presentation that would give us hopes that Iraq has ever intended to fully comply with Resolution 1441. "We see no evidence to indicate that Saddam is voluntarily disarming his nation of its Biological and Chemical Weapons Nuclear capabilities and ballistic missiles. We see no evidence that intends to account for Iraq weapons programme. Without cooperation, disarmament cannot be proven. Without disarmament Iraq cannot comply with Resolution 1441."

In his annual "State of Union address" to the Congress, President Bush had a long impassioned section on Iraq. Turning to Iraq the President portrayed Saddam Hussain as a brutal dictator, with a history of reckless aggression, ties to terrorism, great potential wealth determined to dominate a vital region and a threat to the United States. In terms of the long history of the Iraq crises Bush summarizes "Twelve years ago Saddam Hussain faced the prospect of being the last causality in a war he had started and lost. To spare himself, he agreed to disarm himself of all weapons of mass destruction. For the next twelve years he systematically violated that agreement. He pursued Chemical, Biological and Nuclear Weapons, even while the inspectors were in his country. Bush noted "Almost three months ago the UN Security Council gave Saddam Hussain his final chance to disarm. The job of the inspectors is to verify that Iraqi regime is disarming. It is up to Iraq to show exactly where it is hiding its banned weapons".

In Baghdad during his television interview with President Saddam Hussain, Tony Benn, former British Labour MP and veteran anti war campaigner stated "There is only one truth and therefore I tell you as I have had on many occasions before, that Iraq has no weapons of mass destruction. I would like to tell you directly that we have no relationship with Al Qaeda."[73]

Russian Foreign Minister Igor Ivanov argued ".... the gravity of the issues raised once again shows convincingly that the international inspectors activity has to be continued for they alone can give objective answer to the question of how Iraq complies with Security Council demands."

French Foreign Minister Dominique de Villepin suggested "significant result have already been seen" in the early stages of the inspection process despite. "Grey areas in Iraq's cooperation". The priority henceforth Dominique de Villepin argues, is to boost the inspection process, thereby decreasing Iraq's room for manoeuvre and evasion. "Why go to war if there still exists an unused space in Resolution 1441".

As the United Nations nuclear inspectors fled from Iraq, some of them were angry at the Bush administration for cutting short their work, had mounted their efforts and made false claim about evidence of weapons of mass destruction. The inspectors were scandalized at the way President Bush and Secretary of State Colin Powell among others have politicised the inspection process. The US administration said that the Iraqi aluminium tubes were uniquely suited for centrifuges to make bomb grade Uranium. But UN officials argue that the tubes were possibly designed to become artillery rockets. The US military also used similar rockets known as Hydra 70. The nuclear inspectors trudged through the Iraqi countryside for months. They found Iraqi weapons infrastructure built at a great expense in the 1980s to be in a state of decay. They found no signs of an organized nuclear weapons programme.[74]

The US is not genuinely interested in disarmament. This can be seen from its policy towards Israel. The UN General Assembly Committee on Nov 10, voted 134–2 asking Israel 'not to develop, produce, test or otherwise acquire nuclear weapons and to sign the NPT. The two countries voting against the resolution were Israel and the United States. The US hypocrisy neither begins nor ends with Israel. The US is the only country to have dropped a nuclear bomb on human beings, a country that has the world's largest stockpile of weapons of mass destruction and over the last 50 years installed and supported most dictators the world has seen. To hear officials of this country speak self-righteously of the need to eliminate Iraqi weapons and Iraqi violations of International law should turn anyone's stomach.[75]

Based on the information gathered and analysis conducted by the United Nations Special Commission on Iraq (UNSCOM) and its successor the United Nations Monitoring Verification and Inspection Commission, as well as by the Iraqi Action Team of the International Atomic Energy Agency and other independent sources, it is prudent to assume that Iraq possess at least small stocks of weaponised Chemical and Biological warfare agents and a limited range of delivery system for disseminating Chemical, Biological, Weapons, munitions either in military combats or in terror attacks on civilian populations. Fortunately, however it is extremely unlikely that Iraq possesses nuclear weapons and virtually certain that it possesses far fewer medium range ballistic missiles than it did in 1991.[76]

UN Suspicions

In late 2002, however, a new UN resolution giving Iraq one more chance to implement its pledges led to a new round of inspections by UNMOVIC (UN monitoring, verification and inspection commission). According to the briefing, Iraq's strategy has two key objectives. The first objective is for Iraq to demonstrate ostensible 'compliance' with UN resolutions. This ostensible compliance is an attempt to undermine the credibility of the need for an inspection regime and then further to erode support for continued sanctions. The second objective is to ensure that the UN inspectors will not uncover fully Iraq's, WMD and missile programme. In May 1991, Saddam Hussain formed a concealment operation committee to be supervised by Qusay.[77]

The concealment apparatus has focussed on hiding only critical materials and WMD components. It was reported that these critical components of nuclear biological and chemical missile programmes were dispersed to the environs surrounding Tirkit, Saddam's hometown, where they were concealed in presidential palaces or residence of Iraqi security officials belonging to the special security organisations and special Republican Guards.[78]

The Special Republican Guard is involved in the transportation, concealment and guarding of military facilities and materials. Both Military Industrial Commission and Ministry of Industry and Military industrialisation seek to conceal sensitive activities from UN inspectors.[79] All the individuals involved were brought into the project only after very careful investigations about their personal connections and loyalty to Saddam.[80]

In November, President Bush spoke to the United Nations General Assembly about the importance of all civilised nations uniting to defend themselves against those who pursue terror and violence. The spread of nuclear weapons to additional states not only increases the risk of nuclear war among nations but also increases the risk of nuclear terrorism. Violation of the NPT by Iraq and North Korea and their continued non-compliance with the treaty underscore the dangers to the global community. NPT parties must put such states on notice that the international community will meet a violation of the NPT with swift and firm action. NPT parties who violate the treaty must make a choice. They can either join the vast majority of parties who take their NPT obligations seriously or risk the consequences of being an outlaw nation.[81]

The concealment apparatus has launched a coordinated effort to thwart the full discovery of Iraq's proscribed programmes. Hussain Kammal, Saddam's cousin was instrumental in the creation of ultra elite intelligence agency. This agency also controls Iraq's chemical corps, which is responsible for destroying Iraq's chemical weapons arsenal. The chemical corps in addition to destroying chemical munitions also played a role in salvaging Iraq's chemical weapon capability after 1991 Gulf War.[82] Along with the Special Republican Guard, the special security also had a role in transporting components of Iraq's WMD programme. Their vehicles were disguised, as refrigerated container trucks were responsible for carrying out nuclear material. The destination of these truck convoys would be determined by central command of the special security organisation.[83]

Operation Iraqi Freedom—Disarming Iraq by Force

In his January 28, 2003 "State of Union" address President Bush announced that he was ready to attack Iraq even without a UN mandate. Hans Blix Former International Atomic Agency Director, ordered Iraq to destroy its Al Sal mound 2 missiles by March 1. On February 22, 2003, US, Britain and Spain submitted a resolution to the UN Security Council that states that 'Iraq has failed to take the final opportunity afforded to it in Resolutions 1441 and that it is now time to authorize use of military force against the country." On 24 February 2003, France, Germany and Russia submitted an informal counter resolution to the UN Security Council that stated that inspection should be intensified and extended to ensure that there is a real chance for the peaceful settlement of this crisis and that "the military option should only be the last resort."

The United States was pressuring for the use of force against Iraq. It rejected a plan Canada floated in a bid to give inspectors about another month in Iraq and bridge the divide between Security Council Members whether to go to war.[84] France and Russia threatened to veto the second resolution introduced by the

US in the UN. The US was not able to get any of the six developing countries on the Security Council to vote on a second resolution in Iraq. Then the US withdrew the resolution. Bush issued an ultimatum on March 17 'All decades of deceit and cruelty have now reached an end. Saddam Hussain and his sons must leave Iraq within 48 hours. Their refusal to do so will result in military' conflict.[85] On March 20, 2003 at approximately 5.35 local time, US bombs fell on Baghdad, Iraq.[86] He did this in order to demonstrate the overwhelming superiority of the US to accomplish two primary objectives intimidate all potential nuclear proliferators into abandoning their projects and squash all European ideas of an autonomous political role in the world system.[87]

Secretary Powell told the Security Council that "Saddam Hussain is determined to get his hands on a nuclear bomb and the administration continued to use similarly alarmist rhetoric. National Security advisor Condoleezza Rice, invoked an image of a mushroom of Iraq's nuclear weapons that were not confistcated.[88] In February, Powell stated "Iraq does not intend to use nuclear weapons for peaceful purposes but for aggressive actions against other nations."[89]

To the Bush administration radicals such as Robert Joseph, the National Security Council senior counter proliferation officials and Douglas (Under-Secretary of Defence) nuclear weapons perse not the problem "bad guys" with them are. Rejecting the fundamental premise of the NPT, these officials seek not to create on equitable global regime that actively devalues nuclear weapons and creates conditions for their eventual elimination but rather eradicates "bad guys" or their weapons while leaving "good guys" free of nuclear constraint.[90]

The US government realised that it was necessary to have an international cover for using force against Iraq so it began alleging that Iraq is not complying with Security Council resolutions specially those concerning the inspectors. US administration has elaborated their false allegations by saying that Al-Qaeda organisation would be capable of using weapons it would allegedly get from Iraq to do harm to the US.[91]

US Doctrine of Pre-Emptive Force

The pattern, which is being set by the United States and Britain on the question of disarming a sovereign country i.e. Iraq by force is of a significant nature. Despite getting confirmation from such inspectors that Iraq was cooperating with their mission the United States embarked on a well-formulated plan to seek Regime Change in Baghdad not necessary peacefully but also by force. Paul Wolfwitz the Hawkish conservative military analyst for defence department under Ronald Regan had formulated a new foreign policy with regard to Iraq that is the policy of pre-emption. Pre-emption means to strike first to eliminate threats. The September 11, 2001 terrorist attack on the twin towers brought to life Wolfwitz advocacy of pre-emptive action in Iraq. The question is why the only issue of disarming Iraq has been raised particularly in a situation where there are other countries suspected to be in a possessions of Chemical, Biological, Nuclear and other weapons of mass destruction. Why only Iraq has been singled out? Is there a possibility that after disarming Iraq and changing its regime, America and Britain will target other non-conformist individuals and countries or they will only be contented with Iraq.[92]

America's Dual Policies towards North Korea and Iraq

President Bush has adopted very different policies towards Iraq and North Korea despite having provocatively labelled both countries as part of the "Axis of Evil" along with Iran. In Iraq he has resorted to war to enforce Non-Proliferation norms. But with regard to North Korea he prefers to rely on diplomacy.[93] The Bush administration has set itself as the arbiter of who is and who is not allowed to possess weapons of mass destruction. The US has turned a blind eye to Israel's nuclear programme.[94] The US objective is to remove Saddam and install a pro-American Government which should not oppose Israel.[95] The Bush administration objectives in Iraq kept shifting from disarmament, to regime change, to war against terrorism pointing to Saddam Hussain's connection with Al-Qaeda.[96] The threat of the United States to use nuclear weapons against non-nuclear weapon states party to the nuclear NPT, is a grave violation of US obligations under the provision of Security Council Resolution 255 (1968) and 984 (1995). Paragraph I of the Resolution 255 (1968) recognises that aggression with nuclear weapons or threat of such aggression against a non-nuclear weapon state would create a situation in which Security Council would have to act immediately in accordance to the obligation under the UN Charter Paragraph 3 of Security Council Resolution 984 (1995) "recognises further that in case of aggression with nuclear weapons or threat of such aggression against a non-nuclear state party to the NPT. Any state may bring the matter to the attention of the Security Council to take urgent action to provide assistance in accordance to the charter to the state victim of an act or object of such aggression".

Emerging as a leader of the developing world Dr. Mahathir Mohammad said that wars should be outlawed and a ban imposed on weapons of mass destruction possessed not only by Iraq but also by all countries including the biggest warmonger the United States. The Non-Aligned nations rejected any invasion of Iraq not sanctioned by the United Nations but pressed Iraq to cooperate actively with weapon inspectors.[97]

Iraqi Vice President Taha Yassim Ramadan earlier told at the summit that Baghdad was determined to iron out all its problems over weapons of mass destruction to avert war, but denounced the United States for "trying to dominate the world."

Arms control experts in the Bush administration frequently point that diplomacy is of minimal value for dealing with regimes that are determined to acquire nuclear weapons. The Americans were apprehensive that a nuclear bomb armed Iraq under Saddam Hussain would be undependable so they decided for regime change. As the President put it in a speech in Cincinnati that "we cannot wait for the final proof—the smoking gun that could come in the form of a mushroom cloud.[98]

There is no documented operational link between Iraq and Al-Qaeda. As former National Security Council Advisor Daniel Benjamin has put Iraq and Al-Qaeda are natural enemies. Mr. Hussain would never get involved with a group that cannot be controlled and never give weapons of mass destruction to terrorists that might use it against him.[99]

There was no evidence to suggest that Iraq was on the verge of developing involved or acquiring a nuclear weapon. The IAEA report suggests that Iraq may have been between 6 to 24 months away from developing nuclear weapons in 1991, before the Persian Gulf War in 1991 and seven years of UN weapons inspection.

The Bush administration accused Iraq of buying aluminium tubes, which it felt, would be used to build centrifuges for the production of highly enriched bomb grade Uranium. But independent experts like former UN weapons inspector David Albright emphasised that the tubes had non-military uses and not of the type that would be particularly useful in enriching Uranium. The British government dossier on Iraqi capabilities states that there is no definitive intelligence "linking the tubes to a Uranium enrichment project". In early January, the IAEA reported that inspections in Iraq suggested that the "Aluminium tubes sought by Iraq in 2001 and 2002", were consistent with reverse engineering of rockets as Baghdad had asserted and not directly suitable for building centrifuges to enrich Uranium.[100]

The Nuclear powers have failed to live up to their pledge of more than 30 years to work towards nuclear disarmament. El Baradai's remarks reflect the views of many nations that the five declared nuclear powers that are party to the Nuclear Proliferation Treaty, China, France, Russia, the United Kingdom and the United States have been slow to reduce their nuclear stockpiles as called by the treaty and that such delays undermine efforts to disarm states believed to be developing weapons of mass destruction. He added in an apparent critique of the Bush administration. "Some nuclear weapon states have reversed direction by stressing the continuing value of nuclear weapons in defence of national security interests, including discussion of the feasibility of developing new types of nuclear weapons and scenarios for the use of nuclear weapons against non-nuclear weapon states. The multilateral Non-Proliferation regime has already been attacked on the UN and the inspection process, and the withdrawal of US confidence in the capability of the Security Council to enforce compliance with disarmament agreements.[101]

The Bush administration going war against Iraq was utter contempt for democracy and public opinion. Iraq has hardly defied a Security Council Resolution since the end of the Persian Gulf War in 1991. It has generally cooperated with the dictates of the UN body, although frequently under pretext or with reservations because many of the resolutions involve gross violations of Iraqi Sovereignty. From 1991 to 1998 UN inspectors supervised the destruction of the vast bulk of Chemical and Biological weapons as well as delivery system which Iraq accumulated during the Iran-Iraq war and they also destroyed all of Iraq's facilities for making new weapons.[102] The

International Atomic Energy Agency has categorically stated that Iraq no longer has a nuclear programme.

Bush obviously desires the UN to serve as a rubber stamp for whatever action the United States Government demands under Article 42 of the UN Charter. It is for the Security Council not the US or Britain to decide how Security Council resolutions such as 1441 are to be enforced. The US decision to enforce its interpretation of 1441 regardless of the will of the Security Council is a violation of international law.

Iraq is a non-nuclear nation party to the NPT. It's security interests have been undermined by the invasion which constitutes an important precedent, which declares that the United States has the right to invade sovereign countries and overthrow regimes if they are seen hostile to US interest. There is no legal justification for US military action against Iraq. It has neither nuclear nor chemical, biological weapons otherwise it would have used them in the war. According to Articles 41 and 42 of the United Nations Charter no member state has the right to enforce any resolution militarily unless the UN Security Council determines there has been material breach of its resolution, decides that all non-military means of enforcement have been exhausted, then specifically authorizes the use of military force. The UN inspector's work was twice disrupted due to the arrogant attitude of the US leading to the Persian Gulf War and then by Operation Iraqi freedom. Concerning the withdrawal of the inspectors from Iraq in 1998, Richard Bulter withdrew the IAEA inspectors from Iraq on two occasions, once in November 1998 and another time on 15 December 1998, upon instructions received from senior American Administrative officials and without the authorization of the Security Council or the Secretary General of the UN or even the Director General of the IAEA. These as such refer to the cessation of inspection activities in Iraq, since 16 December 1998 should be remembered as a that fact if they wish to be objective and deal with the causes and consequences of this serious measure that was aimed at facilitating military aggression against Iraq.[103] Britain and the US bypassed the UN the set up a secret team to search for weapons of mass destruction. The new group headed Charles Deuelfer former deputy head of UNSCOM weapons inspectors apparently set up a base in Kuwait a week before the war began.

The coalition tried to find a smoking gun justify the war on Iraq but has so far found no band weapons.[104]

Thus, the Iraqi case is a clear example of a non-nuclear party to the NPT being coerced by a nuclear weapon power for its own economic interest the pursuit of oil attempting to prevent it from emerging as a dominant power in West Asia. This shows the inherently discriminatory nature of the NPT, which imposes no restrictions on the nuclear activity of the sole superpower and forces a non-nuclear state to prove its nuclear innocence at the cost of war and sufferings to the Iraqi people. As far as nuclear weapons were concerned, according to Scott Ritter, the "massive infrastructure" Iraq had built up in its nuclear weapons program had been eliminated by 1995 by the International Atomic Energy Agency.[105] Rosemary Hollis, the head of Middle East programmeme at the Royal Institute of International Affairs, emphasised that Iraq did not have the capacity to build nuclear weapons. It becomes clear that the focus on Saddam's nuclear ambitions were dictated by Washington's plans for a pre-emptive strike on Iraq.[106] The strikes thus were propelled less by the principles of the NPT and more by economic and hegemonic designs.

NOTES

1. David Mutimer, *The Weapon State Proliferation and the Framing of Security*, (USA: Lynne Rcinner Publishers Inc, 2000), p. 95.
2. Stahl A. Shelly, Geoffrey Kemp, *Arms Control and Weapons Proliferation in the Middle East and South Asia*, (Macmillan Academic and Professional Ltd., 1992), p. 113.
3. *Ibid.*
4. Amatizia Baran, Barry Rubin, *Iraq Road to War*, (New York: St Martin Press, 1993), pp. 10-11.
5. See *Iraq Geography and Population*, <http//ICWCh.loc.gov/cgi-bin/query/r/fid/ c...@field (DOCID + iq6026 11/7/02)>.
6. Iraq Report <http://www.rferl.org/iraq-report/index.html>.
7. *Ibid.*
8. Charles Pripp,"The Gulf States and Iraq", *Survival*, Autumn, 1992, pp. 48-49.
9. <www.llnl.gov/nai/default.html>.
10. See David Kay, "Iraqi Inspections: Lessons Learned", Iraq Special Collection, Center for Non-Proliferation Studies, Monterey, USA, 2002, <http://cns.miis. edu/>.

11. Stephen Zunes, Iraq 10 Years After Gulf War, *Foreign Policy in Focus*, Vol. 6, No. 1, Jan 2001, <http://www.foreignpolicy-in focus .org/ breifs/vol 6 /v6 no/Iraq -body html>.
12. A.H.H. Abidi, Changing Politico Security Profile in the Persian Gulf, *Strategic Analysis*, September 1993, Vol. XVI, No. 6, p. 711.
13. James A. Russell, "Searching for a Post Saddam Regional Security Architecture", *MERIA Journal*, Vol. 7, No. 1, March 2003, <http:// meria.idc.ac.il/journal/2003/ issue/jv7nla3.html>.
14. "Iraq Says its Tries UN Says No", *International Herald Tribune*, February 1993, p. 5.
15. Christopher Layne, "Why the Gulf War was not in the National Interest" *The Atlantic Monthly*, July 1991, Volume 268, No. 1, pp. 58-61.
16. Amatizia Baram, "Saddam Hussain Between his Power Base and International Community", *MERIA Journal*, Vol. 4, No. 4, December 2000, <http://www.biu.ac.il/ besa/meria/journal/2000/ issue4/jv4n4a2.html>.
17. Shyam Bhatia, Damiel M.C Gory, *Saddam's Bomb*, <http:// www.rediff. com /news/2003/mar/19specl.htm>.
18. *Iraqi Dossier*, "Iraq's Weapons of Mass Destruction. The Assessment of the British Government", <http/news.bbc.co.UK/noi/shared/spl/ hi/middleeast/02/UK –dossier-on –Iraq/html/full dossier.htm>.
19. Ofra Bergio, "Crossing the Rubicon, Iraq and Arab Israeli Peace Process", *Middle East Review of International Affairs*, Vol. 2, No. 1, March 1998, <http://meria.idc. ac.il/journal/1998/issue1/ jv2n1as.html>.
20. *Ibid.*
21. *Iraq News Agency*, 13 Dec., 1990.
22. David Kay, "Iraq Inspections Lessons Learned", CNS Special Collection in Iraq, Center for Non-Proliferation Studies, USA.
23. Rolf Ekeus, Head of UN Special Commission Estimated that Iraq was 2 Years away from possessing Atomic Bomb, at the time of War.
24. Hibbs, M. "Speculation Rampant While IAEA Compiles Iraqi Helper List"', *Nucleonics Week*, Vol. 32, 10 October, 991, p. 9.
25. "Proliferation Threat of the 1990's". *Hearing Before the Committee on Government Affairs, US Senate*, 24 February, 1993, US Government Printing Office: Washington, DC 1993.
26. Inspectors in Iraq a Background, Carnegie Analysis Briefing, Tuesday 5 March, 2002, < ....\Carnegie Endowment for International Peace, Proliferation Narss and Resources 5/10/02.>.
27. David Albright, "Iraq's Programmes to Make Highly Enriched Uranium and Plutonium for Nuclear Weapons Prior to the Gulf War". October 2002, <http://www. isis-online/publications/iraq/ iraqs_fm_history.html.>.
28. Thomas Shea, International Control and Elimination of Nuclear

Weapons Proceedings of the 45 *Pug Wash Conference in Science and World Affairs*, p. 368.

29. Tracking Nuclear Proliferation, 1998 <....\Carnegie Endowments, Non-Proliferation Project Tracking Nuclear Proliferation 5/10/02>.
30. Gordan Panther, "Way Out on a Limb", 11 January, 2003, <http:// www. worldnet daily.com/news/article.asp? ARTICLE ID = 30445>.
31. K. D. Kapur, *Nuclear Non-Proliferation Diplomacy*, (New Delhi: Lancer Books, 1993), p. 46.
32. Lewis A. Dunn, "New Nuclear Threats to US Security" in Robert D. Blackwill and Albert Carnesale, *The New Nuclear Nations*, (US: Council on Foreign Relations, 1993), p. 22.
33. John Simpson, "NPT Stronger after Iraq", *Bulletin of Atomic Scientists*, October 1991, p. 13.
34. *Ibid.*
35. UN Security Council Resolution 687, April 3, 1991 <http: //www. Un org/docs/scres/1991/687 e.pdf>.
36. Note by Secretary General United Nation, 16 April 1998. <http: // www. un.org/Depts/Unscom/sres98-332.htm>.
37. David Albright, Kevin O'Neil, "The Iraq Maze: Searching for a Way Out", *The Non-Proliferation Review*, Fall-Winter 2001, Vol. 8, No. 3, Monterey Institute of International Studies, <http://cns.miis.edu/ pubs/npr/vol8/83/ab83.htm>.
38. *Ibid.*
39. David Albright, Mark Hibbs, "Iraq's Bomb, Blueprints and Artifacts", *The Bulletin of Atomic Scientists*, Vol. 48, No. 1, January/February 1992, pp. 30-40.
40. "Responding to Iraq's Continuing Nuclear Programme" *Nuclear Control Institute*, Letter to the Security Council <http:// www.nci.org> February 17, 1999.
41. *Ibid.*
42. Leonard Weiss, "Tighten up on Nuclear Cheaters", *The Bulletin of Atomic Scientist* 47, May 1991, pp. 11-12.
43. Joseph F. Pilat, Robert E., Pendley, *A New Beginning for the NPT*, (Los Alamos, New Mexico: Center for National Security Studies, 1995). p. 52.
44. *Ibid.*
45. Statement by the Iraqi Ministry of Foreign Affairs on the Twentieth Anniversary of Iraq's Ratification of the Treaty on the Non-Proliferation of Nuclear Weapons (NPT), Annual Report 1989, Iraqi Atomic Energy Commission, <http:// www.iraqwatch.org/ government/iraq1/IAEC%20/report-1989.htm>.
46. Mohammed A., Al Douri, Annexi to the Letter dated 15 August, 2002 from the Permanent Representative of Iraq to the United Nations Addressed to the Secretary General. <http://www.iraqi-mission.org/ 2002-939.htm>.

47. *Ibid.*
48. Questions Presented to The United Nations Secretary General by Iraq's Foreign Minister, 25 July, 2002, Baghdad, <http:// www.iraqimission.org/202-939.htm>.
49. Comments by the Permanent Representative of Iraq to the United Nations on the Statement of the IAEA Representative, 2000 Review Conference of the Parties to the Treaty on the Non-Proliferation of Nuclear Weapons 10 May, 2000. <http: //www.Iraqi-mission.org/ speech % 2010 % 20 May % 202000.htm>.
50. "Iraq's Cooperation with the IAEA Safeguards", *Republic of Iraq Permanent Mission to the United Nations*, <http://www.Iraqi-mission.org/pr%20April% 2019%202000.htm>.
51. <http: //www.Iraqi mission.org/Pr% 20 April 2019, % 20200.htm, Republic of Iraq, Permanent Mission of the UN, 29 April 2000.>
52. Col. Dan Smith, "Iraq, North Korea and the US Nuclear or Else", <http://www. fpip.org/commentary/2003/0301 nkiraq body.html.>
53. "Security Council Working Hard for Iraq Policy Break Through", *Disarmament Diplomacy*, Issue No. 41, November 1999. <http:// www.acronym.org.uk/dd/dd41/ 41iraq.htm>.
54. Richard Butler, *Saddam Defiant: The Threat of Weapons of Mass Destruction and the Crisis of Global Security*, (Phoenix London, 2000), p. 206.
55. Dilip Hiro, *Neighbours, Not Friends: Iraq and Iran After the Gulf War*, (London: Routlege, 2001), p. 161.
56. Sara Khorshid, "Iraqi Weapons of Mass Destruction: Doubts and Uncertainties", http://www.Islamonlines.net/english/views/2002/ 11/article.04. shtml.
57. Rajeev Srinivasan, "Zen and the Art of Potomac-Watching", <http:/ /www.rediff. com/news//1998/dec/23rajeev.htm>.
58. Laurie Mylroie, "Iraq's Weapons of Mass Destruction and the 1997 Gulf Crisis", *Middle East Review of International Affairs*, Vol. 1, No. 4, December 1997, <http// meria.idc.ac.il/journal/1997/issue 4/jvl/ n4al.html>.
59. Paul Levental and Edwin S. Lyman, "Who says Iraq Isn't Making a Bomb?", *International Herald Tribune*, 2 November 1995.
60. Kenneth M. Pollack, "Current Iraqi Military Capabilities an Assessment", *Meria News*,, 4 February, 1998, <http://meria.idc.ac.il/ news/1998/98news4htm#a1>.
61. Ramnanda Sengupta, "*NPT Falling Apart Warns Non-Proliferation Expert*," <http://www. rediff.com / News 2003/mar/7 sagan.htm.>.
62. "The United States and the Possible War on Iraq", <http:// www.cnduk.org/ briefing/Iraq.htm.>
63. Gordon Prather, "Firing on Fort Sumter", *The Washington Times*, December 24, 2002, <http://www. Washtimes.com/op-ed/2002224-2522323.htm>.

64. "The Catch 22 Inspections", *In Let us Fight the Super Monster,* (Patiala: All India People Resistance, Forum, February 2003), p. 60.
65. Judy Aita, "Weapons Inspectors Begin Analysis of Iraqi Weapons Declaration", <http://US embassy.s html.govt//isalamabad/ www02121 003. html.>.
66. "Material Breach, The Mysterious Phase that could Trigger War on Iraq", in *"Let US Fight the Super Monster"*, (Patiala: All India Peoples Resistance, Forum, February 2003), p. 65.
67. Iraq Inspections Foul to Resolve Crisis as Hourglass Runs Towards War, *Disarmament Diplomacy,* <http: //www.acronym.org.uk/dd/ dd69/69nds /html>.
68. *Ibid.*
69. *Ibid.*
70. *Ibid.*
71. See "IAEA says It has No Evidence of Prohibited Nuclear Activities" *US Embassy Tokyo, Japan,* <http://US Embassy.state.govt./Tokyo/ or wwh20021220 al.htmi>.
72. "US Nuclear Watchdog Sees Post War Role in Iraq", Reuters, 24 March 2003, <http://biz.yahoo.com/rm/030324/Iraq nuclear UN 7.html>.
73. The Saddam Hussain's Interview, <http://www.channel 14.com/ news/2003/02/ weak 1/4 Saddam henn.html 4/3/03>.
74. Dan Stober "Nuclear Inspectors Reportedly Argue Checking False US Leads Wanted Time", *Mercury News,* March 189, 2003.
75. K. Shreeram,"Iraq update," *Guardian,* <http:www.zmag.org/crises cur evts/Iraq/Iraq-update.htm>.
76. Michael Barlitta, Jeffrey Fields and Erik Jorgenson, "Iraq, Nuclear, Biological, Chemical Missile Capabilities and Programmes", *Monterey Center for Non-Proliferation Studies,* September 2001., <http:/ /cns.mlis.edu/research/wrndme/Iraqi. html.>
77. Dilip Hero, *Op cit.,* p. 49.
78. Ibrahim Al-Marashi, "How Iraq Conceals and Sustains Its Weapons of Mass Destruction", *Middle East Review of International Affairs,* Vol. 7, No. 1, March 2003, <http://meria.idc.ac.il/Journal/2003/issue/ Jy 7 nla5.html>.
79. "Jeremy Binnie, *Jane Sentinel Security Assessments: The Gulf States,* (London, Jane's Information group, 2001), p. 219.
80. Andrew Cockburn and Patrick Cockburn, *Out of the Ashes: The Resurrection of Saddam Hussain,* (New York: Harper Collins, 1999), p. 107.
81. Ambassador Wulf, *"Envoy Says Nuclear Non-Proliferation Treaty Important to US"*, <http:US embassy.state.gov/tokyo/wwnse/ 1288.html>.

82. Stephen Hughes, *"The Iraqi Threat and Saddam Hussein Weapons of Mass Destruction"*, (Victoria, Canada: Trafford 2002), p. 98.
83. Shyam Bhatia and Daniel Mc Gory, *Brighter than the Baghdad Sun Saddam's Race to Build the Bomb*, (London: Little Brown and Company, 1999). P. 256.
84. "Iraq Bush Lists Benefits of Taking Action Security Council Resumes Talks", *United Nation Foundation*, <http://www.unfoundation.org/unwir.../display. Stories asp? Objiel = 3227>.
85. Milan Rai, "Latest Confirmation that this War for Regime Stabilization and Leadership Change", March 19, 2003.<www.etext.org ?politics/mim/whas new>.
86. War in Iraq, *Iraq Journal.org*, March 25, 2003.<http://www.Iraq.Journal. org>.
87. Immanuel, Wallestein, *"Bush Gets it All"*, Zet Iraq Watch, <http: // www. Zmag.org./content/show article.cfm? section ID = 158, item/ P = 3297>.
88. John Prados, "Iraq: A Necessary War?", *Bulletin of Atomic Scientist*, Vol. 59, No. 3, May/June 2003, <http://www.the bulletin.org/issues/2003/nj03 pardos. html>.
89. Corland Milloy, "On the Spot, Colin Powell Dissapoints", *Washington Post*, February 26, 2003, p. b 1.
90. George Perkovich, "Bush Nuclear Revolution, A Regime Change in Non-Proliferation", *Foreign Affairs*, March/April 2003, <...//bush-s-nuclear-resolution—a regime- change-in – Non-Proliferation.htm>.
91. Saddam Hussain "Letter to the General Assembly", 19 September, 2002, <http: www. Iraqi-mission.org/president-letter - GA-09-19-02.htm>.
92. Dr. Moonis Ahmar *"Disarming Iraq by Force"*, <http://Jang.com.pk/the news/mar 2003 – daily/18-03-2003/oped/05.htm>.
93. Richard Falk, David Krieger, *"Iraq and North Korea, Meeting the Challenge of Nuclear Weapons Proliferation"*, <http://www. Waging peace.org/articles/a... /o/09 Krieger - Iraq Korea.htm>.
94. Agha Qamar, "The Iraq-US Face off", *The Hindu*, <http://www.hinduonnet. com/thehindu/2002100/2002092700291000. htm>
95. Mohammed A. Aldouri, *"Letter to UN Addressed to Secretary Council"*, June 2002, <http: //www.Iraqi-mission.org/2002-659.htm>.
96. Dr. A.S.M. Enayetullah, "Wars should be outlawed", *The Independent*, <http: //independent – bangaladesh.com/news/February/28/2802 2003.htm. 18 March, 2003>.
97. "Nam Rejects War on Iraq Without UN Approval", *Dawn*, 26 February 2003.
98. "President Outlines Iraqi Threat", Remarks by the President Bush on Iraq, Cincinnati Ohio, Office of White House Secretary, 7 October, 2002.

99. Daniel Benjamin, "Saddam Hussain and Al Qaeda and not Allies", *New York Times*, September 30, 2002.
100. William, D. Hartung, "Prevention Not Intervention, Curbing the New Nuclear Threat", *World Policy Journal*, Vol. XIX, No. 4 Winter 2002/2003 <http://www.worldpolcy.org/journal/articles/wpjo-4/hartung.html>.
101. Jonathan, Dean *"The Post-Iraq Situation"*, March 18, 2003, Global Action to Prevent War, <http://www.cnp.org/global/Dean Post Iraq.htm>.
102. Patrick, Martin, "Twenty Lies of George Bush" 20 March 2003, International Committee of the Fourth International, <http://www.wsws.org/articles /2003/mar 2003/bush.m20.shtml>.
103. Mr. Weajdi, Abass, Director of the Disarmament Section, Ministry of Foreign Affairs 15 April 2002., <http/www.basicint.org/nuclear/NPT/2002 prepcom /reg-iraq.htm.>.
104. *The Hindustan Times*, 13 April, 2003.
105. Scott, Ritter, "Redefining Iraq's Obligations: The Case for Qualitative Disarmaments of Iraq", *Arms Control Today*, June 2000, <http://www.arms control.org/act/2000-06/iraq.asp>.
106. Milan, Rai, *War Plan Iraq*, (London: Verso, 2002), p. 67.

6

Conclusion

The Non-Proliferation Treaty had acquired greater significance during the 1990's, due to the polemic generated over the nuclear programmes of developing nations like India, Pakistan, North Korea and Iraq. These developing nations were situated in a hostile geo-political environment and therefore faced a difficult task in balancing their disarmament goals with their needs for deterrence. The divergence in the rationalisation of nuclear weapons had destroyed the possibility of a meaningful dialogue on Non-Proliferation between the developed and the developing countries. When India and other developing nations proposed the Non-Proliferation Treaty, a global balance of responsibilities and obligations between nuclear and non-nuclear states was envisaged. This however was not operationalized. The transition in the Indian perspective, from being an ardent champion of Non-Proliferation to opposition to the discriminatory regime, emerged out of the compulsions of this dichotomy wherein its own security interests were challenged. The US approach to Non-Proliferation was contested by developing nations like India, Pakistan, North Korea and Iraq. The developing nations' critique of the Non-Proliferation Treaty emanated from the fundamental question of equality. The entire world order was based on unequal tenets and the NPT Regime was a part if this global inequity. The Non-Proliferation Treaty was signed on 1st July 1968; its membership was nearly universal with 188 nations party to it. Only four states India, Pakistan, Israel and now North Korea are outside the Non-Proliferation Regime. The interest of the research community on Nuclear Non-Proliferation was further rekindled recently with North Korea's withdrawal from the NPT on January 10, 2003.

This study attempted to examine the hypothesis that the Non-

Proliferation Treaty does not serve the security interests of developing countries whose compulsions are specific and region oriented. In the strategic and security arena the developing nations have confronted a formidable challenge of conflicts not only from a unipolor hegemonic order but also from powerful regional states. The Western debate over nuclear issues in the developing world had seldom taken into account the psychology underlying the resistance of India and Pakistan to the NPT. The scholarly literature on proliferation had tended to ignore the motives behind nuclear proliferation in the developing world. This study, which attempted to fill this gap, was delimited to four nations namely, India, Pakistan, North Korea and Iraq and their approach towards the NPT.

There was growing realisation in the developing world that the end of Cold War had resulted in the domination of the world by the US. As witnessed, the terrible events of September 11, 2001 were taken as a justification to push forward a total military domination by the US and pressurise the developing nations to dismantle their nuclear weapons and accept the Non-Proliferation norms. The US developed a pre-emptive military strike doctrine and forcibly occupied Iraq. The developing nations feel very insecure and apprehensive about the US intensions in this new millennium. The US Non-Proliferation policy at present is directed towards preventing enemies of US, especially so-called "Rogue States", from acquiring nuclear weapons. US perceived a whole array of new enemies in the form of unruly developing states intent on acquiring Weapons of Mass Destruction. Its dichotomous stand with regard to Pakistan's blatant violation of WMD technology transfers and to Iraq, are clear evidences of its hypocrisy. The Non-Proliferation Treaty is not likely to endure indefinitely if its only concerns are the security interests of nuclear powers. The US retains nuclear weapons for its national security and at the same time denies such weapons to the developing nations, for the sake of global security. The present nuclear security paradigm continues to be patently unjust.

This research attempted to address certain crucial issues.

- A central issue raised in this study was with regard to the challenges faced by developing countries to their security arising out of regional conflicts. A state generally makes a nuclear choice based on the regional security situation. Nuclear weapons provide protection against large-scale military intervention such as pre-emptive attacks by neighbouring countries. India and Pakistan responded to their regional insecurity dilemma by not signing the NPT.

- Secondly, this study focussed on the fact that the Non-Proliferation Treaty was fundamentally discriminatory in nature because it legitimised possession of nuclear weapons by a few states and expected others states, which have security concerns emanating from nuclear dangers, not to acquire similar capability.
- The third major question this research attempted to address was whether the Non-Proliferation Treaty has made any meaningful contribution in containing proliferation over the years or if it has become an instrument of nuclear colonialism over the developing world.
- This study also investigated the schism between nuclear haves and the have-nots in the context of monopoly over the use of nuclear weapons. The new nuclear nations like India, Pakistan and North Korea have protested against the NPT and have gone ahead with nuclearisation in defiance of the treaty. This study was directed towards understanding the sensitivities of four developing nations, India, Pakistan Iraq and North Korea towards the Non-Proliferation Regime established by the great powers. Out of these four nations only Iraq is a party to the NPT. It is ironic that it has been subjected to extreme punitive action. As more developing nations join the Non-Proliferation Treaty, its was essential to assess why these few specific developing nations are reluctant to sign the treaty.
- This study further probed the US projection of military power in the region, which posed problems for political stability of North Korea and Iraq respectively. The new guidelines issued by the Bush administration for the use of nuclear weapons against "Rogue States", have caused alarm in North Korea and Iraq. The US attempts to thwart nascent nuclear programmes of the developing nations and impose export control measures. This development

highlights a disharmony between the US nuclear doctrine and negative security assurances against non-nuclear weapon states party to the NPT. The United States had issued a policy statement in 1978 that it would not use nuclear weapons against any non-nuclear state that was party to the NPT except in the case of attack on the United States by a state allied to a nuclear weapons state. This research raised the important issue of Iraq, a non-nuclear party to the Non-Proliferation Treaty, being subject to US aggression on the suspicion that it possessed Weapons of Mass Destruction. It also noted that the hostile policy of the US towards North Korea was, in significant ways responsible for North Korea's withdrawal from the Non-Proliferation Treaty.

This research work was structured into five chapters. Chapter 1 attempted to explore the concept of proliferation and the historical background of the NPT. This chapter examined the two dominant perspectives about the origin of the NPT. The Western perspective focussed on the need to stop the spread of nuclear weapons to additional nations. The developing nations' perspective emanated from the need to bring about genuine global nuclear disarmament. This chapter endeavoured to bring forth the provisions of the treaty and studied the debates at various review conferences from the perspective of developing world. It was observed that treaty had many loopholes right from the history of its formation. The US and Soviet Union started the treaty process from a position of power and a legacy of secrecy. The main motives of the nuclear weapon states were to retain control of nuclear weapons and profit from the sale of civilian nuclear technology. These ideas were based on Eisenhower's 1953 Atoms for Peace proposals in which the US offered civilian technology to those states that would refrain from nuclear weapons development.

It was observed in the chapter that the basic provisions of the Non- Proliferation Treaty were designed only to prevent the spread of nuclear weapons to additional nations, i.e. to prevent horizontal proliferation and to provide assurance through international safeguards that peaceful nuclear activities of states, which have not already developed nuclear weapons, will not be diverted to making such weapons. The NPT aimed to promote peaceful uses of nuclear energy to include potential benefits of any peaceful application of nuclear explosion technology being made to non-nuclear parties under appropriate safeguards. It was seen that it also expressed the determination of parties that the treaty should lead to progress in comprehensive arms control and disarmament measures.

It was noted in the chapter that the five yearly review conferences as provided in the Article VIII of the Non-Proliferation Treaty, gave an opportunity to developing nations to put forth their grievances and emphasise on the implementation of global disarmament. Developing countries were anxious to stop the vertical proliferation of nuclear weapons. It was noted, however that in all the six review conferences the voice of the developing nations was subdued and the developing nations felt very insecure. The first review conference in Geneva, in May 1975 took up the issue of non-nuclear weapon states but refused to accept the developing nation's proposals. As observed the second review conference in 1980 failed to produce a consensus in the final document. The third review conference was held in August 27th 1985 in Geneva. Its focus was to strengthen peaceful nuclear cooperation. The fourth review conference was held in August 1990 in Geneva, where consensus was achieved on positive and negative security assurances. In accordance to Article X (2) of the Non-Proliferation Treaty a conference was to be held in 1995 to decide whether the NPT should continue in force indefinitely or be extended for an additional fixed period. In May 1995 the NPT was extended indefinitely. It was noted that the voice of developing nations for rolling extensions every twenty-five years was suppressed. North Korea and Iraq had vehemently opposed the indefinite extension of the NPT that would legitimise nuclear weapons forever in the hands of the nuclear weapons nations. The Sixth NPT Review Conference was held in May 2000. The conference expressed its concern with the cases of non-compliance to move to full compliance with their obligations. The conference urged all states not yet party to the treaty, namely Cuba, India, Israel and Pakistan to accede to the treaty as non-nuclear weapons states. Thus, these nations were subject to tremendous pressure to sign the NPT.

The broad issues discussed in Chapter 2 dealt with India's position towards the NPT. For years India has refused to sign the

NPT arguing that NPT protects super power dominance in nuclear weapons and does not address its concerns about regional security threats. India's nuclear threat perceptions include regional as well as extra regional politico-strategic developments. This study has revealed that growing perceptions of a security threat from China and then from Pakistan led Indian decision-makers towards overt weaponisation and the abandonment of the country's posture of nuclear ambiguity. It was noted that the nuclear Non-Proliferation Regime has become an instrumentality of hegemony of big powers. India remains committed to non-discriminatory and universal nuclear disarmament. India was first to criticise the NPT as being highly discriminatory between five nuclear weapon haves and the developing nations. India remained opposed to the indefinite extension of the Non-Proliferation Treaty.

It was observed in the chapter that proliferation of nuclear weapons in India was a part of nuclear chain reactions, which began with China. China's nuclear capabilities were significant and comprised of a strategic triad of long range Bombers, IRBM's and ICBM's. Secondly, China's assistance to Pakistan to develop its nuclear programme posed a grave security threat to India. India opposed the NPT because the NPT as such could not resolve its security threat. China was a key player in South Asian nuclear dynamics. Ever since the border war in 1962 India was very cautious of China and its espousal of no first use principle could not assure the Indians regarding a future breach of faith by China. Both India and Pakistan believed that they needed to bolster their nuclear capabilities in the light of hostile relationships. Pakistan's nuclear arsenals were India-specific and are controlled by the military. Pakistan's refusal to institute no first use policy of nuclear weapons is designated to keep India guessing about when Pakistan might use its nuclear weapons and forms the basis of its policy. On 11th May and 13th May 1998, India conducted nuclear tests in open defiance of the Non-Proliferation Treaty. The emerging nuclear predicament for India was that the world is reluctantly reconciling with the existential reality of India's nuclear weapons status. The South Asian Nuclear tests represented the first serious challenge to the Non-Proliferation Regime. India's position in particular, in conjunction with India's consistent and open refusal to accept the legitimacy of the Non-Proliferation Regime, and espousal of nuclear disarmament as an alternative to Non-

Proliferation, struck at the very roots of the Non-Proliferation Regime. India's perspective strengthened its credentials as a nation that was not against Non-Proliferation but for disarmament on a global scale. Washington rejected India's claims of security threat from Pakistan and China as unpersuasive. President Bill Clinton imposed economic and military sanctions under the Glenn Amendment immediately after the nuclear test. The P-5 nations refused to recognise India and Pakistan as nuclear weapon states pointing to the legality of nuclear status in the NPT, which was, restricted those prior to 1st January 1967. The Indian nuclear doctrine based on no first use, was a defensive doctrine.

It was noted in the chapter that the nuclear Non-Proliferation Regime has become an instrumentality of hegemony of big power. India remains committed to non-discriminatory and universal nuclear disarmament. India was first to criticise the NPT as highly discriminatory between five nuclear weapons haves and the developing nations. India remained opposed to the indefinite extension of the Non-Proliferation Treaty.

The third chapter dealt with Pakistan's approach to the NPT in the context of its geo-political environment, its threat perceptions and attempt to achieve parity with India. It was observed that Pakistan's geo-political environment and its threat perceptions have shaped its approach to the NPT. Located between Iran in the West and India in the East, Afghanistan in the North West and China in the North East, Pakistan faces serious security problems. Pakistan's obsession is to seek parity with India and unwillingness to acknowledge inferior weapon status vis-à-vis India. Pakistan's national interests are based on pragmatism and are security oriented. Pakistan has pursued a nuclear weapon programme for regime survival. In case of Pakistan, traditional threats to its security still remains dominant. The field remains dominated by geo-political threats to its borders especially from India. The memories of partition set the two nations in a confrontational path and led to four wars. The security studies in Pakistan present Kashmir as the core issue and an unresolved problem of partition of the subcontinent. Pakistan was opposed to the discriminatory character of the Non-Proliferation Regime; it wanted to supplement the conventional inferiority vis-à-vis India with nuclear capability. Iran's programme regarding the development of nuclear weapons was seen as another factor that heightened the security concerns of Pakistan.

It was noted in the chapter that the condition put forth by Pakistan for not joining the Non-Proliferation Treaty reflects its consistent desire to keep its nuclear weapons option open. In Pakistan there is a strong national consensus that nuclear programme is essential for national security. Pakistan insists that it would sign the treaty if India does so, conveniently putting all the blame on India for not adhering to the treaty. Pakistan had expressed broad support for proliferation and made proposals to India for the creation of a South Asian nuclear weapon free zone, unlimited inspections of each other's facilities and joint declarations of nuclear arms.

Chapter 3 has unfolded the intersections and concentricity of Pakistan –US foreign policy interests on the NPT. The deftly cajoled global US campaign of Non-Proliferation and the projection of South Asia as a flashpoint of nuclear conflict has been examined in this chapter. This study also reveals that the US pressure on Pakistan has mounted after September 11. This chapter also highlighted the US concern about the diffusion of Pakistan's nuclear technology to terrorist organisation like Al-Qaida.

The fourth chapter has examined North Korea's perceptions towards the Non-Proliferation Treaty. In the first part it was observed that North Korea's security dilemma arising out of deployment of US nuclear weapons in South Korea had motivated former president Kim II Sung to launch a nuclear programme of its own. It was observed in this chapter that North Korea's hostile relations with South Korea, Japan and China and the US were instrumental in the need to develop nuclear weapons as a deterrent. It was noted in the chapter that the disintegration of Soviet Union and its growing cooperation with China has heightened North Korean insecurity.

It was seen that North Korea had signed the Non-Proliferation Treaty in 1985 under Soviet pressure. The main finding in this chapter was that North Korea as a party to the NPT, was disillusioned with the treaty for it had observed that the existing nuclear weapon states, were not interested in genuine disarmament. North Korea refused to sign the safeguards agreement with the IAEA until 1992. Throughout 1992 and early 1993 the IAEA and North Korea continued to clash over full access to nuclear sites. In 1993 North Korea had announced its withdrawal from the NPT and after persuasion from USA and South Korea which also saw an escalation of the situation and North Korea retained the membership of the NPT. It was noted in the chapter that the negotiations with the US ultimately produced the US-North Korean agreed framework of 1994. The research also addressed the failure of the agreed framework due to the deteriorating security environment, which led North Korea to leave the NPT. While US imperialism had threatened sovereign countries like Iraq it became a pragmatic step for North Korea to pursue nuclear weapons as an act of self-defence. North Korea's recent withdrawal from the NPT and its apparent efforts to accelerate its nuclear programme is a response to adverse changes in the external environment. The chapter highlighted the fact that North Korea has taken a series of actions of concern to the international community. It has unfrozen nuclear facilities by removing IAEA surveillance equipment, expelled IAEA inspectors and announced its withdrawal from the NPT and reactivated its nuclear plant in Yongbyong. North Korea asserted that the nuclear issue was a bilateral matter between the US and North Korea and demanded a Non Aggression pact with the US. The US believed that it was an international issue related to the preservation of Non-Proliferation Regime. On April 9, 2003, the Security Council refused to act on a US request to condemn North Korea for pulling out of the NPT. There was a strong opposition from China and Russia who had close ties with North Korea's nuclear programme. The US wished to condemn the country for breach of its international obligations. This confrontation has weakened the Nuclear Non-Proliferation Treaty and may send signals for others that obtaining nuclear weapons has geopolitical benefits. North Korea's main concern was its security. By linking Iraq and North Korea, in the "Axis of Evil", Bush has forced North Korea to a pre-emptive posture in anticipation of what Washington would do after the Iraq crisis when North Korea moves to the top of its foreign policy agenda.

It was observed in the chapter that Pakistan had played a substantial role in the progress of North Korea's nuclear programme. According to a US report, Pakistan gave North Korea high-speed centrifuges to test Uranium triggered nuclear weapons. North Korea has assisted Pakistan's Missile programme. North Korea's trade of missile for highly enriched Uranium technology occurred around 1997, which concluded with Pyongyang's shipment of Nodong missiles to Pakistan. It was noted that though Pakistan was relatively a poor nation, it was determined to keep up with India following its Peaceful Nuclear Explosions in 1974. As Pakistan concentrated its resources in building bombs it also needed a delivery system. The problem was compounded by Pakistan's financial position, which suffered a blow in October 1990 when US suspended over $500 million in aid. The observation that Second tier nations, Pakistan and North Korea have cooperated with each other to nuclear weapons in defiance of the NPT was a new development that has challenged the Non-Proliferation Regime.

In chapter 5 the broad issues investigated were Iraq's approach to the NPT, its opposition to the of Non-Proliferation Treaty and the complete devastation of the sovereign nation by the US on the suspicion of possession of Weapons of Mass Destruction including Nuclear, Chemical and Biological weapons. This study has revealed that when it comes to perceive its strategic interest in the developing world, the US does not hesitate from the use of force. The US chose various ways to deal with the so-called threat from Iraq as a pretext to rationalise and legitimise its persisting urge to dominate the affairs of the world. Iraq became a signatory of the NPT in 1969. It enthusiastically joined the community of nations to put an end to terror brought on the world by nations that invented the atomic bombs. Since the beginning of the NPT the security issues facing the sovereign nation of Iraq have grown. For eight years in 1980's Iraq found itself fighting for its existence with Iran. It had permitted IAEA inspections of OSIRAQ in 1976. The IAEA reported no evidence of Iraqi development of nuclear weapons and had accounted for all Iraq's nuclear material. In 1983, Israel, without justification, attacked one of the nuclear power plants, which was strictly designed for peaceful uses of Atomic Energy. A central point noted in the chapter was that as a country living in an anarchic International system and facing an intense security dilemma Iraq was compelled to expand its programme and identify Israel as a direct threat. In 1990's the Kuwaitis began to extract oil from the oil fields predominantly under Iraqi soil. When Iraq choose to exercise its right to bring the 19th province of Iraq known as Kuwait back to its borders. The Western imperialists with their nuclear weapons and their insatiable appetite for oil invaded Iraq in 1991. As observed in the chapter US illegally established the so-called no fly zones in direct violation of Iraq's sovereignty and then created intolerable conditions for weapons inspections. The Iraqi government fully cooperated with the provisions of UNSCOM without surrendering and compromising its security and sovereignty. However American propaganda gave the world a different impression. The American support to Kuwait and Saudi Arabia were considered by Iraq as grave threats to its national security. Iraq's geo-political situation in Southwest Asia bounded on the East by Iran, on South by Kuwait, Saudi Arabia, on West by Jordan and Syria and on the North by Turkey has accentuated its security concerns. It was seen in this chapter that in 1991 the UK and US attempted to violate the independence, sovereignty and territorial integrity of Iraq. Ever since, the Iraqis were subjected to inspections time and again with the scientists having been psychologically tortured to reveal information about Iraq's nuclear programme. It was evidenced in the chapter, that the IAEA inspectors acted on the instructions of the US. The suspected sites that were visited by the inspection teams were bombed including presidential sites. Iraq hardly violated UN Security Council resolutions, since Gulf War of 1991. It sometimes expressed reservations on some resolutions that involved gross violations of Iraqi sovereignty. As the chapter observed, the Iraqi experience sets a wrong precedent that the US has a right to invade regimes hostile to it.

It was noted in the chapter that the real objective of attack on Iraq was not to stop Saddam from acquiring and using Weapons of Mass Destruction. A primary objective was to secure and control Iraq's oil, which has second largest reserves in the world. The nuclear inspectors trudged through the countryside for months. They found Iraqi weapons infrastructure built at a great expense in 1980 to be in a state of decay. Thus, the chapter argued that for the American military planners, Iraq was merely the easiest target, the more strategic control of Iraq was not an end in itself but the starting point of a programme to redraw the map of Middle East. The claims of mobile biological laboratories were refuted by weapons inspectors, as were claims that Iraq had and was about to get nuclear weapons. The chief UN inspector Hans Blix and Mohammed El Baradei had confirmed that Iraq did not have nuclear weapons. The interesting finding is that the Bush administration tried to assert that only the part of NPT that applied to non-nuclear state is valid and therefore states which violate it, allegedly even without any evidence, like Iraq must be punished for transgression. The Iraqi experience thus shows that the NPT failed to fulfil its major objective to peacefully prevent the future proliferation of nuclear weapons and work towards nuclear disarmament.

The NPT understandably would face many challenges in the years ahead. One of the most serious challenges relates to basic legitimacy of the fairness of the treaty. There is persisting widespread perception in the developing world among the parties that the fundamental NPT bargain is discriminatory. The greatest challenge facing the treaty relates to question that have arisen in context of recent war in Iraq particularly in respect to enforcement. While enforcement concerns existed long before the war, the total disregard to the United Nations has undermined the credibility of the regime. The challenge posed was solved brutally through war and regime change. There are slender chances of nuclear disarmament in South Asia after attack on Iraq.

The eleven nuclear tests by India and Pakistan, in 1998, the two non-NPT states, are a harsh reminder of the treaty's lack of universality. These states opposed the treaty as they saw it as an obstacle in advancing their security interests in a volatile security environment.

Under the terms of the treaty the 188 member nations, have the right to withdraw from the treaty on three months notice after citing extraordinary events that threaten their national interests. The treatment to Iraq was undoubtedly a lesson for other states. North Korea was the first nation to withdraw from the NPT. The argument is that if regime survival is accepted as the overwhelming goal of North Koreans, then their recent actions may be dangerous to international security but is not necessarily irrational from the point of North Korean regime security.

NPT is a discriminatory treaty where the states have variable rights. The nuclear weapon states can defend their sovereignty through possession of nuclear weapons whereas the non-nuclear weapon nations are denied nuclear technology to do the same. The United States of America had built bunker buster bombs especially directed at defiant developing nations. At the same time it condemned India, Pakistan, North Korea and Iraq for developing nuclear weapons. It is thus argued that the NPT had become a vehicle of promotion of nuclear monopoly of nuclear weapons by existing nuclear weapon powers, not an instrument of genuine disarmament. India's nuclear tests in particular in conjunction with India's consistent and open refusal to accept the legitimacy of the Non-Proliferation Regime and India's espousal of nuclear disarmament, would strike at the very roots of the Non-Proliferation.

The study further observed that the treaty did not completely ban the future development of nuclear weapons by those states, which already possessed them. It perpetuated massive military inequality between the super powers and the rest of the world. The "Rogue States" such as North Korea and Iraq are portrayed as irrationally aggressive to suit US foreign policy needs. The fact remains that the only state that has used nuclear bombs on human beings has been the US. Since 1945 America has held to its nuclear arsenals, continues to up-to-date its nuclear technology through computer simulations. It has threatened to reduce North Korea to a charcoal briquette which then prompted North Korea in 1993 to threaten its withdrawal form the NPT. In 1990's the US tried to bargain with Pakistan by telling that it would hand over F-16's if Pakistan restrained from testing its nuclear bombs.

It is further observed that Article I of NPT and Article III are concerned only with keeping nuclear capability away from non-nuclear states. Nuclear states can inspect non-nuclear states to make sure they are not developing nuclear weapons but not *vice versa*. The NPT is a fundamentally discriminatory and unequal treaty. There is a distinction between the five nuclear weapon states as they existed on 1st January 1967 and all the rest of the states.

It is also underlined that the obligations on the nuclear five (USA, China, France, UK and Russia) for nuclear disarmament are loose, ineffectual and not subject to any international supervision. Nuclear weapon states are merely asked to undertake good faith negotiations on the element of nuclear weapons under Article VI, whereas the obligations of non-nuclear states are effective and immediate and supervised by a multilateral body by the International Atomic Energy Agency.

This work highlighted the aspect of the hypocrisy in the NPT. The nuclear weapon states had failed to guarantee that the non-nuclear states would be assured nuclear technology transfers in the civilian field for their developmental needs. The nuclear weapon states transferred out dated technology and that too on a selective basis, much to the disappointment of developing nations.

A serious anomaly existing in the present scenario pertains to the status and recognition of new nuclear states. The newly empowered nuclear capable nations like India and Pakistan are claiming nuclear weapon status while the NPT has failed to accommodate their interests since it has already frozen the nuclear regime to five. In such a situation the NPT has become out dated. Given the present political situation it seems highly unlikely that India, Pakistan and North Korea will relinquish their nuclear weapons and adhere to the NPT as non-nuclear weapon states.

This thesis was directed towards the verification of the hypothesis that the Non-Proliferation Treaty does not serve the security interest of certain developing states whose compulsions are specific and region-oriented. it has been seen in the present world system the security interests of developing nations are determined by many factors, ranging from territorial disputes, stemming from arbitrarily drawn colonial borders, consequences of under development and destabilising policies of great powers. The overall international environment has not been conducive to tension free evolution of developing states and smooth transition into post-colonial societies. The national security concerns of India, Pakistan, North Korea and Iraq are key factors in the process of proliferation of nuclear weapons. The main findings are that Iraq and North Korea had signed the Non-Proliferation Treaty out of their political compulsions, but had grave misgivings about the Treaty. The threat perceptions from the US were the main factors that compelled these nations to defy the Non-Proliferation Treaty. The US hostile policy led North Korea to withdraw from the Treaty. This research aptly shows that the Non-Proliferation Treaty did not provide security even to its non-nuclear members like Iraq. India and Pakistan resisted US pressure and refused to join the Non-Proliferation Treaty. The Non-Proliferation Regime has become fragile after India and Pakistan's nuclear tests on May 1998 and North Korea's withdrawal from the NPT on 10 January, 2002. These nations were placed in difficult geo-political environments had acquired nuclear weapons to meet their security requirements. The US had renewed its right to use nuclear weapons against non-nuclear weapon states and the continued emphasis on first strike policy undermines Non-Proliferation goals. This doctrine of pre-emption pursued by the US will further accentuate nuclear weapons proliferation in the developing world to meet the threat of aggressive use of force. In order to restore the spirit and strength of the Non-Proliferation Treaty it is imperative on the part of the nuclear weapon states to address the proliferation problem globally, assist the developing nations in the use of nuclear energy for peaceful purposes and acknowledge the security problems of the developing nations. It is also imperative that they start with serious disarmament.

Appendix I

Non-Nuclear Signatories of NPT

The Decade of 1960's

1. Ireland	(1 July, 1968)
2. Nigeria	(27 September, 1968)
3. Denmark	(3 January, 1969)
4. Canada	(8 January, 1969)
5. Cameroon	(8 January, 1969)
6. Mexico	(21 January, 1969)
7. Finland	(5 February, 1969)
8. Norway	(5 February, 1969)
9. Ecuador	(7 March, 1969)
10. Mauritius	(8 April, 1969)
11. Botswana	(28 April, 1969)
12. Mongolia	(19 May, 1969)
13. Hungary	(27 May, 1969)
14. Poland	(12 June, 1969)
15. Austria	(27 June, 1969)
16. Iceland	(18 July, 1969)
17. Bulgaria	(5 September, 1969)
18. New Zealand	(10 September, 1969)
19. Syrian Arab Republic	(24 September, 1969)
20. Iraq	(29 October, 1969)
21. Swaziland	(11 December, 1969)

The Decade of 1970's

22. Nepal	(5 January, 1970)
23. Sweden	(9 January, 1970)

24. Iran	(2 February, 1970)
25. Afghanistan	(4 February, 1970)
26. Romania	(4 February, 1970)
27. Paraguay	(4 February, 1970)
28. Ethiopia	(5 February, 1970)
29. Malta	(6 February, 1970)
30. Cyprus	(16 February, 1970)
31. Mali	(10 February,1970)
32. Jordan	(11 February,1970)
33. Laos	(20 February, 1970)
34. Togo	(26 February,1970)
35. Tunisia	(26 February, 1970)
36. Burkina Faso	(3 March, 1970)
37. Costa Rica	(3 March, 1970)
38. Peru	(3 March, 1970)
39. Yugoslavia	(4 March, 1970)
40. Malaysia	(5 March, 1970)
41. Jamaica	(5 March, 1970)
42. Liberia	(5 March, 1970)
43. Somalia	(5 March, 1970)
44. Greece	(11 March, 1970)
45. Maldives	(7 April, 1970)
46. Ghana	(4 May, 1970)
47. Lesotho	(20 May, 1970)
48. Bolivia	(26 May, 1970)
49. Haiti	(2nd June, 1970)
50. Kenya	(11 June, 1970)
51. Lebanon	(11 June, 1970)
52. Zaire	(4th August, 1970)
53. San Marino	(10 August,1970)
54. Guatemala	(22 September, 1970)
55. Madagascar	(8 October, 1970)
56. Central African Republic	(25 October, 1970)
57. Morocco	(27 November, 1970)
58. Burkina Faso	(1970)
59. Senegal	(17 December, 1970)
60. Holy See	(25 February, 1971)
61. Chad	(10 March, 1971)
62. Burundi	(19 March, 1971)
63. Tonga	(7 July, 1971)

64. Dominica Republic (24 July 1971)
65. Cambodia (2 June, 1972)
66. El Salvador (11 July, 1972)
67. Fiji (14 July 1972)
68. Philippines (5 October, 1972)
69. Benin (31 October, 1972)
70. Thailand (7 December, 1972)
71. Australia (23 January, 1973)
72. Nicaragua (16 March, 1973)
73. Cote d'Ivoire (6 March, 1973)
74. Honduras (16 May, 1973)
75. Sudan (31 October, 1973)
76. Gabon (19 February, 1974)
77. Grenada (19 August, 1974)
78. Sierra Leone (26 February 1975)
79. Western Samoa (17 March, 1975)
80. Republic of Korea (23 April, 1975)
81. Belgium (2 May, 1975)
82. Germany (2 May, 1975)
83. Italy (2 May, 1975)
84. Luxemburg (2 May, 1975)
85. Netherlands (2 May, 1975)
86. Gambia (12 May, 1975)
87. Rwanda (20 May, 1975)
88. Libya Arab Jamahirriya (26 May, 1973)
89. Venezuela (25 September, 1975)
90. Singapore (10 March, 1976)
91. Japan (8 June, 1976)
92. Suriname (30 June, 1976)
93. Bahamas (11 August, 1976)
94. Guinea Bussan (20 August, 1976)
95. Panama (13 January, 1997)
96. Switzerland (9 March, 1977)
97. Portugal (15 December, 1977)
98. Liechtenstein (20 April, 1978)
99. Republic of Congo (23 October, 1978)
100. Tuvalu (19 January, 1979)
101. Sri Lanka (5 March, 1979)
102. Yemen (1 June, 1979)
103. Indonesia (12 July, 1979)

104. Bangladesh	(31 August, 1979)
105. Cape Vedre	(24 October, 1979)
106. St. Lucia	(28 December, 1979)

The Decade of 1980's

107. Barbados	(21 February, 1980)
108. Turkey	(17 April, 1980)
109. Egypt	(26 February, 1981)
110. Solomon Islands	(17 June, 1981)
111. Papua New Guinea	(13 January, 1982)
112. Nauru	(7 June, 1982)
113. Vietnam	(14 June, 1982)
114. Uganda	(20 October, 1982)
115. Sao Tom and Principle	(20 July, 1983)
116. Domino	(10 August, 1984)
117. Equatorial Guinea	(1 November, 1984)
118. St. Vincent & the Grenadines	(6 November, 1984)
119. Seychelles	(12 March, 1985)
120. Brunei Darus Salam	(26 March, 1985)
121. Kiribati	(18 April, 1985)
122. Guinea	(29 April, 1985)
123. Bhutan	(23 April, 1985)
124. Antigua and Barbuda	(17 June, 1985)
125. Belize	(9 August, 1985)
126. Democratic Peoples Republic of Korea	(12 December 1985)
127. Malawi	(18 February, 1986)
128. Columbia	(8 April, 1986)
129. Trinidad and Tobago	(30 October, 1986)
130. Spain	(5 November, 1987)
131. Saudi Arabia	(3 October, 1988)
132. Bahrain	(3 November, 1988)
133. Qatar	(3 April, 1989)
134. Kuwait	(17 November, 1989)

The Decade of 1990's

135. Mozambique	(4 September, 1990)
136. Albania	(12 September, 1990)

137. Zambia	(15 May 1990)
138. Tanzania	(31 May, 1991)
139. South Africa	(10 July, 1991)
140. Lithuania	(23 September, 1991)
141. Zimbabwe	(26 September, 1991)
142. Estonia	(7 January, 1992)
143. Latvia	(31 January, 1992)
144. Slovenia	(7 April, 1992)
145. Uzbekistan	(7 May, 1992)
146. Croatia	(29 June, 1992)
147. Azerbaijan	(22 September, 1992)
148. Namibia	(2 October, 1992)
149. Niger	(9 October, 1992)
150. Myanmar	(2 December, 1992)
151. Czech Republic	(1 January, 1993)
152. Slovak Republic	(1 January, 1993)
153. St. Kitts & Nevis	(22 March, 1993)
154. Armenia	(15 July, 1993)
155. Belarus	(22 July, 1993)
156. Guyana	(19 October, 1993)
157. Mauritania	(26 October, 1993)
158. Kazakhstan	(14 February 1994)
159. Georgia	(7 March 1994)
160. Kyrgzstan	(5 July, 1994)
161. Bosnia and Herzegovina	(15 August, 1994)
162. Turkmenistan	(29 October, 1994,)
163. Moldova	(11 October, 1994)
164. Ukraine	(5 December, 1994)
165. Algeria	(12 January, 1995)
166. Marshall Islands	(30 January, 1995)
167. Argentina	(10 February, 1995)
168. Monaco	(13 March, 1995)
169. Eritrea	(16 March, 1995)
170. Macedonia	(30 March, 1995)
171. Micronesia	(14 April, 1995)
172. Federated State of Palau	(14 April, 1995)
173. Chile	(25 May, 1995)
174. Republic of Vanuatu	(24 August, 1995)
175. United Arab Emirates	(26 September, 1995)
176. Comoros	(4 October, 1995)

177. Andorra (7 June, 1996)
178. Angola (14 October, 1996)
179. Djibouti (16 October, 1996)
180. Tajikistan (17 January, 1997)
181. Oman (23 January, 1997)
182. Brazil (18 September, 1998)

The Decade of 2000

183. Cuba (4 November 2002)

Nuclear Weapons States Signatories to the NPT

1. UK (27 November, 1968)
2. US (5 March, 1970)
3. Russian Federation (5 March, 1970)
4. China (9 March, 1992)
5. France (2 August, 1992)

Appendix II

Provisions of the Treaty

The NPT is a collection of eleven articles designed to prevent new countries from obtaining nuclear weapons, to promote disarmament and establishes a system of safeguards and verification. According to the Preamble, the purpose of the treaty was to facilitate and guarantee access to peaceful application of nuclear technology and by products for all parties of the treaty whether nuclear or non-nuclear under the ages is of IAEA.

Article I

Article I of the NPT states that each nuclear weapon state party to the treaty undertakes not to transfer to any recipient whatsoever nuclear weapons or other nuclear explosive devices or control over such explosive directly or indirectly and not in any way to against encourage or induce any non-nuclear weapon state to manufacture or other use acquire nuclear weapons or other nuclear explosive devices or control over such weapons or explosive devices.

Article II

According to Article II each non-nuclear weapon state party to the treaty undertakes not to transfer nuclear weapons or other explosive devices or of control over such weapons or explosive devices directly or indirectly not to manufacture or otherwise acquire nuclear weapons or other nuclear explosive device.

Article III

Each non-nuclear weapon state party to the treaty undertakes to accept safeguards as set forth in an agreement to the negotiated and concluded with the IAEA in accordance with the statute of the International Atomic Energy Agency and the Agency's safeguard system for the exclusive purpose of verification of the fulfillment of its obligation.

1. This has been done with a view to preventing the diversion of nuclear energy from peaceful uses to nuclear weapons on other nuclear explosive devices. Procedures for the safeguards required by this Article shall be followed with respect to special fissionable material whether it is being produced, processed or used in any principal nuclear facility. The safeguards required by this Article shall be applied to all source or special fissionable material in all peaceful nuclear activities within the territory of such state under its jurisdiction or carried out under its control anywhere.
2. Each party to the treaty undertakes not to provide (a) Source or special fissionable material, (b) equipment or material especially designed and prepared for the processing, use or production of special fissionable material to any non-nuclear state for peaceful purposes unless the source of special fissionable material shall be subject to safeguards required by this Article.
3. The safeguards required by this Article shall be implemented in a manner designed to comply with Article IV of the treaty and to avoid hamper of the economic on technological development of the parties or international cooperation or in the field of peaceful nuclear activities including the international exchange of nuclear material and equipment.
4. Non-nuclear weapon states party to the treaty shall conclude agreement with the IAEA to meet the requirements of this Article either individually or together with other states in accordance with the statute of IAEA. Negotiation of such an agreement shall commence within 180 days from the original entry into force of the treaty. For states depositing their instrument of ratification on accession after 180-day's period, negotiation of such agreements shall commence not late than the date of such

deposit. Such agreement shall enter into force not latter than 18 months after the date of initiation of negotiation.

Article IV

Nothing in this treaty shall be interpreted as affecting the inalienable right of all parties to the treaty to develop research, production and use of nuclear energy for peaceful purposes without discrimination and in conformity with Articles I and II of this treaty.

All the parties to the treaty undertakes to facilitate and have the right to participate in the fullest possible exchange of equipment, materials, and scientific and technological information for peaceful uses of energy. Parties to the treaty in a position to do so shall also cooperate in contributing alone or together with other states or international organisation to further development of application of nuclear energy for peaceful purposes especially in the territories of non-nuclear weapons states which are party to the treaty with sole consideration for the needs of developing areas of the world.

Article V

According to Article V each party to the treaty undertakes to take appropriate measures to ensure that in accordance with this treaty, under appropriate international procedures, potential benefits, from any peaceful application of nuclear explosion, will be made available to non-nuclear weapon states, party to the treaty in a non-discriminatory basis and that the charge to such parties will be as low as possible and exclude any change for research and development. non-Nuclear weapon states party to the treaty shall be able to obtain such benefits, pursuant to a special international agreement through an appropriate international body with adequate representation of non-nuclear weapon states. Non-nuclear weapon states party to the treaty so desiring may also obtain such benefits pursuance to bilateral agreement.

Article VI

Each party of the treaty undertake in good faith an effective measures relating to cessation of nuclear arms race at an early date and to nuclear disarmament and a treaty on general and complete disarmament under strict and effective international control.

Article VII

It states that nothing in this treaty affects the right of any group to conclude regional treaties in order to assure the total absence of nuclear weapon in their respective territories.

Article VIII

1. Any party to the treaty may propose amendment to this treaty. The text of any proposed amendment shall be submitted to the depositary governments. All the parties to the treaty to consider such amendments.
2. Any amendment to this treaty must be approved by a majority of the votes of all the parties to the treaty including the votes of all nuclear weapon party to the treaty.
3. Five years after the entry into force of this treaty a conference of parties to the treaty shall be held in Geneva, Switzerland in order to review the operation of this treaty at intervals of five years therefore a majority of the parties to the treaty may obtain, by submitting a proposal to this effect to the depository governments the convening of further conference with the same objectives of reviewing the operation of the treaty.

Article IX

1. The treaty shall be opened to all states for signature. Any state that doesn't sign the treaty before its entry into force in accordance with paragraph 3 of this Article may accede to it any time.
2. The treaty shall be subject to ratification by signatory states. Instruments of ratification and instruments of accession shall be deposited with the governments of Great Britain, USSR, USA, which are hereby, designated the depository governments.

3. The treaty shall enter into force after its ratification by the states, the governments of which are designated depositaries of the treaty and 40 other states signatory to this treaty and deposit their instruments of ratification. For the purposes of this treaty a nuclear weapon state is one, which has manufactured and exploded an explosive device prior to 1 January 1967.
4. For states whose instruments of ratification or accession are deposited subsequent to the entry into force on the date of deposit of their instruments of ratification on accession.
5. The depository government's shall promptly inform all signatories and acceding states of the date of each signature, the date of deposit of each instrument of ratifications, the date of entry into force of this treaty.
6. This treaty shall be registered by the depository governments pursuant to Article 102 of the Charter of the UN.

Article X

Each party shall in exercising its national sovereignty have the right to withdraw from the treaty if it decides that extraordinary events leading to the subject-matter of the treaty have jeopardised the supreme interest of its country. It shall give the notice of such withdrawal to all other parties of, who the treaty have jeopardised the supreme interests of its country. It shall give the notice of such withdrawal to all other parties to the treaty and to the UN Security Council, three months in advance.

Twenty-five years after the entry into force of the treaty, a conference shall be convened to decide whether the treaty shall continue in force indefinitely or shall be extended for an additional fixed period. This decision shall be taken by a majority of parties to the treaty.

Article XI

This treaty the Russian, French, Spanish and Chinese versions shall be deposited in the archives of the depository governments. Duly certified copies of this treaty shall be transmitted by the depository governments to the government of the signatory and acceding state.

Bibliography

Primary Sources

Government Documents

Government of Great Britain, Iraqi Dossier, Iraq's Weapons of Mass Destruction, 2002.

Government of India, Ministry of Defence, Annual Report, 1997-98.

Government of India, Ministry of Defence, Annual Report, 1999-2000.

Government of India, Ministry of Defence, Disarmament and Internal Security, Ministry of External Affairs, Texts and Transcripts of Statement and Debate in Parliament on India's Nuclear Tests in May 1998, New Delhi, September 1998.

Government of India, Ministry of External Affairs, Annual Report, 1998.

Government of India, Ministry of External Affairs, Annual Report, 2001-2002.

United States Arms Control and Disarmament Agency, Documents on Disarmament, 1968.

United States Arms Control and Disarmament Agency, Documents on Disarmament, 1969.

International Atomic Energy Agency Documents

International Atomic Energy Agency, Annual Report, Vienna, 1995.

International Atomic Energy Agency, Annual Report, Vienna, 1996.

International Atomic Energy Agency, Bulletin, Vol. 44, No. 2, Vienna, 2002.

International Atomic Energy Agency, Bulletin Vienna, Vol. 45, No. 1, June 2003.

International Atomic Energy Agency, Bulletin, Vienna, Vol. 45, No. 2, December 2003.

Non-Governmental Reports

Korean Peninsular, Energy Development Organisation, Annual Report, 1996.

Korean Peninsular, Energy Development Organisation, Annual Report, 1997.

Korean Peninsular, Energy Development Organisation, Annual Report, 2001.

Acronym Report No. 13, "Non-Proliferation Treaty Challenging Times", Acronym Institute, London, February 2000.

Parliamentary Publications

Lok Sabha Debate, Session 11, Indrajit Gupta, "Discussion on Recent Nuclear Test", 29 May, 1998.

Lok Sabha Debate, P.V. Narshima Rao, "Nuclear Capping not Discussed", 13 June, 1994.

Lok Sabha Debate, Jaswant Singh, "Nuclear Non-Proliferation and Pakistan", 6 September, 1991.

Lok Sabha Debate, Session 11, Sri Atal Bihari Vajpayee, "Evolution of Nuclear Policy", 27 May 1998.

Rajya Sabha Debate, Suresh Kalmadi, "CTBT and NPT", 14 December, 2000.

Rajya Sabha Debate, "Opposition Assails Rao on NPT", 6 May, 1994.

Rajya Sabha Debate, "India Against US Arms to Pakistan", 17 May, 1995.

Rajya Sabha Debate, "Rao to Brief US on Pakistan", 11 May, 1994.

Rajya Sabha Debate, Jaswant Singh, "Indo-US Dialogue", 16 December, 1998.

United Nations Documents and Speeches

United Nations, Conference on Disarmament, Statement of Arundhati Ghose on Nuclear Disarmament, 22 May, 1997.

United Nations, Conference on Disarmament, Statement of Arundhati Ghose on Nuclear Disarmament, 9 September, 1997.

United Nations, Conference on Disarmament, Statement of K. Natwar Singh, "Nuclear Disarmament and Action Plan", 14 February, 1989.

United Nations, Conference on Disarmament, Geneva Munir Akram,

Statement of Permanent Representative of Pakistan, 14 May, 1994.

United Nations, General Assembly, A. B. Vajpayee, 'Non-Proliferation of Nuclear Weapons', 26 October, 1995.

United Nations, General Assembly, Arundhati Ghose, 'Non-Proliferation Treaty', 14 November, 1995.

United Nations, General Assembly, First Committee, M. Chandra, 'Non-Proliferation Treaty', 12 November, 1992.

United Nations, General Assembly, Disarmament Rajiv Gandhi, 'A World Free of Nuclear Weapons, An Action Plan', 9 June 1998.

United Nations, General Assembly, Saddam Hussain Letter to the General Assembly, September 19, 2002.

United Nations, General Assembly, 53 Session, Statement of Nawaz Mohammed Sharif, Prime Minister of Pakistan, 23rd September 1998.

United Nations, General Assembly, Statement by Indian Representative Trivedi to The First Committee of the General Assembly, 31 October, 1966.

United Nations Report, K. Sharma, India's Permanent Representatives Statement to the United Nations, May 14, 1998.

United Nations, Security Council, Secretary General's 16th Quarterly Report, United Nations Monitoring Verification and Inspection Commission, 27 February, 2004.

United Nations, Security Council, 1284(S/2004/160) 16th Report, David Kay, The Former Head of The Iraq Survey Group, Testimony Before The US Senate Armed Services Committee on 20 January 2004, 16th Report under UNSCR.

United Nations, Security Council, Mohammed A. Aldouri, 'Letter to UN', June 2002.

United Nations, Document S/22986, 28 August, 1991.

Secondary Sources

Books

Abraham, Itty, "*The Making of The Indian Atomic Bomb, Science Secrecy and Post-colonial State,* (New York: Zed, 1998).

Adele, E. Wick, *Strategy for Managing Nuclear Proliferation Economic and Political Issues,* (Lexington: Heath, 1983).

Ahmed, Samina, David, Cortright, *Pakistan and the Bomb, Public*

Opinion and Nuclear Option, (Norte Dame, Indiana: Norte Dame Press, 1998).

Alam, Aftab, *US Policy Towards South Asia*, (Delhi: Raj Publication, 1998).

Alam, Mohammed, B., *"Essays on Nuclear Proliferation"*, (Delhi:Vikas Publishing House, 1995).

Ali, Akhtar, *Pakistan's Nuclear Dilemma*, (New Delhi: ABC, Publishing House, 1984).

— *South Asia: Nuclear Stalemate or Conflagration*, (Karachi: Research on Armament and Poverty, 1987).

Andrew, Mack, *Asian Flashpoint: Security and the Korean Peninsula*, (Australian National University, 1993).

Avi, Baker, *Disarmament Without Order the Politics of Disarmament at the UN*, (Westport: Greenwood Press, 1988).

Babu, D. Shyam, *Nuclear Non-Proliferation Towards a Universal NPT Regime* (Delhi: Konark Publishers Private Limited, 1992).

Banerjee, Dipanker, *Security in The World Order*, (New Delhi: IDSA, 1994).

Baran, Amatizia and Rubin, Barry, *Iraq Road to War*, (New York: Macmillan Press Limited, 1992).

Benjamin, Frankel, *Opaque Nuclear Proliferation, Methodological and Policy Implications*, (London : Frank Class,1991).

Bhatia, Shyam and Daniel, M.C., Gory, *Brighter than the Bagadad Sun, Saddam's Race to Build the Bomb*, (London: Little Brown and Company, 1999).

Bhatia, Shyam, *India's Nuclear Bomb*, (Delhi: Vikas Publishers, 1979).

Bhola, P.L., *Pakistan's Nuclear Policy*, (New Delhi: Sterling Publishers, 1993).

Bhudiana, Rajpal, *India's National Security Dilemma, the Pakistan Factor and India's Policy Response*, (New Delhi: Indus Publishing Company, 2001).

Bhutto, Zulfikar, Ali, *The Myth of Independence*, (London: Oxford University Press, 1969).

Bhutto, Zulfikar, Ali, *If I am Assassinated..*, (New Delhi: Vikas Publishing House, 1979).

Bidwai, Praful and Achin, Vanaik, *South Asia on a Short Fuse*, (New Delhi: Oxford University Press, 2001).

Bruce, and Robert, H., *Nuclear Proliferation: South Asia and the Middle East*, (Australia: Indian Ocean Centre for Peace Studies, 1992).

Burrows, William, E., and Windrem, Roberts, *Critical Mass,* (New York: Simon and Schuster, 1994).

Butler, Richard, *Saddam Defiant: The Threat of Weapons of Mass Destruction and Crises of Global Security,* (Phoenix: London, 2000).

Butler, Richard, *Fatal Choice Nuclear Weapons and Illusions on Missile Defence,* (Colorado: Westview Press, Boulder, 2001).

Burki, S.M., *Pakistan's Foreign Policy, An Historical Analysis,* (Karachi: oop, 1973).

Buzan, Barry, *People States and Fear, The National Security Problem in International Relations,* (Brighton: Sussex, Wheatsheaf Book Ltd., 1983).

Carnesale, Albert, *The New Nuclear Nations,* (USA: Council of Foreign Relation, 1993).

Chari, P. R., *Indo-Pak Nuclear Standoff: The Role of United States,* (New Delhi : Manohar: 1995).

Caroline, Thomas, *In Search of Security the Third World in International Relations,* (Britain: Wheatsheaf Books Ltd., 1987).

Chari, P. R. Pervaj, Iqabal, Cheema and Iflekharuzzam (Ed.) *Nuclear Proliferation in India and Pakistan,* (New Delhi: Manohar, 1996).

Chellaney, Brahma, *Securing India's Future in the New Millennium,* (New Delhi: Sage Publications, 2000).

Chellaney, Brahma, *Nuclear Proliferation; The US-India Conflict,* (New Delhi: Orient Longman Ltd., 1993).

Chengappa, Raj, *Weapons of Peace, The Secret Story of India's Quest to be a Nuclear Power,* (New Delhi: Harper Collins Publishers, 2000).

Chitkara, M.G., *Nuclear Pakistan,* (Delhi: APIJ, 1996).

Cockburn, Andrew and Patrick, Cockburn, *Out of the Ashes, The Resurrection of Saddam Hussein,* (New York: Harper Collins, 1991).

Cohen, Stephen, Philip, P. (Ed.), *The Security of South Asian: Asian and American Perspectives,* (Urbana: University of Illinois, 1987).

Cohen, Stephen, P. (Ed.) *Nuclear Proliferation in South Asia: The Prospects for Arms Control,* (New Delhi: Lancer International, 1991).

David, Albright and Kevin, O. Neill, *Solving the North Korean Nuclear Puzzle,* (Washington DC: Institute of Science and International Security, 2000).

Davis, S. Zachary and Benjamin, Frankel, *The Proliferation Puzzle, Why Nuclear Weapons Spread and What Results*, (London: Frank Class, 1993).

Desai, Jatin, *Nuclear Diplomacy The Art of the Deal*, (New Delhi: Commonwealth Publishers, 2000).

Dewitt, David, (Ed.) *Nuclear Non-Proliferation and Global Security*, (London: Croom Helm, 1987).

Fischer, D. A. V., *The Nuclear Non-Proliferation Regime*, (New York: United Nation Institute for Disarmament Research, 1987).

Fischer, David, *Stopping the Spread of Nuclear Weapons: The Past and Prospects*, (London: Routledge ,1992).

Forsberg, Randall, William, Driescoll, Gregory Webb and Thomas Dean, *Non-Proliferation Primer, Preventing the Spread of Nuclear, Chemical and Biological Weapon*, (Cambridge: The MIIT Press, 1995).

Frankle, B. (Ed.) *Opaque Nuclear Proliferation: Methodological and Policy Implications*, (London: Frank Cass & Co., 1991).

Francine, Frankle, (Ed.), *Bridging the Non-Proliferation Divide*, (Ianhum M D: University Press of America, 1995).

Ganguly, Sumit, and Greenwood, Ted, (Ed.), *Mending Fences Confidence and Security Building* Measures *in South Asia*, (Delhi: OUP, 1997).

Garner, Gary T., *Nuclear Non–Proliferation A Primer*, (London: Lynne Reiner Publication, 1994).

Greenwood, Ted, Fevison, Harold, A. and Taylor, Theodore B., *Nuclear Proliferation: Motivation, Capabilities and Strategies for Control*, (New York: Mc Graw Hill Company, 1977).

Goldblat, Jozeph, (Ed.) *Non-Proliferation the Why and Wherefore*, (Great Britain: Taylor and Francis, 1985).

Goldblat, Jozeph, *Twenty Years of the Non-Proliferation Treaty: Implementation and Prospects*, (Oslo: International Peace Research Institute, 1990).

Gupta, Bhabani Sen, *Nuclear Weapons? Policy Options for India*, (New Delhi: Sage Publications, 1983).

Devin, T. Hagerty, *The Consequences of Nuclear Proliferation Lessons from South Asia*, (Cambridge: Belfer Center for Science and International Affairs, 1998).

Halliday, Von & Bruce, Cummings, *Korea the Unknown War*, (New York: Pantheon, 1988).

Harrison, Selig, S. and Kemp, Geoffrey, (Ed.), *India and America after the Cold War*, (Washington DC: Carniege Endowment for International Peace, 1992).

Hart, David, *Nuclear Power in India Comparative Analysis*, (New Delhi: Select Book Service, 1983).

Henry, D. Sokoloski, *Best of Intentions America's Campaign Against Strategic Weapons Proliferation*, (USA: Prager Publishers, 2000).

Hiro, Dilip, *Neighbours Not Friends, Iraq and Iran After the Gulf War*, (London: Routledge, 2001).

Imai, R. and Press, *Nuclear Non-Proliferation Failures and Prospects*, (New York and London: International Consultative Group on Nuclear Energy, 1980).

Jain, B.M., Eva, Maria, Hexamer, (Ed.), *Nuclearisation in South Asia*, (New Delhi: Rawat Publications, 1990).

Joek, Neil, *Strategic Consequences of Nuclear Proliferation in South Asia*, (London: Frank Cass Co. Limited, 1986).

Kanwal, Gurmeet, *Nuclear Defence Shaping the Arsenal*, (New Delhi: IDSA Knowledge World, April 2001).

Kapur, Ashok, *India's Nuclear Option*, (New York: Prager Publishers, 1976).

Kapur, Ashok, *Pakistan's Nuclear Development*, (New York: Croom Helm Limited, 1987).

Kapur, K.D., *Nuclear Non-Proliferation Diplomacy*, (New Delhi: Lancers Books, 1993).

Kapur, K.D., *Nuclear Diplomacy in East Asia, US and Korean Nuclear Crises Management*, (New Delhi :Lancers Book 1995).

Karnard, Bharat, *Future Imperilled; India's Security in the 1990's, and Beyond*, (New Delhi: Viking Penguin India ,1994).

Kaushik, Brig, Mohan, O.M. Mehrotra, *Pakistan's Nuclear Bomb*, (New Delhi: Sopan Publication House,1980).

Kevic, Lorne, J., *India's Quest for Security Defence Policies 1947-1965*, (Berkeley LA: University of California Press, 1967).

Khan, Saira, *Nuclear Proliferation Dynamics in Protracted Conflict Prone Regions Comparitive Study of South Asia and the Middle East*, (England: Ashgate Publishing Limited, 1988).

Khan, S. Agha, (Ed.), *Nuclear War Nuclear Proliferation and Their Consequences*, (Oxford: Clarendon Press, 1986).

Khan, Zulfiqar, Ali, *Pakistan's Security : The Challenge and Response*, (Lahore :Progressive Publishers, 1998).

Kheli, Tahir, Shirin, *The United States and Pakistan the Evolution of an Influence Relationship*, (New York :Prager ,1982).

Kilhani, R.K., *Nuclearisation of South Asia*, (New Delhi: Commonwealth Publishers, 2000).

Kreption, Michael and Amit, Sevak, *Crises Prevention Confidence Building and Reconciliation in South Asia*, (Delhi: Manohar ,1996).

Kunju, N., *Indo-Pak Nuclear Cold War*, (New Delhi: Reliance Publishing House, 2002).

Kokoski, Richard, *Technology and Proliferation of Nuclear Weapons*, (New York :Oxford University Press, 1995).

Maharaj, Sanjay, Badri, *The Armageddon Factor, Nuclear Weapons in the Indo-Pakistan Context*, (New Delhi: Lancers Publishers, 2000).

Marwah, Onkar and Shulz, Anne, (Ed.), *Nuclear Proliferation and Near Nuclear Countries*, (Cambridge: MA Ballinger Publishing Company, 1975).

Matòo, Amitab, *India's Nuclear Deterrent Pokharan II and Beyond*, (New Delhi: Har Anand Publishers, 1999).

Menon, Raja, *A Nuclear Strategy for India*, (New Delhi: Sage Publications, 2000).

Moshaver, Z., *Nuclear Weapons Proliferation in the Indian Sub-continent*, (London: Macmillan , 1991).

Molty, Jamesclay, Alexander, Y., Mansourov, *The North Korean Nuclear Program, Security, Strategy and New Perspectives from Russia*, (New York: London: Routledge, 2000).

Mukherjee, Amitava, *India's Policy Towards Pakistan*, (New Delhi: Associated Book Centre, 1983).

Mutimer, David, *Proliferation and the Framing of Security*, (USA: Lynne Reinne Publishers, INC 2000).

Nanda, Colonel, Ravi, *Indo-Pak Detente*, (New Delhi: Lancers Books, 1989).

Nanda, Prakash, *Nuclearisation of Divided Nations*, (New Delhi: Manas Publications, 2001).

Nair, Vijai K., Brig, (retd), *Nuclear India*, (New Delhi: Lancer International, 1999).

Nazmi, Haider, K., *The Roots to Rhetoric, The Politics of Weapons in India and Pakistan*, (New Delhi: India Research, 2001).

Neil, Joek, *Strategic Consequences of Nuclear Proliferation in South Asia*, (London: Frank Cass and Company Limited, 1986).

Nicole, Ball, *Security and Economy in the Third World*, (Princeton University Press, 1988).

Palit, D.K. Maj, General, Namboodri, P.K.S., *Pakistan's Islamic Bomb,* (New Delhi: Vikas Publishing House, 1979).

Pande, Savita, *Pakistan's Nuclear Policy,* (New Delhi: D.K. Publishing Corporation, 1991).

Pathak, K.K., *Nuclear Policy of India, A Third World Perspective,* (Delhi: Gitanjali, 1980).

Perkovich, George, *India's Nuclear Bomb and the Impact on Global Proliferation,* (New Delhi: Oxford University Press, 2000).

Peter, Hayes, (Ed.), *Countering Proliferation and Use of Weapons of Mass Destruction,* (New York: Mc Graw Hills, 1998).

Pilat, J. and Pendley, R.E., (Eds.), *Beyond 1995, The Future of the NPT Regime,* (New York: Plenum Press, 1990).

Poulose, T.T. (Ed.), *Perspective of India's Nuclear Policy,* (New Delhi: Young Asia Publications, 1978).

Poulose, T.T., *Nuclear Proliferation and the Third World,* (New Delhi: ABC Publishing House, 1982).

Rajan, M.S., Ganguly, Shivaji, (Eds.) *Great Power Relations and World Order and the Third World,* (New Delhi: Vikas Publishing House, 1981).

Reiss, Mitchel, *Without the Bomb: The Politics of Nuclear Proliferation,* (New York: Columbia University Press, 1988).

Reiss, Mitchell, *Nuclear Proliferation After the Cold War,* (Washington DC: John Hopkins University Press, 1990).

Roberts, Brad, (Ed.), *Weapons Proliferation in the 1990's*, (Cambridge: MIIT Press, 1995).

Shahi, Agha, *Pakistan's Security and Foreign Policy,* (Lahore: Progressive Publishers, 1988).

Sharma, Dhirendra, *India's Nuclear Estate,* (New Delhi: Lancers Publishers, 1983).

Schmidt, Gold, Bertrand, *The Atomic Complex, A World Wide Political History of Nuclear Energy,* (La Grange Park III: American Nuclear Society, 1980).

Simpson, J. (Ed.), *Nuclear Non-Proliferation: An Agenda for the 1990's,* (London: Cambridge University Press, 1987).

Singh, P.B., and Subrahmanyam, R.R., *Nuclear Pakistan: Atomic Threat to South Asia,* (New Delhi: Vision Book, 1980).

Sokolski, Henry, D., *Best of Intentions Americas Campaign Against Strategic Weapons Proliferation,* (USA: Prager Publishers, 2000).

Spector, Leonard, S., and Smith, Jacqueline, R., *Nuclear Ambitions the Spread of Nuclear Weapons 1989 –1990,* (Boulder: Westview Press, 1990).

Specter, Leonard, S., *Nuclear Ambitions: The Spread of Nuclear Weapons 1989-1990*, (Boulder: Westview Press, 1990).

Subrahmanyam, K., and Singh, Jasjit, (Ed.), *Security Without Nuclear Weapons: Indo-Soviet Dialogue*, (New Delhi: Lancer International, 1986).

Stephen, P. Cohen, (Ed.), *Nuclear Proliferation in South Asia The Prospects for Arms Control*, (Boulder and Westview Press, 1994).

Thakur, Ramesh, *The Politics and Economics of India' s Foreign Policy*, (Delhi: Oxford University Press, 1994).

Thappar, Usha, Mangesh, Kulkarni, (Ed.), *India in World Affairs Towards the 21st Century*, (Mumbai: Himalaya Publishing House, 1999).

Thomas, Raju, G.C. Amit, Gupta, *India's Nuclear Security*, (New Delhi: Vistaar Publication, 2000).

Tellis, Ashley, J., *Stability in South Asia, Prospects of Indo-Pak Nuclear*, (Dehradun: Natraj Publishers, 2000).

Tellis, Ashley, J., *India's Emerging Nuclear Posture*, (New Delhi: Oxford University Press, 2001).

Winderm, Robert, *"Critical Mass:The Dangerous Race of Superpowers" in the Fragmented World*, (London: Simon and Schuster, 1995).

Articles

Abidi, A. H. H., "Changing Politico Security Profile in the Persian Gulf", *Strategic Analysis*, Vol. XVI, September 1993.

Adler, Emanuel, "Opaque Nuclear Proliferation and the Political Selection of Arms Control Concepts", *Journal of Strategic Studies*, 13(3) September, 1990.

Albright, David, "The Shots Heard Around the World", *The Bulletin of Atomic Scientist*, Vol. 54, No. 4, July/August 1998.

Albright, David, Kevin, O'Neil, "The Iraq Maze : Searching for a Way Out", *The Non-Proliferation Review*, Vol. 8, No. 3, Monterey Institute of International Studies, Fall-Winter, 2001.

Albright, David , Mark, Hibbs, "Iraq's Bomb, Blueprints and Artefacts", *The Bulletin of Atomic Scientists*, Vol. 48, No. 1, January/February 1992.

Albright, David, "How Much Plutonium Does North Korea Have," *Bulletin of Atomic Scientist*, Educational Foundation for Nuclear Science, September/October 1994.

Al-Marashi, Ibrahim, "How Iraq Conceals and Sustains its

Weapons of Mass Destruction", *Middle East Review of International Affairs*, Vol. 7, No. 1 March, 2003.

Babar, Farhtullah, "Nuclear Non-Proliferation Issues", *Strategic Studies*, 10(40) 11 (1) Summer, 1987.

Bergio, Ofra, "Crossing the Rubicon Iraq and Arab Israeli Peace Process", *Middle East Review of International Affairs*, Vol. 2, No. 1, March 1998.

Beri, Ruchita, "Challenge of Proliferation and Existing Control Regime", *Strategic Analysis*, Vol. XVI, No. 10, January 1994.

Binnie, Jeremy, "The Gulf States", *Jane Sentinel Security Assessments:* (London: Jane's Information Group, 2001).

Blix, Hans, "IAEA Safeguards New Challenges", *Disarmament*, A Periodic Review by United Nations, Vol. XV, No. 2, 1992.

Bok, Dang, Lee, " The Status of North Korean Nuclear Program", *Korea Focus*, Vol. 3, No. 6, November/December 1995.

Bull, Hedly, "Rethinking Non-Proliferation", *International Affairs*, Vol. 51, April 1975, p.175.

Carroll, Eugene, "The-NPT Review Last Chance", *The Defence Monitor*, Vol. XXIX, No. 3, Centre for Defence Information, 2000.

Chari, P.R., "India's Nuclear Doctrine Confused Ambitions", *The Non-Proliferation Review*, Fall, Winter 2000.

Cheon, Seongwhum, "North Korea's Nuclear Program Heading Towards the End", *Korea and World Affairs*, Vol. XXVI, No. 4, Seoul Research Centre for Peace and Unification of Korea, Winter 2000.

Chellaney, Brahma, "South Asia's Passage to Nuclear Power," *International Security*, Vol. 16, Issue 1, Summer, 1991.

Cohen, P. Stephen, "The Economic and Geo Strategic Stakes in South Asia", *Oxford Analytica*, Daily Brief, March 23, 2000.

Cirincione, Joseph, How will Iraq War Change Global Non-Proliferation Strategies, *Arms Control Today*, Vol. 33 , No. 5, April 2003.

Choudhary, Rahul, Roy, "Regional Stability and Weapons Proliferation in South Asia", *Strategic Analysis*, Vol. XV, No. 7, October 1992.

Cummings, Bruce, "A Monstrous Idea", *The Bulletin of Atomic Scientists*, Educational Foundation for Nuclear Science, September/October 1994.

C.H. John, and Gubel, M. Ruth, "The North Korean Nuclear

Weapon Crisis the US and its Policy Options", *Korean Observer*, Institute of Korean Studies, Vol. XXVI, No. 1, Spring, 1995.

Datt, Savita, "NPT and Non-Nuclear Weapon States: Options and Non-options", *Strategic Analysis*, Vol. XV, January 1993.

Dhanpala, Jayantha, "Disappointment in the Third World", *The Bulletin of Atomic Scientist*, Vol. 46, The Education of Nuclear Science, January 1990.

Dunn, A. Lewis, "High Room for the NPT", *Arms Control Today*, Washington DC, Arms Control Association, July / August 1995.

Dunn, A. Lewis, "Non-Proliferation the Next Steps", *Arms Control Today*, 17(a), November 1987.

Epstein, William, "Indefinite Extension with Increased Accountability", *The Bulletin of Atomic Scientist*, The Educational Foundation of Nuclear Science Chicago, January 1995.

Fischer, David, Muller, Harald, "The Fourth Review of the NPT", *SIPRI Year Book*, 1991.

Fischer, David, "Towards the 1990 NPT Review Conference, Preparations and Problems", *Disarmament*, 13(3), 1990.

Garrett, Banning, Bonnie, Glaser, "Looking Across the Yalu, Chinese Assessment of North Korea", *Asian Survey*, Vol. XXXV, No. 6, June 1995.

Gerson, Joseph, "Key Problems", *Asia Pacific and Security Issue*, Vol. 2, No. 10, January 1997.

Ganguly, Sumit, "The Sino-Indian Border Talks 1981-1989, A View from New Delhi", *Asian Survey*, 29 : 12 (December, 1989).

Hammad, Fawzi, "Taming the Trigger Happy", *Al. Ahram Weekly*, Issue No. 481, Cario, 11-17 May, 2000.

Harries, Jack, "Horizontal Proliferation, Who will Stop the Bomb? *New Scientist*, 113(1542), 8 January 1987.

Hathaway, M. Robert, "Confrontation and Retreat: The US Congress and South Asian Nuclear Tests", *Arms Control Today*, January-February 2000.

Hewitt, Vernon, "Containing Shiva India Non-Proliferation and the Comprehensive Tests Ban Treaty", *Contemporary South Asia*, 9(1) 2000.

Hibbs, M. "Speculation Rampant While IAEA Compiles Iraqi Hit List," *Nucleonics Week*, Vol. 32, 10 October, 1991.

Ho, Shun, Lee, "North Korea's Development of Weapons of Mass Destruction", *Korean Focus*, Vol. 4, No. 2, March-April 1996.

Iroie, Laureny, "Iraq's Weapons of Mass Destruction and The 1997 Gulf Crises" *Meria Journal*, Vol. 1, No. 4, December 1997.

Jetly, Nancy, "India's Security Challenges: Perspectives and Prospects", *Strategic Analyses*, Vol. XXI, No. 9, December 1997.

Johnson, Rebeca, "Rouges and Rhetoric", The 2003 NPT Prep Com Slides Backward, *Disarmament Diplomacy*, Issue No. 71, June-July 2003.

Kapur, Ashok, "Dump the Treaty", *The Bulletin of Atomic Scientist*, Vol. 46 No. 7, The Educational Foundation of Nuclear Science, Chicago, August 1990.

Kapur, Ashok, "Nuclear Proliferation South Asian Perspectives", *Pacific Affairs*, 57(2), Summer, 1984.

Kie, Byung, Yong, "Changes in North Korea's Military Policy and East Asian *Security*", *Korea Focus*, January-February 2003.

Krauthammer, Charles, "The Unipolar Moment", *Foreign Affairs*, Vol. 7, No. 1, 1991.

Kucia, Christine, "NPT Meeting to Control New Nuclear Threat", *Arms Control Today*, Arms Control Association, June 2003.

Layne, Christopher, "Why the Gulf War was Not in the National Interest", *The Atlantic Monthly*, Vol. 268, No. 1, July 1991.

Levental, Paul, Lyman, S. Ewin, "Who Says Iraq isn't Making An Bomb?", *International Herald Tribune*, 2 November 1995.

Lee, Joo, Tae, Yang, Maeng, Ho, "Half a Century Evolution of US Non-Proliferation Policy", *The Korean Journal of Defence Analysis*, Vol. XV, No. 1, Spring 2003.

Mack, Andrew, "The Nuclear Crisis in the Korean Peninsula", *Asian Survey*, Vol. XXXIII, No. 4, April 1993.

Nair, K. Vijai, "Nuclear Proliferation US Aims and India's Response", *Studies in Conflict and Terrorism*", 1994.

Namboodri, P.K.S., "NPT Regime in Trouble", *Mainstream*, 24 November, 1985.

Nye Joseph S., "NPT, The Logic of Inequality", *Foreign Policy*, 59, Summer 1985.

Ispahni, Mahnaz, "Pakistan's Dimension of Insecurity", *Adelphi Papers*, International Institute for Strategic Studies, 246, Winter 1989/1990.

Oh, C.H. John, Grubel, M. Ruth, "The North Korean Nuclear Weapons Crises, The United States and its Policy Options", *Korea Observer*, Vol. XXVI, No. 1, The Institute of Korean Studies, Spring, 1995.

Oknim, Chung, "Outlook for Bush Administer North Korea Policy", *Korea Focus*, Vol. 9, No. 2, March-April 2001.

Paik, Haksoon, "Steering Between Red Basis A South Korean View", *Arms Control Today*, Arms Control Association: Washington DC, Vol. 33, No. 4, May 2003.

Pande, Savita, "NPT Export Controls and Nuclear Trade" *Strategic Analysis*, Vol. XXI, No. 6, IDSA, September 1997.

Pande, Savita, "NPT Extension and Review Conference", *Asian Strategic Review* 1994-1995, IDSA, September 1995.

Pattnaik, Smurti, S., "Pakistan's Nuclear Strategy", *Strategic Analyses*, IDSA Vol. 27, No.1 January-March 2003.

Perkovich, George, "Bush Nuclear Revolution, A Regime Change in Non-Proliferation", *Foreign Affairs*, March/April 2003.

Poulouse, T. T., "Atomic Colonialism", *Bulletin of the Atomic Scientist*, October 1978.

Pripp, Charles, "The Gulf States and Iraq", *Survival*, Autumn 1992.

Rauf, Tariq, "View Point, Preparing for April 1997 NPT prep.com", *The Non-Proliferation Review*, Winter, 1997.

Ritter, Scott, "Redefining Iraq's Obligation: The Case for Qualitative Disarmaments of Iraq", *Arms Control Today*, June 2000.

Russell, A. James, "Searching for a Post-Saddam Regional Security Architecture", *MERIA Journal*, Vol. 7, No. 1, March 2003.

Sen, Gupta, Bhabani, "Nuclear Non-Proliferation in South Asia Problem and Prospects", *Strategic Studies*, Summer and Autumn, 1987.

Sethi, Manpreet, "Post Cold War Nuclear Proliferation, Pattern and Possibilities", *Asian Strategic Review*, New Delhi, Institute for Defence Studies and Analysis, 1997-98.

Sethi, Manpreet, "NPT Review Conference 2000: What Lies in Store", *Strategic Analyses*, Vol. XXIV., No. 1.

Simpson, John, "NPT Stronger After Iraq", *Bulletin of Atomic Scientists*, October 1991.

Singh, Jasjit, "Developing, Countries and Nuclear Issues", *Strategic Analysis*, February 1986.

Singh, Jasjit, "India's Nuclear Policy a Perspective", *Strategic Analysis*, Vol. XII, No. VII, November 1989.

Singh, Jasgit, "India, Europe and Non-Proliferation, Pokhran-II and After", *Strategic Analysis*, 22-28 November, 1998.

Sigal, V. Leon, "The North Korean Nuclear Crises : Understanding the Failure of Crime and Punishment Strategy", *Arms Control Today*, The Arms Control Association, May 1997.

Sigal, V. Leon, "Averting a Train Wreck in North Korea", *Arms Control Today*, The Arms Control Association : Washington DC, November-December 1998.

Song, Sum, Young, "The Korean Nuclear Issue", *Korea and World Affairs*, Fall 1991.

Spector, S. Leonard and Smith, R. Jacqueline, "North Korea: The Next Nuclear Nightmare?", *Arms Control Today*, 21: 2 March 1991.

Stober, Dan, "Nuclear Inspectors Reportedly Argue Checking False US Leads Wanted Time" *Mercury News*, March 18, 2003.

Subrahmanyam, K., "Fighting the Nuclear Cult", *Mainstream*, 24 Annual, October 1985.

Subramanyam, K., "NPT Review Conference, Strategy for the Non-agreed", *World Focus*, 6 June, 1985.

Sullivan, L.O. Meghan, "Replacing the Rogue Rhetoric, A New Label Opens the Way to a Better Policy", *Brooking Review*, The Brooking Institution, Washington DC, Vol. 18, No. 4, February 2000.

Thakur, Ramesh, "Envisioning Nuclear Futures", *Security Dialogue*, Vol. 31 (1) : Sage Publications, 2000.

Tow, William, "Reassessing Deterrence on the Korean Peninsula", *Korean Journal of Defence Analysis*, 3 : 1, Summer 1991.

Vinod, M.J., "Nuclear Proliferation in South Asia: Current and Future Trends", *Strategic Analysis*, Vol. XVIII, No. 12, March 1996.

Wagner, Alex, "Bush Labels North Korea, Iran Iraq as Axis of Evil", *Arms Control Today*, (Washington DC: Arms Control Association, March 2002).

Walker, William, "International Nuclear Reactions After India and Pakistani Nuclear Explosions", *International Affairs*, Vol. 74, July 1998.

Weiss, Leonard, "Tighten Up on Nuclear Cheaters", *The Bulletin of Atomic Scientist*, 4 May 1991.

Woon, Byoung, Choi, "Prospect of Social Reform and Disarmament in North Korea", *Korea Focus*, Vol. 9, No. 3, May-June 2001, Seoul, Korea Foundation.

Wook, Jang Lee, "North Korea's Nuclear and Missile Ambitions", *Korea Focus*, Vol. 9, No. 5, September-October 2001.

Wrenn, B. Catherine, "The Korean Nuclear Crisis: Nuclear Non-Proliferation Treaty in Retrospect, The Case of North Korea", *Bulletin of Concerned Asian Scholars*, Vol. 6, No. 1-2, Philadelphia Routledge, January-June 1994.

Zunes, Stephen, "Iraq 10 Years After Gulf War", *Foreign Policy in Focus*, Vol. 6, No. 1, January 2001.

Zoman, Iftehharuz, "Emerging Trends in South Asia", *Bangladesh Institute of Strategic Studies*, Vol. 3, No. 3, 1992.

Zuberi, M., "NPT-Nuclear Inequality–An Imperialist Ploy", *World Focus*, (6), June 1985.

News Papers

Anderson, John, Ward and Kamran, Khan, "Pakistan Sets off Nuclear Blasts", *Washington Post*, 29 May, 1998.

Beg, Aslam, Mirza, General, "Pakistan-Nuclear Program, A National Security Perspective", *The Nation*, Lahore, June, 22-23, 1993.

Bender, Bryan, "US Considers Helping Pakistan", *Boston Globe*, 20 September, 2001.

Benjamin, Daniel, "Saddam Hussain and Al Qaeda and Not Allies", *New York Times*, 30 September, 2002.

Bhusan, Bharat, "F-16's Promised in Return for Capping N-plan", *Indian Express*, 17 March, 1994.

"BJP for Consensus on NPT Issue", *The Hindu*, 31 March, 1994.

Brahma, Chellany, "The Talbot Visit and the Arms Race", *Indian Express*, 6 April, 1994.

"China's North Korean Test", *The Economist*, 11-17 June, 1999.

Datta, Sujit, "Perpetuating of the Divide", *The Pioneer*, 17 May, 1995.

Dixit, Abha, "US and South Asia", *The Hindustan Times*, 13 May, 1994.

Ghose, Arundhati, "Taming India", *Times of India*, 26 February, 1999.

Gordon, R. Michael, *New York Times*, 25 October, 1989.

Harrison, Selig, "Idea of a Nuclear Bargain Between India and US" *Asian Age*, 9 December, 1997.

Hoagland, Jim, "Thinking about Korean War II", *Washington Post*, 12 May, 1994.

"India May Be Forced to Consider N-Option", *Indian Express*, 17 March, 1994.

"India Reaffirms Stand on NPT", *The Times of India*, 23 March, 1994.

"Iran Says All its Nuclear Plants are Open to Inspection", *Dow Jones Newswire*, 13 December, 2003.

"Japan has the Ability to Make Nuclear Bombs, Hata Admits", *The Japan Times*, Tokyo, 18 June, 1994.

Jehl, Douglas, "US Seeking UN Pressure to Compel North Korea to Honour the Treaty", *New York Times*, 13 March, 1993.

"Joint statement by the Chairman of the Atomic Energy Commission and The Scientific Adviser to the Defence Minister", *The Hindu*, 18 May, 1998.

Khan, Munir, Ahmed, "Understanding Pakistan's Nuclear Plan", *The News*, Islamabad, 8 March, 1995

Matoo, Amitabh, "India's Nuclear Doctrine in Search of Strategic Autonomy", *Times of India*, August 1999.

Menon, N.C. "North Korean Conundrum" *Hindustan Times*, 12 March, 1994.

Menon ,"Non-Proliferation to be High on Clinton's Agenda", *The Hindustan Times*, 15 May, 1994.

Minaz, Merchant, "The NPT Game is Up; India Should Set the Agenda Now", *The Times of India*, 16 June, 1998.

Mitra, Nirmal, "NAM Countries Take a Tough Stand on NPT", *Hindustan Times*, 6 May, 1995.

Mohan, C. Raja, "The Bully has its Way", *The Hindu*, 14 May, 1995.

Mohan, C. Raja, "Nuclear Balance in Asia", *The Hindu*, 11 June, 1998.

"North Korean Official Threatens War", *Times of India*, 24 March, 1994.

"North Korea Rejects UN's Statement", *Times of India*, April 5, 1994.

"North Korea Pyongyang Pulls Back", *Far Eastern Economic Review*, June 1993.

"Pakistan Not to Roll Back Nuclear Plan", *The Hindustan Times*, New Delhi, 21 March, 1994.

Poulose, T.T., "Non-Proliferation – Brokering a Deal", *The Hindustan Times*, 6 April, 1994.

"Pyongyang may Transfer N-tech to Middle East India's NPT Stand Conveyed to Raphel", *The Times of India* 25 March, 1994.

Qazi, Jehangir, Ashraf, "An Unwanted Attack on Pakistan", *Washington Post*, 29 October, 2002.

"Reactor Deal with France Stalled by NPT Status", *Nuclear News*, August 1999.

"Scientist Affirms Pakistan Capable of Uranium Enrichment Weapons Production", *Naw-E-Waqt*, Lahore, 10 February, 1984.

"Sino Korean Talks Prove Futile on North's N-plant", *Hindustan Times*, 29 March, 1994.

Smith Jeffry, "Report Sites China-Pakistan Missiles Links, "*Washington Post*, 13 June, 1996

Srinivasan, "Nuclear Realities", *The Hindu*, 6 April, 1994.

Subramanium, R.R., "Time to Call Pakistan Rebuff", *The Hindustan Times*, 18 December, 1987, p. 11.

"Talks on Kashmir, NPT Today, Raphel Arrives Amid Protests", *Hindustan Times*, 23 March, 1994.

Taylor, Gregg, M., "Pakistan: Going it Alone at KANUPP", *Nuclear News*, March 1990.

"US Acknowledge India's Stand an NPT", *The Hindustan Times*, 13 May, 1994.

"US Allies Agree on Phased Curbs Against North Korea", *The Hindustan Times*, 13 June, 1994.

"US to Press India for Regional NPT", *The Hindustan Times*, New Delhi, 28 May, 1994.

Usmani, "Pakistan to Review Policy if India Refuses to Sign the Treaty", *Pakistan Times*, 17 July, 1968.

Periodicals/Journals

Al Ahram Weekly (Cairo)
Arms Control Today (Washington DC)
Asian Strategic Review (Delhi)
Asian Survey (California)
Brooking Review (Washington DC)
Bulletin of Concerned Asian Scholars (Philadelphia)
Contemporary South Asia
Disarmament
Disarmament Diplomacy (London)
Foreign Affairs (Washington DC)
Foreign Policy (Washington DC)
India Today (New Delhi)
International Security (Massachusetts)
Jane Sentinel Security Assessments (London)

Journal of Aerospace Defence Industry News
Korea and World Affair (Seoul)
Korea Focus (Seoul)
Korea Observer (Seoul)
Mainstream (Delhi)
Middle East Review of International Affairs (Tel Aviv)
Nucleonics Week (New Jersey)
Pacific Affairs (Vancouver)
Security Dialogue (Oslo)
Strategic Analysis (Delhi)
Survival (London)
The Atlantic Monthly (Boston)
The Bulletin of Atomic Scientist (Chicago)
The Defence Monitor (Washington DC)
The International Affairs (London)
The Korean Journal of Defence Analysis
The Korean Journal of International Studies (Seoul)
World Focus (Delhi)

News Papers

Asian Age (Delhi)
Boston Globe (Massachusetts)
Indian Express (Delhi)
International Herald Tribune (Paris)
Los Angeles Times (California)
Naw-e-Waqt (Lahore)
New York Times (New York)
News Week
Nuclear News
Pakistan Times (Rawalpindi)
People's Daily (Beijing)
The Hindu (Madras)
The Japan Times (Tokyo)
The Korean Herald Times
The Nation (Lahore)
The News (Islamabad)
The Pioneer (Delhi)
Times of India (Delhi)
Washington Post (Washington DC)

Websites

<http://www.acronym.org.uk>
Acronym Institute is a non-governmental research centre in London (UK), working on disarmament and arms control.

<http://www.arms control.org>
The Arms Control Organisation is a non-governmental organisation in Washington (USA).

<http://www.basicint.org>
British American Security Information Council is a non-governmental research centre in London (UK).

<http://www.brook.edu>
The Brooking institution was established in Washington in 1996 is an independent non-partisan organisation devoted to research and analysis on foreign policy.

<http://www.ceip.org>
Carnegie Endowment for International Peace is a non-government organisation in Washington (USA).

<http://cnduk>
Campaign for nuclear disarmament in England is an organisation that campaigns non-violently to rid the world of nuclear weapons.

<http://cns.miis.edu>
Centre for Non-Proliferation studies was established in 1989 at Monterey Institute of International Studies is a non-governmental organisation of the US.

<http:disarmament.un.org>
United Nations department for disarmament affairs was established in January 1998 by General Assembly resolution 52/12. The department promotes the goal of nuclear disarmament and Non-Proliferation.

<http://www.freeman.org>
Freeman Centre for Strategic Studies was founded in Houston, Texas in 1992. It conducts extensive research on military and strategic issues.

<http://www.fpip.org>
Foreign Policy in focus was established in Washington DC in 1995. This organisation provides useful analysis of international affairs.

<http://www.iaea.org>
This is the website of International Atomic Energy Agency in Vienna (Austria).

<http://www.idsa.india.org>
The Institute for Defence Studies and Analysis New Delhi, India was established in November 1965.

<http://www.ieer.org/reports>
Institute for Energy and Environmental Research was established in Maryland (USA) in 1987. It deals with environmental and security aspects of nuclear weapon production and nuclear technology.

<http://www.iraqi mission.org>
Permanent mission of Iraq to United Nation in New York.

<http://www.jamaat.org>
Jamaat-e-Islami is an organisation of Pakistan.

<http://www.kas.org.ia>
Konard Adenaver sifting is an organisation of South Africa.

<http://www.mtholyoke.edu>
Mount Holyoke College Massachusetts was founded in 1837.

<http://www.mid.ru>
The Ministry of Foreign Affairs of Russia.

<http://www.nti.org>
Nuclear threat initiative was established in January 2001 with a mission to strengthen global security.

<http://reaching critical will.org>
Reaching for a critical mass of political will for nuclear disarmament is a disarmament project of the Women's International League for peace and freedom created in 1999.

<http://www.wsws.org>
The World Socialist Website.

<http://www.undir.org>
The UN institute for disarmament research.

<http://www.uno.org>
This is the website of the United Nations.

Index